D1633936

£3.99

9b/42

THE
GEORGIAN
VILLA

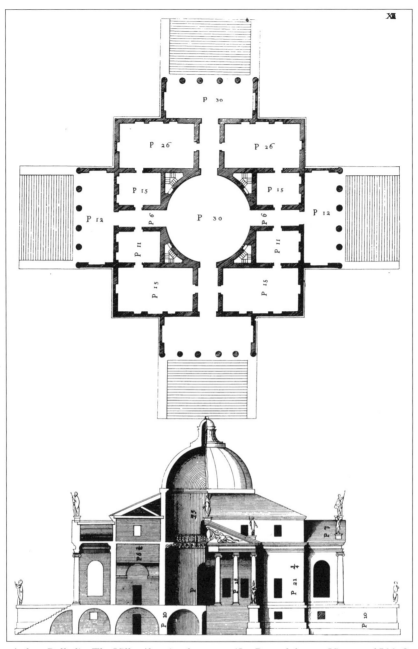

Andrea Palladio, The Villa Almerico, known as 'La Rotonda', near Vicenza, 1566–9.
From Palladio, I quattro libri dell'architettura, *Venice, 1570, book II, p. 19.*

THE GEORGIAN VILLA

EDITED BY DANA ARNOLD

SUTTON PUBLISHING

First published in the United Kingdom in 1996 by
Alan Sutton Publishing Limited, an imprint of Sutton Publishing Limited
Phoenix Mill · Thrupp · Stroud · Gloucestershire GL5 2BU

Paperback edition first published in 1998

Copyright © texts the authors, 1996

All rights reserved. No part of this publication may be reproduced, stored in a retrieval system, or transmitted, in any form or by any means, electronic, mechanical, photocopying, recording or otherwise, without the prior permission of the publishers and copyright holder.

A catalogue record for this book is available from the British Library

ISBN 0 7509 2022 X

This book is based on papers given at a two-day conference organized jointly by the Georgian Group and the Paul Mellon Centre for Studies in British Art held on 17–18 February 1995.

    The conference drew together the latest research on the Georgian villa and provided a forum for discussion on the subject. The contributors and those who attended the sessions acknowledge the valuable opportunity for the study of the Georgian villa made possible by the collaboration of these two organizations. The generous support of the Royal Academy and English Heritage for the conference receptions was greatly appreciated by all.

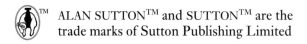 ALAN SUTTON™ and SUTTON™ are the
trade marks of Sutton Publishing Limited

Typeset in 11/12 Ehrhardt.
Typesetting and origination by
Sutton Publishing Limited.
Printed in Great Britain by
Butler & Tanner, Frome, Somerset.

Contents

Contributors

Dana Arnold is Senior Lecturer and Director of the Centre for Studies in Architecture and the Decorative Arts, Department of Fine Art, University of Leeds. She is course leader for the Centre's MA degree in Country House Studies. Dr Arnold is the author of *The Georgian Country House; Architecture, landscape and society*, Sutton 1998 and her forthcoming publications include *Re-presenting the Metropolis: Architecture, urban experience and social life in London 1800–1840*, and a volume of essays *The Metropolis and its Image: Creating identities for London*. She is the Associate Editor of *Art History*.

Lindsay Boynton was Reader in History, Queen Mary and Westfield College, University of London. His publications include *The Elizabethan Militia* and *Gillow Furniture Designs 1760–1800*. Dr Boynton died in 1995.

Julius Bryant is Director of Museums & Collections at English Heritage. He was formerly Director of Historic Properties (London Region) and Head of Museums Division. The author of guidebooks to English Heritage historic houses and exhibition catalogues, his most recent works are *London's Country House Collections* and *Turner: Painting the Nation*.

Michael Davis is Secretary of the Architectural Heritage Society of Scotland. His published work includes *Castles and Mansions of Ayrshire*, and he is currently working on an examination of the Scots Baronial Revival.

Ian Gow is Curator of The National Trust for Scotland. He is also an Honorary Curator of the Royal Incorporation of Architects in Scotland. He has written widely on the decorative arts and architecture of Scotland, including *The Scottish Interior*.

John Harris is the former Curator of the RIBA Drawings Collection, and author of *The Revival of the Palladian Style: Lord Burlington and his House and Garden at Chiswick*, and curated the 1995 Royal Academy exhibition on the subject.

Deborah Howard is a Fellow of St John's College, Cambridge, and Reader in Architectural History in the Faculty of Architecture and History of Art, University of Cambridge. She is the author of *Jacopo Sansovino*, *The Architectural History of Venice* and *Scottish Architecture from the Reformation to the Restoration, 1560–1660*.

Sally Jeffery is Architectural Historian to the Corporation of London, and author of *The Mansion House*.

Seán O'Reilly is Director of the Architectural Heritage Society of Scotland, and author of *Irish Houses and Gardens: from the archives of Country Life*. Dr O'Reilly has lectured and written extensively on post-medieval architecture and its content, and is editor of the Irish Georgian Society's journal, *Irish Architectural and Decorative Studies*, formerly the *Bulletin*.

Professor Alistair Rowan FRSE is Principal of Edinburgh College of Art and author of *Designs for Castles and Country Villas by Robert & James Adam*.

Frank Salmon is a Lecturer in the Department of Art History and Archaeology, University of Manchester. He works primarily on eighteenth- and early nineteenth-century British architects, particularly with regard to their connections with Italy. He has also published on eighteenth-century painting, literature and landscape, and on Michelangelo's Laurentian Library.

Philippa Tristram is Reader Emeritus in English at the University of York. She has published on a range of subjects, including medieval art and literature, nineteenth- and twentieth-century literature, and politics. Her most recent book, *Living Space in Fact and Fiction*, explored the use made by novelists of architecture and interior design. She is at present writing on the portrayal of China in England prior to the Macartney Embassy of 1793.

David Watkin is a Fellow of Peterhouse, Reader in the History of Architecture, University of Cambridge, and Vice-Chairman of the Georgian Group. He is author of *Sir John Soane: Enlightenment Thought and the Royal Academy Lectures*.

Introduction

Dana Arnold

The villa remains one of the most potent architectural forms in western culture. Its appeal has endured from antiquity to the present day. Yet during this time the villa has, in terms of both its physical form and intellectual concept, progressed through many important changes. Many of these developments took place in the Georgian period.

This book considers the architectural and cultural development of the classical villa in eighteenth- and early nineteenth-century Britain. The chapters are based on papers given at a conference held 17–18 February 1995. This was the first major conference to consider the villa in the British Isles during the Georgian period. The conference was convened as it was felt there was a need to re-examine the architectural history of the Georgian villa and to establish the cultural significance of its transformation from a rarefied symbol of an aristocratic appreciation of antiquity to the beginnings of the suburban family house.

There is no doubt of the importance of architectural treatises, especially Andrea Palladio's *I quattro libri dell'architettura* (1570), for the spread of the villa ideal. Many of the chapters address this issue and reveal a complex relationship between design theory and practice. Buildings must meet the needs of occupants. As the social fabric of Britain changed so did the form and location of the villa. As cities grew the villa was drawn away from its rural setting and given an urban context to provide suitable dwellings for the growing ranks of the middle class. This stage in the history of the villa still has resonance today not only in the suburban home but also in the demographic patterns and urban plan of many towns and cities across the British Isles.

This new study re-evaluates two orthodoxies about the architecture of the villa: the typology of the villa, and the rise of the villa tradition in Britain as being equated with the rise of Palladianism. These concepts are interrelated. The identification of a villa type is problematical on several levels. First, the grouping together of buildings under the heading of a type implies a uniformity of form and function that may not be wholly accurate. Stylistic uniformity suggests that there are a limited number of sources for the villa. These are assumed to be classical, if not uniquely Palladian. But villas exist in a variety of architectural styles. Moreover, this adherence to type might also imply a uniformity of planning that is frequently assumed to be symmetrical and hierarchical – again a Palladian concept. Type can also suggest there is no development of form. But there is a distinct difference between the villas of antiquity and those of the Renaissance, just as there is marked variation between those of early eighteenth- and early nineteenth-century Britain. Here, although scale remains compact, changes of plan and the social significance of space betray the democratization of the villa as it moves from being an aristocratic diversion specific to one generation to a family home in continual occupancy.

These variations of form raise the question of the function of the villa which is equally problematical. The ideal of a rural retreat for relaxation and contemplation has endured from antiquity to the present day. But the significant changes in the physical form of the villa, patterns of use and the social and economic circumstances of its occupants must, in some ways, challenge this acknowledged function of the villa. Outside the framework of the villa 'type' it is perhaps at first difficult to see the connection between Chiswick Villa (below) by Lord Burlington and The Grove (opposite) by Decimus Burton in Regent's Park. Chiswick draws on Roman and Italian models and may not initially have been residential. The villa was set in an elaborate, privately owned landscaped garden. The Grove derives largely from ancient Greek religious architecture and was the sole residence of its occupant. The small private grounds constituted part of a large public park. But the idea of these villas as having a connection with nature and offering some kind of shelter from the rigours of urban life is common to both. It is this idea of the villa rather than any prescriptive form that justifies the use of the term in Georgian architecture. The variety of form, location and occupant demonstrated in the texts shows that the villa was to some extent a state of mind in the Georgian period. It is the response of the onlooker, the occupant or indeed the historian that identifies a villa rather than a set of predetermined, if not inflexible, principles of design and function.

The influence of Palladio, especially his *Quattro libri*, is generally seen to dominate the tradition of villa building throughout the period. Several of the chapters clearly demonstrate that the villa is more varied than the Palladian model in both the Renaissance

Lord Burlington, Chiswick Villa, 1723 onwards. Courtesy of English Heritage.

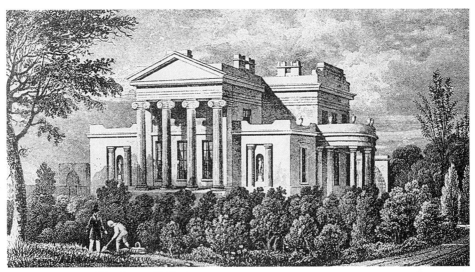

Decimus Burton, The Grove, 1822–4.

and Georgian periods. The rigour of Palladio's illustrations of his own work to some extent stifled the villa tradition in eighteenth-century Britain. Palladio's ordered representations met an intellectual need of the thinkers of the Enlightenment and imposed the need for order and rule in villa designs. This in turn has influenced architectural historians' formulations of the idea of the villa. For many Georgian architects Palladio was merely a stepping stone into the architecture of antiquity, including the villa culture of antique and Renaissance Italy. The great variety of architectural ideas around at the beginning of the eighteenth century is explored to show how alongside Palladio the work of Inigo Jones and English Baroque architects helped shape architectural thinking.

If the dominance of Palladio is challenged then so surely must be the judgement of what makes not only a villa but good architectural practice. This leads to a challenging of the Palladian canon in many of the chapters and a reassessment of what is meant by regionalism in architecture. It is clearly demonstrated that at the beginning of the eighteenth century Palladio and his English follower Inigo Jones were only a part of the rich supply of sources for early Georgian architecture. Even Lord Burlington is demonstrated to have broken away from the rigours of Palladianism to produce his own distinct style of architecture. This puts a very different complexion on the notion of the Palladian villa in eighteenth-century Britain and Burlington's role in the spread of Palladio's architectural ideas. The development of the villa in Ireland, for instance, bears stronger relationship to the architecture of ancient and Renaissance Rome. Many of the chapters challenge further the preconceptions about the architectural and cultural significance of the villa. This is especially the case in the discussion of the villas of Georgian Edinburgh and Glasgow. In both cases the more modest villas are shown to be as much an important part of the villa culture of the city as their grander counterparts. Perhaps most importantly, in these chapters and elsewhere, the villa is discussed in its urban context, which has previously received little attention.

These new lights on the Georgian villa allow it to be examined without the rubrics of classification and value judgement employed by some architectural historians. An early eighteenth-century villa designed on non-Palladian lines is not necessarily second-rate. If it is outside the Thames valley it is not necessarily provincial in the pejorative sense of the word. It might instead challenge the canon of perceived excellence which is often endorsed by architectural historians. This is based on a scholastic preference for Palladianism and London rather than any contemporary evidence for considerations of quality. Moreoever, the texts show the versatility of the villa. The idea of a villa transcends stylistic fashion and social strata, as it meets a need to relate to nature which still exists today.

This book is intended to complement the existing literature on the villa. Most relevant to this subject is Sir John Summerson's fundamental essay 'The Idea of the Villa: The Classical Country House in Eighteenth-century England', *Journal of the Royal Society of Arts*. Pierre de la Ruffinière du Prey takes this further in his consideration of 'Soane's Place in the Genesis of the "Villa"', in *Sir John Soane: The Making of an Architect*. James Ackerman's rich survey of the villa from antiquity to the present day, *The Villa: Form and Ideology of Country Houses* is an essential reference work for the study of the villa. More recently, more specialized studies have been published which give valuable insights into specific areas of Georgian villa culture which are beyond the scope of this volume. The exhibition and catalogue, both by John Harris, *Lord Burlington and his Villa and Garden at Chiswick,* is a thorough study of perhaps Britain's best-known villa. A more unusual but very rewarding approach to the subject is taken in the recently published study by William L. MacDonald and John A. Pinto, *Hadrian's Villa and its Legacy* (Yale, 1995), which examines the influence of Hadrian's villa at Tivoli on subsequent designs and the variety of attitudes and interpretations of it made by architects and visitors from antiquity to the present day. This is a new way of examining the predominance of villa culture in western society, and an important new direction in architectural history.

A book such as this is not possible without the hard work and commitment of others. I must first thank Dr Brian Allen, Director of the Paul Mellon Centre for Studies in British Art, for his encouragement and support from the outset of my idea of staging a large-scale conference on the Georgian villa. The realization of this idea was made possible through the financial support offered by the Paul Mellon Centre and the Monument Trust which funded my post at the Georgian Group. Throughout the two years it took to organize the conference I was working as Education Secretary for the Group. I would like to thank the staff and members of the Executive Committee, and especially the Group's chairman Lord Crathorne, for their support and appreciation of the project. My initial ideas were refined and enhanced by the conference committee: Dr Brian Allen, Julius Bryant, Professor J. Mordaunt Crook and Professor Alistair Rowan, all of whom tolerated rigorous breakfast meetings and considerable demands on their time with good humour and grace. The conference was administered by Kasha Jenkinson and Emma Scrase of the Paul Mellon Centre, whose patience and efficiency was appreciated by everyone. The expertise and professionalism of the speakers came across forcibly over the two days of the conference. I am grateful to all of them for their excellent papers and for their continued support of the project by agreeing to contribute to this volume. Finally, I am greatly indebted to Ken Haynes for his understanding and indulgence of my obsession with the Georgian villa.

PART I

THE LEGACY OF THE RENAISSANCE

1 The Italian Renaissance Villa: The Reconciliation of Nature and Artifice

Deborah Howard

Definition

This chapter attempts to identify those salient characteristics of the Italian Renaissance villa that made the type such a potent model for later European architecture. We shall begin with a simple question of definition: what is a villa? In the Veneto a villa was not a type of *building* but a country estate. In his *Quattro libri* Palladio described the villa as a place where the owner could retire from the city to oversee the agricultural activity, to take physical exercise and, through study and contemplation, to restore the soul, fatigued by the tumult of the city.[1] For Palladio the villa was much more than a house, or even a house with a garden. The owner's residence itself was merely the 'casa di villa', to be designed according to the owner's domestic requirements like a city house: 'si fà come si usa nella città'.[2] The villa was not even simply an economic and administrative unit. Above all, Palladio explains, it was also a cultural centre, conceived on the model of the academies of the ancient philosophers.[3] Paradoxically, in the suburbs of Rome, where the term *vigna* (vineyard) was applied to the type, this was little more than a memory of the estate's earlier productive status.[4]

Classification

In Italy in the fifteenth and sixteenth centuries, various attempts were made to classify villas, in a self-conscious recognition of their remarkable qualities. Palladio divided his own villas according to the identity of the patrons – Vicentines, Venetians and, of course, the ancients.[5] For Alberti, Serlio and Doni, as for Palladio, ownership was also the main criterion, but for these writers the classification depended on a hierarchical gradation, ranging from the villas of the kings and princes to simple peasants' huts.[6] The villas of rulers, remarked Doni, 'are made so beautiful, rich and comfortable that they are no different from the palaces and beautiful structures within the City'.[7] The largest villas, such as the huge Farnese seat at Caprarola, or Federico Gonzaga's suburban retreat known as the Te, outside Mantua, were even called 'palazzi' rather than villas. At the opposite end of the spectrum, the peasants ('the first villa dwellers', according to Doni) 'enjoy the Villa by necessity . . . and there', he adds romantically, 'they labour with joy'.[8]

Villas can also be classified according to function, regardless of the status of the owner, though here, too, a continuous gradation exists between the two polarities – the working farm and the suburban pleasure villa. Palladio recognized the duality between farming and recreation, although he evidently considered that his own villas fulfilled both roles.[9] The exception was the Villa Almerico (see frontispiece), now known as the Rotonda, which he classed as a town house because it had no agrarian role and was so close to the city.[10] One cannot discuss Palladio's villas except in the context of the elaborate programme of land drainage and economic improvement in which his patrons were engaged.[11] On the other hand, all his patrons lived primarily in the city, and spent only short periods on their estates, which were managed by resident factors.

Symbiosis with the city

It is essential to remember that the existence of the villa is fundamentally dependent on the city. Not only is it the pressure of city life (not to mention, in the case of Italy, the summer heat) that creates the need for escape: it is in the city that villa owners establish their status, operating within tightly defined political, religious and cultural networks. In Renaissance Italy, activities such as trade and banking generated capital for investment on the land. Some of the most splendid villas, such as the Sienese banker Agostino Chigi's suburban retreat on the banks of the Tiber, now known as the Farnesina, were financed through the profits of banking[12] (fig. 1.1). The ostentatious display of wealth was a primary function of Chigi's villa. At a legendary banquet on the banks of the Tiber, he is said to have ordered all the silverware to be thrown nonchalantly into the river, only to be fished up with nets after the guests had left.[13] On another occasion he entertained the Pope to dinner in his stables, which were so magnificent that his Holiness was amazed when a curtain was raised to reveal the horses' stalls.[14]

Herrschaftsarchitektur

If the city often generated the wealth that funded the building of country villas, the villa extended the hegemony of the city across subject territory in a quasi-colonial fashion.[15] We should remember that Italy was not united until 1871. In the Renaissance period political boundaries were fluid, and the maintenance of

*Fig. 1.1   Baldassare Peruzzi, Villa Chigi, known as 'La Farnesina', Rome, 1505/8–1511.
Photograph courtesy of Conway Library, Courtauld Institute of Art.*

political control across the countryside depended not only on efficient administrative structure and patterns of investment, but also on the projection of the ruling urban culture across the territory. The landowner was a visible symbol of authority, whether overseeing the grape-picking or hunting in the hills; and in his absence the villa symbolized his dominant role in a permanent, highly conspicuous way. A villa should be *visible*, says Palladio: a site hidden in a valley was not only unhealthy but also lacked 'degnità'.[16] In the Renaissance period villas were more effective extensions of *local* political control than rural abbeys or monasteries, which were more international in their administration. The early Medici, however, recognized that the religious orders could be marshalled to support their own authority, through the patronage of abbeys or monasteries near their country properties, as at Fiesole (fig. 1.2) and Cafaggiolo.[17]

The villa and its public

It is important to remember that, despite the appeal of retreat, villas communicated their values to a *public*, not just to the villa owner and his family. The audience comprised not only the subject population, but also the owner's friends. Hospitality in the country was as ritualized as in the town, even if the myth of informality prevailed. At his Tuscan villa the younger Pliny had enjoyed not having to wear a toga or endure visits from the neighbours.[18] Similarly Falcone, in his book on villa life of 1559, took a childish pleasure in being able to

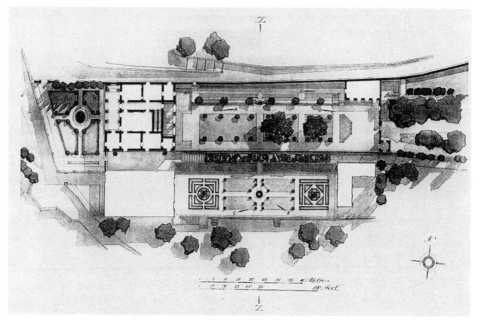

Fig. 1.2 Michelozzo di Bartolomeo, Villa Medici, Fiesole, c. 1458–62, from J.C. Shepherd and G.A. Jellicoe, Italian Gardens of the Renaissance, *London, E. Benn, 1925.*

eat plenty of onions and garlic when in the country, and in not having to wash his hands before meals.[19] The important thing was not the freedom from the rules of etiquette, but rather the right to make one's own rules. Friends were invited, but they were carefully chosen for their intellectual stimulation and enjoyable company. Alberti advised against choosing too accessible a site, so that 'your family life will not be plagued by visits from acquaintances who are passing by'.[20]

The villa was a private realm from which one could exclude unwanted guests by the mere authority of the place, not necessarily by remoteness or elaborate security. In 1552 the Sienese ambassador complained that he could never speak to the Pope, Julius III, because 'His Holiness goes so often to the *vigna*'.[21] Palladio remarked that the academies of the ancients, which he envisaged as the prototype of the modern villa, were enhanced not only by buildings, gardens and fountains, but above all by the *vertù* – the moral and intellectual stature – of those who visited the villa.[22] In other words, the villa provided a setting for a restricted inner circle of friends, where one could create a unique cultural environment, articulated by the physical context of the buildings and gardens, which organized and codified its particular social routines.

Private and public space

Even within the seclusion of the villa there were gradations between private and public space. In a Palladian villa, the central hall was used for receiving business callers, as well as for parties and receptions, whereas the apartment on each side provided gradations of privacy.[23] The most exclusive retreat possible in the Italian princely villa was the *giardino segreto*, usually intended for intimate sexual encounters. For example, the 'appartamento della grotta' at the foot of the garden of the Palazzo Te outside Mantua offered elegant seclusion to Federico Gonzaga and his mistress. A hanging garden – evocatively known as a *giardino pensile*, or garden for contemplation – was hidden from public view, yet offered a view to the world outside. This one-way visibility is exemplified by the walled terrace in Federico da Montefeltro's Palazzo Ducale at Urbino, which enjoys a panorama over the town below and, beyond, to the rolling hills of the Marche. The outlook over the landscape would itself become the object of contemplation. Thus Pius II in his family palace at Pienza described the view over the countryside to Monte Amiata in overtly Plinian terms, as if to give physical reality to a familiar literary trope.[24]

Interior and exterior

The opening up of the domestic space to incorporate the natural world marks a turning point in the design of the villa that deserves closer attention. The earlier Medici villas, Cafaggiolo, Trebbio and Careggi, retain the castellated form of the feudal tower house, however delectable the surroundings.[25] A document of 1468 describes Cafaggiolo as 'hedificato a ghuisa di fortezza'.[26] By now the use of gunpowder artillery had invalidated the defensive function, but the architectural language still signified lineage and feudal authority. By contrast, in Michelozzo's hillside villa at Fiesole, commissioned by Cosimo il Vecchio for his son Giovanni in about 1458, the boundary between inside and outside became blurred.[27] Here a spacious loggia opens on to a hanging garden, which projects the alignment of the villa into the landscape and offers extensive views over Florence below. An area far greater than the sphere of Medici ownership is appropriated into the conceptual realm of the villa, both by the views from within and by the conspicuousness of this innovatory white cubic block on the hillside.

Ambiguity in defining the limits of interior and exterior space becomes more subtle as the period progresses. In the loggia of Chigi's Roman villa, the so-called Farnesina (fig. 1.1), Raphael painted a pergola hung with tapestries in about 1518; and in Peruzzi's own murals in the Sala delle Prospettive upstairs, painted two or three years earlier, views over Rome dissolve the boundary between inside and outside.[28] In his frescoes for the Villa Imperiale at Pesaro, executed *c.* 1529–32, Giovanni Genga, renowned for his skill in depicting country scenery for the stage, opened up the rooms to a fictive world of pergolas and gardens.[29]

Theatre

It is no coincidence that in the sixteenth century villas acquired a theatrical role in the literal as well as symbolic sense. Alvise Cornaro's suburban villa in Padua was not called the Odeo Cornaro by chance. It was here that plays by Cornaro's protégé, the dramatist Ruzante, were performed in the open air, in Paduan dialect.[30] In 1533 the Venetian diarist Marin Sanudo attended a performance that lasted from 9 p.m. to 4 a.m.![31] The gardens of Peruzzi's Farnesina (fig. 1.1), Bramante's Cortile del Belvedere and Genga's Villa Imperiale all had theatrical functions; and Raphael's unfinished Villa Madama was intended to have a Roman-style theatre built into the hillside behind.[32] Not only did theatre add to the menu of recreational delights, but it also extended the limits of the fictional artificiality which characterized villa life.

Patronage

In his penetrating study *The Villa*, Ackerman remarked on the self-conscious modernity that has characterized villa design through the ages.[33] The very nature of the *genre* encouraged architectural invention. The surroundings offered few constraints, and the patrons belonged to a wealthy and culturally ambitious élite. Even a woman could have a decisive role, as we can see from the remarkable case of Eleonora Gonzaga, Duchess of Urbino, who organized the building of the new extensions to the Villa Imperiale as a retreat for her husband, Francesco Maria della Rovere, in the interludes between his military campaigns.[34] As the daughter of another celebrated Renaissance patron, Isabella d'Este, Eleonora freely imposed her wishes over the architect, Girolamo Genga (described by Pietro Bembo as 'a great and rare architect'[35]), as well as over the import of rare plants for the garden.

Each villa was intended as a self-conscious representation of the identity of the patron and his family, artfully manipulated and deliberately innovatory. It is this quest for cultural individuality that makes it difficult to define a consistent theoretical framework. While one can classify the villas, the categories are slippery and exceptions abound. More seriously, we still know very little about the actual way of life in the villa. We know little about how spaces were used, or which members of the household occupied which rooms. Women and children evidently did inhabit villas, especially in summer, but the treatises are silent about where they spent their time.[36] Alberti, a noted misogynist, thought women best kept out of the way, and advised that 'the prattling and noisy hordes of children and housemaids should be kept well away from the men, as should the servants with their uncleanliness'.[37] Agostino Chigi, on the other hand, lived openly with his mistress at the Farnesina, and even accommodated Raphael's mistress too, in an attempt to speed up the artist's work, if we are to believe Vasari.[38]

Sacred allusions in villa design

Although the secular, hedonistic emphasis of villa culture is often highlighted, the role of the villa as a setting in which to seek to understand the mysteries of God's creation should not be overlooked. After all, many of the most celebrated Renaissance villas – such as the Villa Giulia outside Rome or the Villa Rotonda – were created for popes, cardinals or other ecclesiastics. Wittkower's recognition that the use of harmonic proportions, canonic since the time of Vitruvius, could reflect the harmonies of the cosmos is only one aspect of the penetration of religious thought into villa design.[39] Alvise Cornaro wrote of 'santa agricoltura', as if farming were almost an act of worship in itself.[40]

The link between paradise and the villa did not escape the commentators of the time. Cosimo il Vecchio told Ficino that he went to Careggi 'not to cultivate my field but my soul'.[41] Bembo called the villa of Queen Caterina her 'barco', a name derived from the Greek word for paradise.[42] Palladio asserted that, in the idyllic surroundings of their academies, the ancients achieved the most blessed life that one could find 'quà giù' (on this earth).[43] Through the use of the temple front in his own villas from the 1550s onwards, he articulated the sanctity of the internal space, and conveyed the solemnity of the act of entry. With its overt references to the Pantheon (also known at the time as La Rotonda), the Villa Almerico alludes even more directly to its quasi-sacred status, as the villa of a retired cleric.[44]

The first temple front on a Renaissance villa was to be seen at Lorenzo il Magnifico's villa at Poggio a Caiano, begun about 1485 by Giuliano da Sangallo[45] (fig. 1.3). This seminal villa embodied another principle that was to inform Palladio's villa designs, namely its completely symmetrical plan, a feature then more characteristic of sacred spaces than of domestic planning. This early

Fig. 1.3 Giuliano da Sangallo, Villa Medici, Poggio a Caiano, begun c. 1485. Detail of view by Giusto Utens, 1599. Courtesy of Museo di Firenze com'era.

expression of Albertian *concinnitas* was begun just as Lorenzo was having the text of Alberti's treatise on architecture printed, as if Lorenzo hoped to inform a wider audience of the theoretical justification for the design. He had bought the estate in 1474 from his banking rival Giovanni Rucellai, himself the author of an evocative document on the pleasures of villa life.[46]

Text and image

This observation reminds us of the textual dimension that is so crucial to Renaissance villa design. A literary text to accompany a design, as a consciously mimetic recollection of the letters of the younger Pliny, could be produced either by the patron (as in the case of the commentaries of Pius II),[47] or by the architect (as in Raphael's letter describing the Villa Madama).[48] In each case the text became a renowned work of literature in its own right, not merely a factual information sheet. The pastoral idylls of Virgil and Ovid were echoed in the Renaissance in the poetry of Poliziano and Bembo, written in the setting of the villa under the patronage of Lorenzo il Magnifico and Queen Caterina Cornaro respectively.[49]

The transmission of villa designs across wide expanses of time or space operated primarily through books and illustrated texts. Literary texts were the main source of information about the villas of the ancients, with the exception of a few conspicuous archaeological remains such as Hadrian's villa. Pompeii and Herculaneum were, of course, still unexcavated. The lack of physical evidence, paradoxically, stimulated the artistic imagination, particularly through Pliny's emphasis on the villa's effect on all five senses, rather than merely on the eye. (Curiously, Pliny's delight in seaside views had little appeal to the Renaissance – the Villa Imperiale, for example, lies tantalizingly close to the sea, yet sits firmly on the landward side of the hill.) And it was through the medium of text (though in this case illustrated books), that the Italian villa was transmitted to England. By an accident of history, Serlio's volume on domestic architecture remained in manuscript until our own times;[50] otherwise the history of the English villa might have taken a very different course. It was the very individuality of the villa that was lost in Palladio's standardized, idealized presentation. The polite conformity of the English Palladian version seems far removed from the infinitely varied range of Palladio's buildings themselves.

Nature and artifice

As we have seen, the villa offered exceptional scope for architectural virtuosity and experiment. Design was ostensibly rooted in the laws of nature, but its manipulation was highly artificial and contrived. Through artifice, nature could be recreated in an idealized and imaginative way, in order to provide protection from the elements and control over the surroundings. In antiquity, Tacitus had remarked of the Golden House, newly excavated in the early sixteenth century, that 'with their cunning and impudent artificialities, Nero's architects and contractors had outbid nature'.[51]

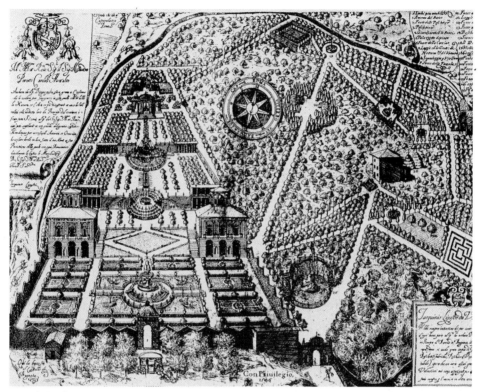

Fig. 1.4 Giacomo Barozzi, il Vignola (attrib.), Villa Lante, Bagnaia, begun 1568. Engraving by Tarquinio Ligustri, 1596. Courtesy of the Bibliothèque Nationale, Paris.

In its formal purity the house could itself become a geometrical abstraction, a quality we noticed in the Medici villa at Fiesole. It is this quality of the Renaissance villa that fascinated modernist critics, from Rudolf Wittkower to Colin Rowe.[52] Although a continuum between wild nature and the interior of the house may be established, the architectural formality of the core of the house and the technically daring terracing of the hillside at Fiesole assert man's control over nature. When the humanist Filelfo went to visit Giovanni de' Medici at Fiesole in 1455, he found him 'rusticating, absorbed in his building'.[53] It was the house rather than the countryside that preoccupied him.

Quasi-natural elements – the grottoes and wildernesses in the gardens, and the use of rusticated stonework in the buildings – reflected the growing understanding of the natural world.[54] In the confidence of its comprehension, nature could be harnessed to surprise, to perplex or to shock. The new hydraulic virtuosity of the sixteenth century, in particular, fostered the ostentatious waterworks of the Mannerist garden that excited visitors such as Montaigne.[55] The humanist Claudio Tolomei remarked of such fountains in 1543 that 'one cannot distinguish whether they are the work of art or of nature'.[56] Significantly, engraved views of the Villa d'Este or the Villa Lante at Bagnaia (fig. 1.4) give prominence to the garden at the expense of the house.[57] Indeed, the villa at

Bagnaia is reduced to two little pavilions on either side of the garden. Palladio remarked that the gardens and orchards, not the house – that is, the realm of nature – were the *anima* or soul of the villa.[58] A surprising number of villas have gardens at the heart of the design, with two separate buildings at either side. One could cite not only Bagnaia, but also Palladio's perplexing Villa la Ripeta,[59] or the villa of the Venetian Grimani family in Rome,[60] or the Cornaro Villa on the island of Murano, consisting of two buildings a quarter of a mile apart.[61] Two villas offered the flexibility of summer and winter quarters, male and female orbits or apartments for two brothers, as in Palladio's Villa Thiene at Quinto.[62]

Conclusion

This chapter has explored the inherently contradictory nature of Renaissance villa culture and its symbiosis with the city. Its basis lies in the reconciliation of opposites – public and private, formality and informality, work and play, town and country, sacred and profane, inside and outside, truth and fiction, modernity and nostalgia, nature and artifice. It is perhaps the artistic and cultural freedom that best characterizes the development of the Italian villa from the mid-fifteenth century onwards. An inscription in the Sacro Bosco at Bomarzo records that the garden 'resembles only itself and nothing else'.[63] The Renaissance villa in Italy was an affirmation of cultural individuality, not a typology governed by the rules of politeness and architectural canons.

PART II

CONTEMPORARY ATTITUDES TO THE GEORGIAN VILLA

2 Villa Views and the Uninvited Audience

Julius Bryant

A current concern among scholars of eighteenth-century domestic architecture, particularly villas, is the reconstruction of period perceptions. We are assured that owners and their educated guests could read buildings like books, not only in terms of I-Spy sources and spot the mathematical proportions, but in unravelling the iconography that links classical motifs into specific messages. Beyond the association between aesthetic and moral principles that underpins the Platonic philosophy of connoisseurship lies a political dimension that could be specific, topical and concealed.

Chiswick House has attracted the greatest debate as an early example of speaking architecture. To James Ackerman, for example, 'Burlington and his associates were less interested in taste or in controlling the art world than in political, moral and aesthetic principles that could be expressed through buildings and landscape designs'.[1] To Jane Clark, Chiswick is 'a symbolic miniature palace, waiting for the King who never came: a temple to the restoration of Augustus in the form of the House of Stuart'.[2] To David Solkin, Richard Wilson's view of the Thames at Marble Hill House is a translation of Alexander Pope's vision of Twickenham: 'Pope and his later eighteenth century admirers dressed Twickenham in the literary garb of Roman antiquity . . . as a new Parnassus, the home of the Muses, as an English Arcadia . . . . Wilson's picture mediated these same values for the identical public . . . . Marble Hill House could claim kinship to both the great Palladio himself and the architectural heritage of ancient Rome.'[3]

Despite modern reconstructions of the ideological framework in which to view villas, how far did visitors actually think in terms of Horace's Sabine farm, the letters of Pliny the younger or Virgil's *Eclogues* and *Georgics*, let alone Palladio,

Scamozzi and the use of the architectural orders? If 'the first Palladian villas . . . were vehicles for stating a point of view'[4] how far did that point get across? These may have been the creative context for the owner, his architect and their immediate circle. But the original meaning of the building lies as much in its place in the popular imagination of its time, in how it was perceived by visitors, be they guests or the uninvited audience of passers-by, and the artists and engravers who catered for the onlooker market.

In pursuing the intellectual context of the owners, will we really come to know why most people looked at villas, who they were or what they thought about? It seems unlikely that villa viewing was predominantly a sport of the well educated. There were uninvited guests, who brought their own concerns, and villas evoked ideas and associations for them without any reference to the designer and his sources of inspiration. To understand their responses fully, we need to know who let them in, how far they got and who got left outside. We need to explore the extent to which their responses to the same villa and garden changed over generations, and hence how the villa's identity changed with time. It is debatable to what extent and end villas and their gardens were conceived, positioned and designed for display to this more general and diverse public.

Even more so than country houses, villas were caught up in the jostling of middle and upper social classes coming to call, and in the resultant redefinition of protocol. From about 1700 house viewing involved a shift in social convention from the antiquarian or virtuosi travellers being admitted by the owner as unexpected guests, to the establishment, largely in the first half of the nineteenth century, of routine opening times and income-earning guided tours by housekeepers and butlers. These access arrangements became formalized in response to demand from a greater and wider public for admittance, for similar hospitality and even for unintended souvenirs. The rise of architectural connoisseur-ship in the eighteenth century and the related spread of house viewing can be linked to the urge to develop and demonstrate one's 'taste' in an age when new wealth and titles left fewer means of indicating one's social rank.[5]

Villas were particularly affected by these changes on account of their relative ease of access to a wider public than country houses. Villas were closer to population centres and were built closer to streets and rivers, partly as a consequence of not being in the midst of vast estates, but also to fulfil their purpose of being built for show. Villas were also the focus of a mix in social outlook from within, on the part of the owners, for they were often self-made individuals themselves. The capital's villas were at the forefront of changes in visitor access arrangements, in rewriting the unwritten codes of conduct for house viewing, their greater numbers of visitors placing them at the forefront of changes in tourism.

In this chapter an eighteenth-century villa is regarded not as an architectural type defined primarily by its plan, elevation, ornament and descendance from Inigo Jones's Queen's House. Rather, a villa is defined by its use, which usually determined the primary considerations: location and scale. Its characteristic function is as an occasional brief retreat from the demands of public and business life. Not a principal residence, it is neither a family seat nor the primary source of income through farming. Planned for pleasure, compact and convenient, it may also be a place of secrecy, for private meetings to satisfy political or sexual ambitions or for matchmakers to sew up their marital schemes. With these uses, the villa can be modest in scale, with no vast wings for family or servants, but with a smart reception suite leading to rooms for the secluded study of books, for gossip or informal breakfasts, plus a stately 'great room' for elegant receptions for people of influence. The characteristic contents are not ancestral portraits and heirloom furniture such as old courtiers' perquisites, but the most fashionable pieces, ideally unique and designed for the great room as proof of the patron's taste.

How can we reach back into the past and identify the more popular alternative period responses to villas, to the attitudes that attracted viewers less familiar with the vocabulary of architectural connoisseurship and the classics? The main resource supporting this chapter is illustrative topographical engravings. The quantity of engravings of villas, particularly from periodicals and tour books, is evidence of their popularity among sightseers. The difference in audience and attitudes may be illustrated by comparing Richard Wilson's view of the Thames at Twickenham of 1762 (fig. 2.1) and the engraving published after Augustin Heckell's drawing in 1749 (fig. 2.2), and its many pirated derivatives. The contrast is not simply between two artistic traditions, of Claudian landscape

Fig. 2.1 Richard Wilson, The Thames near Marble Hill, Twickenham, *c. 1762. Marble Hill House. Courtesy of English Heritage.*

painting and topographical recording (Heckell's view is also idealized, in concealing the tenant farms that helped to fund the fallen mistress's retreat). The answer lies beyond the artistic frame of reference in different ways of looking at the same scene, and in catering for different viewers.

As a more overtly commercial art form, illustrative topographical engravings have, arguably, some advantage over the genre of painted house portraiture as evidence of period attitudes, being relatively less subject to the whims of single patrons or the personal preoccupations of artists. The relative anonymity of illustrative engravings, acquired for their subject matter rather than as the work of a particular artist, makes them potentially a more direct mirror of their market's interests. Engravings also have the distinct advantage over house portraiture in that they were often published with some accompanying text (in addition to the printed titles) from which they have become divorced. Tracing engraved views back to where they first appeared in periodicals, tour books, county histories and elsewhere, reveals text, and general context, as tangible evidence of the growing audiences for villa viewing, their responses and rival diversions.

Views of three London villas can serve as case studies, namely Alexander Pope's villa, Marble Hill and Kenwood. Having identified the variety of viewers and their ways of responding to these villas in the eighteenth and early nineteenth centuries this chapter will end by looking in this light at Jacques Rigaud's unengraved views of Chiswick. These four villas were, with Strawberry Hill, the most fashionable, accessible and most viewed and engraved villas of all.

The most celebrated home of an individual in eighteenth-century Britain was Pope's Twickenham villa, which prompted over thirty different views by 1811[6]

Fig. 2.2 James Mason after Augustin Heckell, The Countess of Suffolk's House near Twickenham, *1749, engraving. Marble Hill House. Courtesy of English Heritage.*

Fig. 2.3 After Augustin Heckell, Pope's Villa, *c. 1750, watercolour. Guildhall Library, City of London. Heckell's view of Pope's villa was first published in 1749.*

(fig. 2.3). By 1720 it had been remodelled by James Gibbs, and with its gardens and grotto the villa was promoted through Pope's own writings. By 1736 arrangements were in place for opening the house and garden to visitors by servants. The first guidebook appeared in 1746, two years after the poet's death. Pope certainly reinforced through his writings the classical ideal of his villa as a place for pastoral retirement and promoted it as representing an alternative to those great country houses (such as Houghton and Blenheim) which were based on mercantile, military and political success. But judging from the engravings and their inscriptions, interest was more in the home of a genius and man of fame.

In 1744, on Pope's death, the villa was purchased by a brother of the 4th Earl of Chesterfield and Heckell's view, published in 1749, was a popular subject for copying in watercolour.[7] The previous year the villa had appeared as the frontispiece to the *Newcastle General Magazine* and in 1760 it featured in a series of engravings in the *Royal Magazine* on houses in and near London, published in response to requests from subscribers. By 1807 demands to view Pope's villa had become so frequent and irritating to the owner, Lady Howe, that she had it torn down – possibly the worst case of visitor wear and tear! This did not stop J.M.W. Turner from painting in the following year his *View of Pope's Villa at Twickenham During its Dilapidation* (Walter Morrison Settlement) when it served as a symbol of the transience of genius and fame. Views continued to be produced when there was nothing to see but a new house, the arch of Pope's grotto and a descendant of the poet's willow tree. Clearly, something less tangible than the architecture of James Gibbs remained as the prevailing attraction.

Horace Walpole provides a neighbour's perspective on Pope's villa. The view from the terrace of Strawberry Hill that he commissioned from William Pars was engraved in *A Description of the Villa of Mr Horace Walpole*, published in 1784. Walpole disliked the villa as Pope had known it, and hung in his Green Closet Samuel Scott's view of it after the next owner had removed Gibbs's portico and added wings. He remarked to Horace Mann of Sir William Stanhope's improvements, that Pope's villa was 'so small and bad, one could not avoid pardoning his hollowing out that fragment of the rock Parnassus into habitable chambers'.[8] This concern over practical comforts and lifestyle in modish new villas echoes the famous early criticisms of Chiswick House made by Lord Hervey and Lord Chesterfield. Walpole is more concerned about Stanhope's alterations to Pope's garden. There is even a sense of the heritage landscape conservationist about his indignant response to the clearance across the river: 'some monuments of our predecessors ought to be sacred . . . if the muses wanted to tie up their garters, there is not a nook to do it in without being seen'.[9]

Walpole established increasingly strict controls on his housekeeper to limit access to his own villa. Visitors had to produce initially a written note, then from 1774 a signed and dated printed ticket, and by 1784 a printed page of rules annotated at the bottom with the name, date of visit and number of visitors to be admitted. His rules were necessary, they state, 'as the villa is situated so near to London and in so populous a neighbourhood'.

No more than four people could enter at once and 'They that would have tickets are desirous not to bring children.'[10] One reason for the excessive number of visitors which prompted the introduction of these rules was probably the income gained by his housekeeper Margaret from giving guided tours. Her earnings prompted Walpole to write in 1783, the year before, 'that I have a mind to marry her and so repay myself that way for what I have flung away to make my house quite uncomfortable to me'.[11]

This reality of Twickenham as a popular area for sightseers is of course not conveyed by ideal images such as Richard Wilson's arcadian view of the Thames near Marble Hill. When Marble Hill first makes its appearance as a published engraving, in the third volume of *Vitruvius Britannicus* in 1725, before being built, it is as an anonymous design labelled simply 'A house in Twitnam'.[12] Heckell's view published in 1749, with its barges and dray horses, seems by comparison like a souvenir of the whole area. Heckell's publisher's catalogue, *Perspective Views in and about London*, describes 'a collection of pleasant views of the most noted places in London and the adjacent parts drawn in Perspective'. It boasts how they are held 'not only in esteem for furniture in frames and glasses, but are much used in proper colours without frames, for viewing in the Diagonal Mirror, in which method of looking at them, they appear with surprising beauty, and in size but little inferior to the real places'.[13] Villas could be suitable subjects for amateur artists to copy or to colour in, and then view through some form of camera lucida.

Seven years later some idea of who would do such a thing can be found in Henrietta Pye's *Short Account of the Principal Seats in and about Twickenham*. Miss Pye writes in her introduction 'I have observed, that ladies in general, visit those places, as our young gentlemen do foreign parts, without answering any other end, than barely saying they have been there. . . . These little excursions being commonly the only travel permitted to our sex, & the only way we have of becoming at all acquainted with the Progress of Arts, I thought it might not be improper, to throw together on paper, such remarks as occurred to me.'[14] Villa viewing may not be a feminist issue as yet, but here is tangible evidence of the pastime as a kind of stuck-at-home sisters' Grand Tour, with the difference being that these young women see the latest fashionable fruits of 'the Progress of Arts'.

Such a view of Marble Hill, both in life and reproduction, could have had a more overtly political dimension. Following the Countess of Suffolk's fall from favour as the mistress of King George II and her early retirement to Marble Hill in 1734, her renown as a focus for opponents of the first minister Sir Robert Walpole endowed the villa with more specific connotations. Alexander Pope lamented 'there is a greater court now at Marble Hill than at Kensington and God knows where it will end'.[15] The display of a coloured and framed print of the disgraced royal mistress's villa could thus have implied one's opposition to Walpole, just as Pepys in 1669 had commissioned Danckerts to paint 'the four houses of the King' for his lodgings in the Navy Office to demonstrate his loyalty to his employer.[16]

The main alternative form of villa engraving to the perspective view suitable for colouring and framing was the book illustration. *A New Display of the Beauties of England*, published in 1773, is an early pocket-sized tour book, and includes views of Marble Hill and Kenwood. The text confirms the pastime of viewing villas to sketch. It boasts 'a greater number of Noblemen's and Gentlemen's seats . . . than can be met with in any other publication', and seeks to provide 'an agreeable companion for those who may occasionally visit different parts of England, in order to take a view of the many fine palaces and seats with which this Kingdom abounds'.[17] The other source is periodicals, such as the *Gentleman's Magazine* which in 1794 referred to Mrs Howard's house in terms of its literary associations as 'the celebrated and beautiful villa of Marble Hill, a classic spot, immortalized by Pope and Swift'.[18]

The appeal of villa viewing to amateur landscape painters is one market which seems to have prompted Britton and Brayley's *Beauties of England and Wales* of which the Middlesex volume of 1815 includes views of Marble Hill and Kenwood, both nestling cosily between clouds and foliage. Twickenham was of course the home of generations of artists, and the nursery of English naturalism. However, the traditional literary and historical associations prompted by the sight of Marble Hill were eclipsed in the popular imagination not by the preoccupations of landscape painters, but by a chapter in Walter Scott's *Heart of Midlothian*, published in 1818. In the crucial scene in this historical novel Jeanie Deans pleads with Queen Caroline for the life of her half-sister before Mrs Howard, as a lady-in-waiting, intervenes. The avenue of elms was long mistakenly sought out at Marble Hill by onlookers instead of in Richmond Park, as *The Builder* magazine pointed out in 1890, even though 'thousands have scanned curiously from the deck of a river steamer'.[19]

Scott's mix of historical fiction and real places kindled the imagination of tourists keen to bring houses back to life. They did not need Scott's help to create another historical legend for Marble Hill. According to James Thorne's *Environs of London* of 1876 'it was rented by Mrs Fitzherbert whose irregular marriage ceremony with the Prince of Wales, afterwards George IV, it has been said was performed here'.[20] The publication of Mrs Howard's letters in 1824 was one response to this historical attitude behind villa viewing, as was the reissue of engravings after Heckell, Joli and others.[21] The introduction by Queen Victoria of free admission to Hampton Court in 1838 (following the death of the housekeeper who had made her living from charging) further increased tourism along this stretch of the Thames and a larger market prompted more basic pocket books. Arthur Freeling's *Picturesque Excursions* of 1839, for example, illustrates Marble Hill not as anything to do with Palladian architecture, but as a house 'built by Lady Suffolk, the mistress of George II. Here Swift, Pope, Gay and many others of the wits and literati of their day often met.'[22] This suggests how literacy had spread well into the middle classes, encouraging Sunday tourism. It also raises the question of the relative literacy of today's villa viewers and the extent to which their predominantly architectural response is a consequence of the absence from our general education of the poets of the Augustan age and of Walter Scott.

The major association of villas at the end of the nineteenth century was as survivors against the sprawl of suburban London. At Marble Hill, Chiswick and Kenwood it was the estates rather than the architecture that really saved them, thanks to the faith in fresh air and exercise as moral forces to reduce political unrest and drunkenness. In 1901, while the Cunard family were busy felling trees and laying roads and drains across the 66.5 acres of Marble Hill that Pope and Bridgeman had designed, a local patron cursed 'the demon builder . . . with his exhibition of latter-day villadom'.[23] Marble Hill Park was established the following year, with the house serving as a footballers' changing room, park keeper's flat and café.

Turning to Kenwood as a third case study, we enter a very different part of outer London. Hampstead Heath was something one gazed across rather than through when admiring the shining capital. This was not 'classic ground' like Twickenham, and not the kind of neighbourhood of elegant villas where young women might admire, from the safety of some ferry, the progress of the arts. In 1714 an observer wrote of Hampstead 'Its nearness to London brings so many loose women in vampt-up old Cloaths to catch the City Apprentices, that modest Company are ashamed to appear here.'[24] Even so, successful lawyers chose to dwell in the clean air of Highgate and Hampstead, travelling by road to the Inns of Court and Westminster Hall. The early house views are paintings giving a proprietorial view, presumably for hanging in their owner's town houses. Kenwood first appears in the background of Ramsey's view of Heath House of 1755 (private collection),[25] the year after Kenwood was acquired by Alexander Pope's protégé, the young Attorney General, William Murray. But its inclusion depends on artistic licence and reinforces the privacy of this prospect, for it would only be visible to guests enjoying the panorama from the leads of the wing to Heath House.

Likewise in the same year, John Wootton's view from the terrace at Kenwood (private collection)[26] suggests an area to look over, or rather, that seems to be part of an estate leading all the way to St Paul's Cathedral. Sketches from the following two years, 1756 and 1757, by Murray's friend Mrs Delany, are the exceptions that underline the rule.[27] Whereas the villas of fashionable Twickenham were well engraved by this time, the public did not view Kenwood, it seems, until Robert Adam wanted them to.

The earliest known engraving relating to Kenwood is a political caricature entitled the *Excursion to Caen Wood* published in the *Oxford Magazine* of 1771 (fig. 2.4). Even then the image may have been some twenty years old. It reveals an awareness of the villa as a place of secrecy and intrigue as Murray rides with the Princess Augusta on a broomstick propelled by demons. It would have been about this time that Jeremy Bentham, a young lawyer at Lincoln's Inn, studied his hero in action at the Court of King's Bench as the self-made 1st Earl of Mansfield and Lord Chief Justice. Bentham later recalled how 'He kept, as a great treasure, a picture of him, and frequently went to Caen Wood, as a lover to the shrine of his mistress, in the hope that chance might throw him his way.'[28] This frame of mind when admiring a villa is not so far removed from the hopes of today's connoisseurs on the Hollywood homes tour bus.

Presumably Bentham was not alone in his excursions to Kenwood, but it is not until Adam's remodelling of the south front that an engraving appears in *A New*

Fig. 2.4 *Anon*, The Excursion to Cain Wood, *engraving, published in the* Oxford Magazine *in 1771. Iveagh Bequest, Kenwood. Courtesy of English Heritage.*

Display of the Beauties of England, a traveller's pocket companion to gentlemen's seats, published in 1773. Adam's second part of volume one of his collected works, devoted to Kenwood, appeared in 1774. Adam did not publish the country houses by which he is more often illustrated today, such as Kedleston, Osterley or Newby, and one reason for his preference may have been the greater prominence of Kenwood as the London villa of the Lord Chief Justice. If so, then one wonders to what extent this characteristic visibility of a London villa (compared to a country house) could influence an ambitious young architect in his designs, as he built to advertise.

Kenwood was only really visible from the south, from high ground across a high wall along Millfield Lane, as it appears in George Robertson's view of 1780, published by Boydell in 1781 in a set of *Six Views of Gentlemen's Seats near London* (fig. 2.5). The artistic gentlemen sketching in the foreground give no hint of the fact that in the same year, 1780, the Lord Chief Justice's town house was looted and gutted by fire by the Gordon Rioters who then marched to Kenwood. Again, the celebrity of the resident and his political connections cannot have been absent from the minds of these picturesque villa viewers.

A view of the north front facing Hampstead Lane, after a sketch by Conrad

Fig. 2.5 Wilson Lowry after George Robertson, A View of Kenwood, the Seat of the Earl of Mansfield, *1781, engraving. Iveagh Bequest, Kenwood. Courtesy of English Heritage.*

Fig. 2.6 James Heath after Conrad Metz, North Front of Caen Wood, *1788, engraving, published in* The Copper Plate Magazine *and in* The British Magazine and Review. *Iveagh Bequest, Kenwood. Courtesy of English Heritage.*

Metz, appeared in the *British Magazine and Review* in 1782 (fig. 2.6), but the raised viewpoint from Prospect Hill and the absence of gates suggests an openness that is belied by a less elegant contemporary view that gives the emphatic portico a very different character.[29] An engraving published by Robert Sayer in 1792 similarly emphasizes the high, solid wall of this conspicuous, yet very private house. The following year Joseph Farington recorded in his diary 'strange additions' being made to the house, seen from the raised vantage point of his horse as he took a morning's ride from London around Hampstead and Highgate.[30]

Unlike Pope's villa or Marble Hill, Kenwood was not situated where ladies might sketch in safety or seek inspiration to colour in engravings for viewing in the 'diagonal mirror'. Like Marble Hill, Kenwood's architecture was admired but the fame of its resident and the political associations seem to have been more prominent. Diaries and correspondence from the 1770s record servants showing visitors around the house, but it is the gardens that hold the greater appeal, the more so in the following century after the improvements made according to Humphry Repton's designs. J.C. Loudon in his *Suburban Gardener, and Villa Companion* of 1838 reminds us of another category of uninvited visitors. Lamenting that the estate was not then shown to strangers, he comforts his readers with the thought that 'Gardeners, however, can always visit gardeners.'[31]

As with Marble Hill, the historical novel added to this awareness of Kenwood, and three years after Loudon's publication there appeared Dickens's *Barnaby Rudge* in which Kenwood narrowly escapes destruction during the Gordon Riots. The looting and burning of the Lord Chief Justice's town house was later illustrated at the Royal Academy of 1879 by Seymour Lucas and published in the *Art Journal* of 1887. As at Marble Hill, in the final years of Kenwood as a private residence it is valued as a safe haven for wildlife from the encroachment of suburban sprawl, but also as a haven from the cockney pleasure ground of ''Appy 'Ampstead' that followed the railway's arrival in 1860. Nevertheless, like Marble Hill, Kenwood found itself being parcelled up for developers until it was saved primarily to provide 'lungs for London'.

To summarize the evidence from these case studies, villa viewers did not confine their responses to the intellectual realms of architectural connoisseurship or the rural ideology evoked by classical writers. These may have been the primary concerns of owners and their architects, but villas attracted a wider audience whose diverse responses reflect a variety of values, motivations and attitudes. Compared to country houses, the proximity of villas to the urban population of the capital, and their relative visibility from public rights of way, ensured less select uninvited viewers. In addition to the dedicated virtuosi and travellers in pursuit of the picturesque, there came, as today, day trippers including students and servants seeking out the latest novelty in fashionable design, celebrity homes, settings from historical novels, havens from suburban sprawl and rallying points for political (and even conservationist) protest. Villa viewing is coloured by these other preoccupations of the city dweller.

An ambitious architect could make a villa that not only pleased his patrons but

Fig. 2.7 Jacques Rigaud, Chiswick View from in front of the Burlington Lane Gate at the Rond-point with Obelisk, *1733, watercolour. Courtesy of the Trustees of the Chatsworth Settlement.*

played to the crowd, knowing that the growth of the market for engravings would multiply interest. The major precedent for Adam's self-publicity stunt at Kenwood may be Burlington's use of Chiswick. The wealth of engravings of Chiswick nearly included the most vivid and evocative images of villa viewers, namely Jacques Rigaud's set of eight drawings of Chiswick of 1733–4 (fig. 2.7) which were never published. John Harris questions the abundance of human activity, and suggests that we are looking at standard staffage, presumably lifted from a copy-book, as in one of Watteau's *fêtes galantes*.[32] The quantity of figures – one image contains forty – warrants caution, but these celebrations of the house and gardens cannot have sprung from the artist's imagination alone.

Against the likelihood of their validity is the quantity of topographical inaccuracies and the fact that, after Rigaud claimed a higher fee, Burlington, according to George Vertue 'sent him away like a lying ras..l'.[33] This is also a very different world from the Chiswick painted by Pieter Andreas Rysbrack and George Lambert with their more solitary meandering promenaders (whose elegant seclusion may be equally exaggerated) and more so from the Chiswick in which Kent sketches himself and his dog peeing, and happy bunnies dancing by moonlight. Nevertheless Rigaud, as an established draughtsman for the engraving market, could have followed his successful formula and peopled his views with potential customers.

There is ample evidence to suggest that Chiswick was the most visited London villa. In 1732 Alexander Pope wrote to Burlington of the 'privilege your lordship allows me of bringing it admirers'.[34] But on 13 November 1733 (the year of Rigaud's commission) a newspaper satirized the unusual practice of charging entry to Chiswick.[35] Rocque's map of Chiswick (published three years later) is the visual equivalent of a gardens guidebook, with its border of thirteen postcard-like views, while the description of Chiswick in the 1738 edition of Daniel Defoe's *Tour through . . . Great Britain* must have added to the curiosity prompted by Pope's *Epistle to Lord Burlington on Taste* of 1731. As John Harris points out, the 1741/2 catalogue of the Chiswick library contains detailed directions for those 'not acquainted with this library', implying its use by strangers. Horace Walpole's notes from his visit in 1760 seem to echo a guided tour[36] and in 1761, Dodsley's *Environs of London* provided a room-by-room guide to 168 paintings in the villa.

Texts accompanying illustrative engravings of Chiswick from later in the same century complain of tickets and rules, and one even assumes the fosse before the Orangery trees to have been built 'to prevent their being injured by the Company admitted to walk in the Gardens'.[37] The international list of royalty, politicians and writers who visited Chiswick is lengthy and where such celebrities went, the villa viewers followed. Visual evidence of early tourism includes the sheer quantity of railings immediately surrounding the villa (in the engravings by Rocque and Donowell, and in Rigaud's drawings) which seem far too sturdy to keep out just the duck, turkey and guinea fowl visible in Rysbrack's paintings. Indeed, Burlington's reclusive life at his Yorkshire seat, Londesborough, may have been partly prompted by the realization that he had built his ideal villa too near to town to avoid uninvited company.

It is tempting to draw a parallel between Chiswick in 1733 (the year of Rigaud's commission and the admission charge) and Vauxhall Gardens, which reopened under Jonathan Tyers's management the previous year. Tyers only introduced a charge at the gate in 1736, to keep out 'the inferior sort' after crowds on the twelve-acre site proved too dense, a demand which led to the opening of Ranelagh Gardens in 1742.[38] In the interim, Chiswick could have given some of Tyers's customers somewhere else to go, particularly in the daytime. This idea of Chiswick as a themed pleasure garden may not be so far fetched, whether Burlington intended it or not. One was Italianate Palladian, the other French Rococo; one was presided over by statues of Burlington's architectural heroes Palladio and Inigo Jones, the other by a statue of Burlington's musician Handel, and both could be identified with opposition to Sir Robert Walpole's government.

Perhaps the best evidence for believing Rigaud provided the nearest thing to portraits of early villa tourists is close comparison with figures in other works by Rigaud. In his views of Stowe (for which he was brought to England by Charles Bridgeman in February 1733) the types may be similar but there are no direct models for the Chiswick crowds. In his views of Versailles the social reportage of courtiers in their finery seems worthy of *Life* magazine, and is totally different from his visual account of company at Chiswick.

In the absence of evidence to the contrary, the intellect may at least indulge in the thought that Rigaud is introducing us to the ancestors of today's villa visitors. For they are all here – from the connoisseurs to the courting couples, from families on a day out to local dog walkers. We may never get inside their minds and see villas afresh through their eyes. But in Rigaud's views more than any others, we are reminded how villa gardens were open to visitors. Indeed, we can almost sit down next to them, on one of the many comfortably cushioned garden seats he records, and simply turn and ask, 'what do you think of the place?'

Far from being the preserve of residents and their educated guests, villa viewing was a popular recreation, involving a web of ideas, associations and attitudes that reached beyond architectural connoisseurship and sophisticated political allusion. The early tourists' reasons for coming and their ways of responding to villas may be less intellectual, but they are no less valid a dimension of the villa phenomenon.

3 Jane Austen's Aversion to Villas

Philippa Tristram

Jane Austen rarely describes houses. Furthermore, she almost never mentions villas. A discussion of Jane Austen and the villa therefore requires an explanation.

Houses are rarely described in fiction before the time of Dickens for several reasons. Georgian novelists do not usually take their readers into houses which would be unfamiliar to the 'visiting card classes'; Victorian novelists drop in at every social level. In *Bleak House* we range from the great house, Chesney Wold, to the slums of Tom-all-Alone's and the shacks of the brickmakers. In *Emma*, characters visit the poor, but we do not. Even when Harriet calls on Robert Martin's sisters in his pleasant farm, the reader waits with Emma at the gate. Dickens, given the architectural variations of his day, does not assume that readers will even know what well-bred houses look like. Jane Austen, who (like Shaftesbury) assumed a consensus both classical and moral, makes the courteous assumption that they will. In her novels, a phrase like 'modern built' does not mean 'new built' but 'Georgian'; a word like 'taste' speaks for itself, requiring no more definition than the designation 'gentleman'. The Gothic novel, which reached its apotheosis in Jane Austen's time, is an exception because the English are not supposed to be familiar with the curious amenities of foreign castles – like dungeons, secret passages and oubliettes. Antiquity in itself is unfamiliar. For that reason, Jane Austen has more to say about old houses, like Elizabethan Sotherton or Northanger Abbey. But the majority of houses in her novels are 'modern-built'; that is, Georgian or Classical in style. To detail their appearance and contents would be bad manners, both in life and art. 'Your descriptions are often more minute than will be liked,' she warns her niece Anna, one of four aspiring novelists in the next Austen generation.[1] Similarly, in *Pride and Prejudice*, Mr Collins displays bad manners in his parsonage at Hunsford, when he draws to Elizabeth's attention 'every article of furniture . . . from the sideboard to the fender', and points out every prospect from his garden 'with a minuteness which left beauty entirely behind'.[2]

But although Jane Austen does not describe most of her houses, it does not follow that they are unimportant. As Chapman comments in the context of her letters, she has the ability to describe without description: Miss Beaty, for example, 'is good-humour itself, & does not seem much besides'.[3] Houses have almost as much presence as characters in her fiction, and in both cases a great deal which she does not make explicit may be condensed into a single word or phrase. Not only are two of her six novels – *Northanger Abbey* and *Mansfield Park* – named from houses, but for readers her characters are inseparable from their domestic context. Charlotte Brontë's reaction to *Pride and Prejudice*, though negative, is nonetheless a good example. 'No fresh air, no blue hill, no bonnie beck,' she complained to Lewes. 'I should hardly like to live with her ladies and gentlemen in their elegant but confined houses.'[4] Blue hills and bonnie becks are uncommon in Hertfordshire, and Jane Austen, as her letters show, was almost obsessively accurate in matters of fact. Fresh air there is – even in the Brontë novels, it is hard to think of any character who walks as often as Elizabeth. But while Charlotte Brontë does not seem to have inhaled all that fresh air, she has a very clear impression of those houses – 'elegant but confined' – although Longbourne and Netherfield, where readers spend most of their time, are never formally described.

Jane Austen is even more reticent when it comes to villas. In all her published writing, she employs the word just twice: once in *Northanger Abbey* and once in her juvenilia. Yet the houses in her novels are often set in places where one would expect some villas. Emma's Highbury, for example, is in Surrey, sixteen miles from London, nine from Richmond. Frank Churchill nips up to London, ostensibly to have his hair cut, actually to order a piano. Nonetheless, Highbury does not boast a villa. Neither does Sanditon – the resort development between Hastings and Eastbourne which features in Jane Austen's last, unfinished novel – although in other respects Sanditon is very modish with its terrace, new seaside houses, cottages *ornées* and plans for a crescent.

There are, however, quite a number of houses in her novels which her contemporaries would have described as villas. For example, in 1803 Richard Elsam distinguishes between the town house and the villa by 'a material difference in the style of decoration' for 'the grave, sober, serious ornaments of the city mansion would ill become the country villa'.[5] In an unfinished novel, probably written in 1804 and later named *The Watsons*, Jane Austen makes a similar distinction:

> Mr E[dwards] lived in the best house in the Street, & the best in the place, if Mr Tomlinson the Banker might be indulged in calling his newly erected House at the end of the Town with a Shrubbery & sweep 'in the Country'. Mr E[dwards']s house was higher than most of its neighbours with two windows on each side the door, the windows guarded by posts and chain, the door approached by a flight of stone steps.[6]

But one notices that Mr Tomlinson, like Mr Edwards, has a 'house'; he does not have a 'villa'. Mr Tomlinson, as a banker, is of course at the lower social end of the villa scale. However, many rather more dignified rural houses, inhabited by those of independent means, sometimes acquired in trade and sometimes not, also feature in Jane Austen's home counties. Longbourne, Cleveland and Hartfield, for example, answer to Loudon's later definition of a villa 'as a country residence, with land attached, a portion of which, surrounding the house, is laid out as pleasure ground . . . with a view to recreation and enjoyment, more than profit'.[7] Given the many putative villas in her novels, one is led to wonder why she avoids the word itself, for that avoidance cannot be accidental. As I have indicated, Jane Austen's detail repays minute attention, and her omissions can sometimes reveal as much as her inclusions. By seeking, in the rest of this chapter, to discover *why* she avoids the term 'villa', I hope to put it in its place, both from a social and a moral point of view.

The first explanation is too simple in isolation: Jane Austen does not use foreign words for English objects. Significantly, her two usages of the word *ornée*, attached respectively to Uppercross Cottage in *Persuasion* and to Sir Edward's speculation in 'Sanditon', are both disparaging. Because she followed her sailor brothers by means of books and maps from China to the Barbados, she knew a surprising amount about the wider world, but remained at heart a chauvinist. She had a respect for Sweden, but only because 'I have always fancied it more like England than many Countries.'[8] When her nephew returned from France, however, she remarked, 'He is . . . thinking of the French as one could wish, disappointed in everything.'[9] The term 'villa' may therefore have struck her as an affected word for an English house. Moreover, in the case of the *nouveaux-riches* at least, villas and affectation had been connected some twenty years before Jane Austen's birth. In 1753 one satirist proposed a garden suburb crammed with villas on the Essex marshes.[10] Another commented on 'the vast multitude of grotesque little villas' that 'swarm' round London, adding 'If one wished to see a coxcomb expose himself in the most effectual manner, one would advise him to build a VILLA; which is the chef-d'oeuvre of modern impertinence, and the most conspicuous stage which folly can possibly mount to display herself to the world.'[11]

A second explanation of Jane Austen's avoidance of villas lies in the naming of houses. She was particularly attentive to the suggestiveness of names. 'The name of Rachael is as much as I can bear,' she protests in a letter, but Anna's fictional village, Newton Priors, 'is really a Nonpareil', for the name in itself evokes her favourite subject, '3 or 4 Families in a Country Village'.[12] Important houses are commonly referred to in her novels by their names, and acquire presence through reiteration. Acceptable names are resolutely Anglo-Saxon and combine the features of an English countryside: Mansfield, Longbourne, Hartfield and Cleveland are examples. Only houses of importance have a right to names. Thus in *Emma* the reader is told that Hartfield, 'in spite of its separate lawn and shrubberies and name', really belongs to the 'large and populous village' of Highbury,[13] for its land is limited to 'a sort of notch in the Donwell Abbey estate'.[14] But since the Woodhouse family is well-connected, has an income that equals Mr Knightley's and has lived at Hartfield for several generations, the right of their house to a name is not questioned further. Conversely, although today we invariably refer to 'Chawton Cottage', Jane Austen herself did not dignify it with a name, but always gave her address simply as 'Chawton'.

It may well be that 'jumped-up' houses give themselves away both by claiming names, and by the names they claim, rather than by the more ambiguous designation 'villa'. For a category which could include, on the one hand, the house of Mr Tomlinson the banker, and, on the other, Longbourne, Cleveland and Hartfield, would seem to Jane Austen woefully imprecise. Satire is probably contained in the name Maple Grove, so often cited by the egregious Mrs Elton. 'Maple' is distinctly transatlantic, and 'Grove' a shade poetic. Mrs Elton may discover similarities between Hartfield and Maple Grove, where her brother-in-law, a Bristol merchant, has lived for a mere eleven years, but the reader is surely meant to sense the difference. There is certainly satire in the name Trafalgar House, built on a windy cliff top by Mr Palmer, the developer of Sanditon, to replace his 'honest old Place' (note the word 'honest'): 'Our Ancestors, you know always built in a hole.'[15] His wife, however, prefers the hole – 'those dreadful Nights . . . literally rocked in our bed' – and even Mr Palmer regrets the name Trafalgar since 'Waterloo is more the thing now'. This reminds one of Cobbett's comment on Cheltenham just eight years later: 'There is . . . the "NEW SPA"; there is *Waterloo-house*! Oh, how I rejoice at the ruin of the base creatures!'[16] To name one's house after oneself is even worse. In *Pride and Prejudice* Sir William Lucas makes himself ridiculous when, on receiving his knighthood, he abandons an honest trade and retires to a house a mile from Meryton, 'denominated from that period Lucas Lodge, where he could think with pleasure of his own importance'.[17] Lucas Lodge is probably a villa, for Willmot Lodge, the 'Beautiful Villa' in Jane Austen's juvenilia, is owned by Mr Willmot, who 'possessed besides his paternal Estate, a considerable share in a Lead mine & a ticket in the Lottery'.[18] Probably Maple Grove and Trafalgar House are villas too, but it is their names that give them away as 'jumped-up' houses. They are transient and modish, not enduring.

I do not want to suggest that Jane Austen is a snob. In *Pride and Prejudice*, Elizabeth's uncle and aunt, the Gardiners, although in trade, make a much better impression than her landed parents when she introduces them to Mr Darcy: 'It was consoling, that he should know she had some relations for whom there was no need to blush.'[19] When the Coles – 'very good sort of people . . . but . . . of low origin, in trade' – build themselves a dining room and invite 'the best families' of Highbury to dinner, Emma is clearly in the wrong when she determines to refuse their invitation.[20] For the Coles, like the Gardiners, are 'unpretending' people. Their house at Highbury is probably a villa, since they have another one in town, but like its owners it assumes no false importance and does not have a name. It is Emma, not the Coles, who has to learn her lesson, namely to value 'truth and sincerity' above all else in social relations. Houses, like people, are at their best when honest and unpretentious.

This brings me to the third and final reason for Jane Austen's aversion to villas, but this must be explained by a digression into cottages, on the subject of which she has much more to say. My suspicion that Jane Austen classed the smaller villa with the cottage as an example of architectural insincerity is borne out by her second allusion to villas, which occurs in *Northanger Abbey*. Isabella Thorpe is quite as insincere as Mrs Elton. She is a shameless husband-hunter, who gets her claws into James Moreland and later jilts him for a better prospect. But in her romantic phase with James, Isabella pooh-poohs the modesty of his fortune: 'Where people are really attached, poverty itself is wealth: grandeur I detest: I would not settle in London for the universe. A cottage in some retired village would be extasy. There are some charming little villas about Richmond.'[21] A great deal is condensed into that casual aside. Neither a cottage nor a villa is an appropriate dwelling for the parson James is to become. Both are seen as façades which mask restricted means. The cottage suggests that its occupants have chosen to embrace the simple life; the villa that they have a major residence in town. One also notices that Isabella makes a rapid removal upmarket, from the cottage to the villa.

Jane Austen's account of Barton Cottage in *Sense and Sensibility* suggests that it is exactly the type of dwelling which, according to Ruskin, 'ruralizing cheesemongers' imagined to be a villa.[22] Contemporary designers also saw the two as overlapping at their extremes, the larger cottage being scarcely distinguishable from the small, plain villa. Jane Austen's objections to the cottage and the villa, though differing, are certainly related, and her explicit disapproval of the one may thus illuminate her implicit rejection of the other. By 'cottage' I mean of course the cottage, *ornée* or not, of the middle classes, for Jane Austen gives her readers only glimpses of the genuine cottage of the labourer, usually noting that picturesque enthusiasms do nothing to promote decent accommodation. The village cottages at Sotherton are described by Maria Bertram as 'really a disgrace', but this leads her merely to rejoice at the distance between the great house and the village.[23] The reader perceives that, until Mr Rushworth has improved his village, he should not be planning to employ Repton to redesign his grounds. When it comes to middle-class cottages, however, Jane Austen appears to have two distinct objections.

The first of these is found in *Sense and Sensibility*. This novel was given its final revision, thought to be chiefly concerned with matters of fact, shortly after Jane Austen moved to Chawton in 1809. Although her niece, Fanny Knight, does refer to Chawton as a 'cottage', in distinction to the Great House owned by her father, Jane Austen herself never uses the term, either as an address or in her letters, where she always refers to it as their 'house' or 'home'. There are, however, close resemblances between Chawton and Barton Cottage in *Sense and Sensibility*: both contain the same number of residents, of servants and of rooms which are even disposed in a similar way; the income on which both households subsisted is the same. Jane Austen writes: 'As a house, Barton cottage, though small, was comfortable and compact; but as a cottage it was defective, for the building was regular, the roof was tiled, the window shutters were not painted green, nor were the walls covered with honeysuckles.'[24] As a house, it is perfectly frank, declaring that those who live there, though gentlefolk, have straitened means. But relatives, friends and acquaintances – like John Dashwood, Willoughby and Robert Ferrars – who romanticize it as a cottage, are wilfully concealing from themselves the uncomfortable realities of pinched incomes. When Willoughby declares he will demolish the mansion he is to inherit and recreate Barton, Eleanor comments, 'with dark narrow stairs, and a kitchen that smokes, I suppose'.[25] When Robert

Ferrars dismisses Bonomi's villas on the grounds that 'every comfort may be as well enjoyed in a cottage as in the most spacious dwelling', she does not consider he even deserves 'the compliment of rational opposition'.[26]

Like Eleanor Dashwood at Barton, Jane Austen was both positive and realistic about Chawton, as verses addressed to her brother Frank reveal:

> Our Chawton home, how much we find
> Already in it, to our mind;
> And how convinced, that when complete
> It will all other Houses beat
> That ever have been made or mended,
> With rooms concise, or rooms distended.[27]

Her eldest brother James and his wife, who occupied the spacious parsonage at Steventon where she spent her early years, do, however, have a certain resemblance to Mr and Mrs John Dashwood. Not unnaturally, Jane Austen has little time for those who make themselves comfortable with the discomforts of others by romanticizing 'rooms concise' as 'cottages'.

Insincerity, both architectural and social, assumes a different form in *Persuasion* when Jane Austen describes the village of Uppercross:

> Uppercross was a moderate-sized village, which a few years back had been completely in the old English style; containing only two houses superior in appearance to those of the yeomen and labourers, – the mansion of the 'squire . . . and the compact, tight parsonage . . . but upon the marriage of the young 'squire, it had received the improvement of a farm-house elevated into a cottage for his residence; and Uppercross Cottage, with its viranda, French windows, and other prettinesses, was quite as likely to catch the traveller's eye, as the more consistent and considerable aspect and premises of the Great House, about a quarter of a mile farther on.[28]

Here it is the occupants themselves who, like Isabella, use architecture to disguise their actual status. The transformation expresses Mary Musgrove's insistence that, as the daughter of a baronet, she takes precedence over her mother-in-law at the Great House, from which the cottage deliberately distracts attention. Jane Austen finds those 'prettinesses' impractical, particularly the 'viranda' which is 'black, dripping and comfortless' on a 'dark November day' of 'small thick rain'.[29] But her main objection to Uppercross Cottage undoubtedly lies in its attempt to confuse the traveller. As Ruskin puts it (but in the context of the villa), it seeks to draw attention to itself: 'What a pretty place! whose can it be?'[30]

One may argue from those two instances that Jane Austen's objection to the villa was primarily to its social imprecision. As Pocock suggested in 1807, the villa was more versatile than the cottage because it could be elevated to a mansion or depressed to a building 'scarcely exceeding a Cottage in simplicity of appearance, and only to be distinguished therefrom by the magnitude of the dimensions'.[31] In Jane Austen's view, a building with a claim to be a mansion *was* a mansion, and had a name which signified its landed status. Smaller middle-class dwellings were simply houses, with dimensions which corresponded to the occupant's income. It is when such houses attempt to disguise their status, like putative villas which flaunt unmerited names, that her narrative acquires satiric edge.

In concluding, I would like to observe that it is partly through the architectural landscape in her novels that Jane Austen registers the increasing pace of social change and leads her readers to discriminate. For she was much too intelligent either to welcome change for its own sake, or to condemn it out of hand. When in *Persuasion* Admiral Croft, who has made his fortune at sea, rents Kellynch Hall from the well-descended but trivial Baronet, Sir Walter Elliot, her heroine, Anne, though dispossessed, 'could not but in conscience feel that they were gone who deserved not to stay, and that Kellynch-hall had passed into better hands than its owners'.[32] Conversely, when in *Mansfield Park*, Henry Crawford advises Edmund to give his parsonage at Thornton Lacey 'such an air as to make its owner be set down as the great land-holder of the parish, by every creature travelling the road', Fanny's finer moral sense is registered in her 'quick negative'.[33] Edmund is a parson, not a landowner; his house is a parsonage, not an ancestral mansion; his income is to be counted in hundreds, not in thousands. Henry Crawford has no business to be suggesting, under the guise of improvements, fabrications which belie those truths.

One suspects that Jane Austen would not have sympathized with Ruskin's statement that the villa has a close connection 'with the character of its inhabitant',[34] although it would have been perfectly acceptable to Dickens whose houses are always expressions of rampant individualism. To her, society, at least in its outward expression, had paramount claims, and architecture was expressive of society. Villages and novels for Jane Austen resembled each other in more than one respect: a village, like a good novel, should be readable. Occupants may change, as they move upwards in society, or downwards; houses should not. The traveller, like the reader, should be able to interpret what he sees. A mansion should be a mansion; a parsonage, a parsonage; a cottage, a cottage. And a villa with no claim to be a mansion? – neither a cottage nor a villa; just a house.

PART III

RESPONSES TO PALLADIO

4 John James: An Early Disciple of Inigo Jones

Sally Jeffery

Responses to Palladio by English architects began to appear in the seventeenth century, and the work of Inigo Jones must be the most impressive response of all. Through him, others absorbed the principles set out by Palladio in his treatise, and because of his official position as Surveyor of the King's Works to Charles I, his buildings had the greatest possible impact on both court circles and those involved in designing buildings for King, Queen and courtiers. Responses to Palladio are also, in England, responses to Jones.

Jones was held in high esteem not only in royal circles and by courtier patrons but also by those with whom he worked. His assistant and colleague John Webb carried the personal influence of Jones through the great disturbances of the Civil War and the Commonwealth and on into the 1660s, when he was contender for the post of Surveyor under the restored Charles II. He died in 1672. Similarly, Sir Roger Pratt carried his personal knowledge of Jones's architecture into the building world of the later seventeenth century. He died in 1685. All of those who occupied posts in the Office of Works at this time must have heard first-hand accounts of Jones as a personality and would have been well acquainted with his work at Whitehall and Greenwich.

Roger North, writing in the late 1690s, spoke of the high regard in which Jones was held at this time:

> few ages can bragg of a good surveyor of building, or such as wee call architects. Inigo Jones was one, who did all things well and great . . . [Since, there had been Pratt, Webb and Wren] . . . dexterous men . . . but have not the grand maniere of Jones. His plaineness, seen in the repair of Pauls, Convent Garden, and the Banquetting house, hath more majesty then any thing done since. There must be a peculiar soul, to inspire a good builder; it is not daubing on of ornament which graceth, but a good disposition or profile.[1]

John James would have been trained in this tradition by Matthew Banckes, the King's Master Carpenter,[2] to whom he was apprenticed in 1690, when Banckes was nearing the end of a career which stretched back to the 1650s. Banckes was apprenticed to John Scott, who was carpenter to the Ordnance Office, and may well have known Webb personally. He had extensive contacts not only with the Office of Works but also in the City of London where he was a lifelong member of the Carpenters' Company and a freeman of the City. He worked on a number of the City churches in the 1670s, and certainly knew John Oliver, who was not only one of the City's surveyors for the post-Fire rebuilding but also held a post at the Office of Works. Through Oliver, he may have seen the collection of drawings by Jones and Webb, including those for St Paul's Cathedral, the Banqueting House and Whitehall Palace, which was eventually acquired by Lord Burlington. Jones would have been a powerful legend for Banckes, and he passed on the impact of this experience to his apprentice, James, who was thus predisposed to be receptive to a revived interest in the old master.

James completed his apprenticeship with Banckes and was made a freeman of the Carpenters' Company and of the City of London in 1697, but he probably stayed on with Banckes for a while after this, since he later wrote that he received 'Ten Years Instruction in all the practical parts of Building by Mr Banks, who was well known in their Majesty's Works.[3] James would have been about seventeen when he was bound apprentice and about twenty-four when he was made free. He must have worked with Banckes as a carpenter on Hampton Court Palace, Chelsea Hospital and Eton College.

One of the buildings constructed by Banckes while James was with him was New Park, a house for Lawrence Hyde, Earl of Rochester, at Petersham in Surrey. Two contracts survive, dated November 1692 and January 1693 respectively, with four drawings – an elevation and three plans – annotated in Banckes's hand. The details were to be to the standard of those of Ranelagh House, Chelsea, the property of Richard Jones, Earl of Ranelagh, who was to act as arbitrator in the event of any dispute. The building accounts refer to work carried out for Banckes.[4] Although suggestions have been made that Robert Hooke was involved, because he was acquainted with the Earl of Rochester, there was little about the house which would make an attribution to Hooke very convincing, and there are the contracts, accounts and drawings which point to Banckes, who was very capable of doing such work and designed buildings elsewhere.[5] New Park was, in fact, a conventional house for its time, and was the type of domestic architecture with which James became familiar during his training.

In a letter to John Sheffield, 1st Duke of Buckingham,[6] John James made a most revealing statement about his architectural philosophy. He wished to work as one of the surveyors to the Commissioners of New Churches appointed under the Act of 1711, and wrote that if he got the post 'I may once in my life have an Opportunity of Shewing that the Beautys of Architecture may consist with the greatest plainness of the structure' – a virtue which he said had 'scarce ever been hit by the Tramontani unless by our famous Mr Inigo Jones'.

From the foregoing, it might seem that James would aspire to produce designs for buildings which would resemble those by Jones, but this was far from being so. Although he clearly admired Jones's work, and especially its 'plainness', this was interpreted by him according to his own experience, and what emerged were buildings which could be described as 'plain' but which bore little direct relationship in terms of proportion or indeed of detailing to those of Jones, although their provenance was clear. Neither did they bear much resemblance to the work of Banckes. In fact, he developed his own interpretation.

He did not get the job he was applying for in 1711, although he was given carpentry contracts for some of the new churches, but in 1716 he succeeded James Gibbs to become co-surveyor with Nicholas Hawksmoor to the church commissioners. Hawksmoor was by then a colleague of long standing. They had worked together at Greenwich from at least 1698,[7] and possibly earlier; Hawksmoor was there as Wren's personal clerk from 1696. James had been employed as a carpenter in the St Paul's Cathedral works from 1701, and was Master Carpenter at St Paul's from May 1711; Hawksmoor was paid a regular salary at St Paul's from 1691 until *c.* 1711 so their paths crossed there too. They must have known each other very well. Perhaps also significantly, James had contacts with Hawksmoor in Oxford, where he would have seen some of the new buildings which heralded renewed interest in Jones, such as Aldrich's Peckwater Quad of 1706 at Christchurch College. Hawksmoor's influence was just as significant in James's formation as a designer as that of Banckes. The fact that we know that James and Hawksmoor were working together very closely from the late 1690s onwards makes their parallel development all the more interesting, and it can be studied in two houses – Herriard and Easton Neston.

James was employed by Thomas Jervoise of Herriard, near Basingstoke, Hampshire, to supervise the building of his new house (demolished 1965) which was dated 1704 on the rainwater heads. There are payments to him from 1702 to 1705, and he wrote letters which reveal his close association with the building work. That he was also responsible for the design is now beyond reasonable doubt.[8]

The Herriard designs are interesting for the light they throw on the close relationship between James and Hawksmoor. One set, dated 1696, includes a very beautiful elevation of the side of the proposed house (fig. 4.1).[9] It is in many ways more dramatic than anything James designed subsequently. The style is unique in his oeuvre and, I think, elsewhere – I have never come across a drawing of this period so strikingly executed in shades of grey wash against a black background. It seems to have been inspired by the fashionable Baroque style of Hawksmoor, and particularly of his Easton Neston, although less complex, plainer and astylar. It emerges that Easton Neston was a house which James knew well.

The Herriard documents reveal that Hawksmoor and James apparently worked together at Easton Neston, built for Sir William Fermor, Baron Leominster, between *c.* 1695 and 1710. James's role there is not clear – he may have had the carpentry contract or he may have been acting as assistant or clerk of works for

Fig. 4.1 Side elevation of a project for Herriard House, Herriard, Hampshire, of 1696, attributed to John James. Courtesy of Jervoise of Herriard Collection, Hampshire Record Office.

Hawksmoor. The only firm information is contained in a letter from James to Thomas Jervoise of Herriard of August 1703, about the glass for Herriard, in which he discusses the disadvantages of Newcastle glass compared to Crown glass, 'for we find at My Ld Lempsters its very easily discernd . . .'.[10] The 'we' implies an associate, probably Hawksmoor. It seems likely that Hawksmoor asked his assistant at Greenwich, who was not very well established in the years 1700–3, to work with him on Easton Neston, which was nearing completion by 1703.

The drawing has been attributed to both Talman and Hawksmoor. The documentary evidence now makes it clear that James was the designer of the house built at Herriard, and the hand and technique support his authorship. Although Hawksmoor used a wash technique on many occasions, his style was usually freer, and it is rare to find one of his drawings without a touch of freehand detail somewhere. James, by contrast, hardly ever drew freehand, and in this drawing even the short lines of hatching in the shadow cast by the pediment are carefully ruled, as are the details of the Doric triglyphs and of the steps. He used this kind of careful draughtsmanship throughout his career, and it may be observed in his designs for the Mansion House of 1735.[11] Nevertheless, this is an unexpected *tour de force* for a young man not yet out of his apprenticeship, and it seems that James could not have accomplished it without his knowledge of Hawksmoor's work and drawing technique. It is likely that in this, probably his first sortie into independence, he was leaning quite heavily on his colleague.

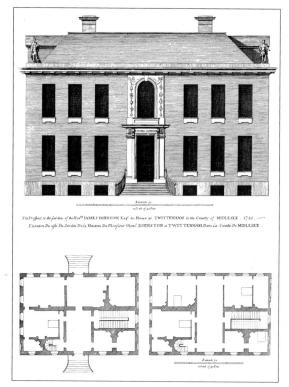

Fig. 4.2   Garden façade of Secretary Johnston's House at Twickenham, Middlesex, 1710, by John James, as published in Vitruvius Britannicus, *vol. 1, 1715.*

Herriard House bears very little resemblance to the work of Jones, whose plainness James admired so much in 1711, and it appears that his ideas underwent a change at about that time.

The house James designed for James Johnston, Secretary of State for Scotland, at Twickenham in *c.* 1710 was plainer than Herriard, and less indebted to Hawksmoor (though still reflecting Easton Neston distantly in its plan) (fig. 4.2). It could conceivably have been thought of as a 'villa' since it was just outside London in a country situation and surrounded by a productive garden, but there is no evidence that James regarded it as such, and in spite of his developing interest in Jones, he was never, it seems, particularly interested in exploring the villa form.

John Macky described Twickenham in 1714 as 'a Village remarkable for (its) abundance of Curious seats' and commented that Johnston 'for the Elegancy and Largeness of his Gardens, his Terras on the River, and the Situation of his House, makes much the brightest figure here'.[12] The house, built *c.* 1710, was demolished in 1926 but the Octagon Garden Room by James Gibbs of 1715–20 remains (fig. 4.3). The gardens were established by 1705.

The house, which was attributed to James by Colen Campbell in *Vitruvius Britannicus*, vol. 1 (1715), was very plain, with little ornament compared to other houses of the period. It was of brick with stone dressings, and presented a seven-bay façade to the river. Campbell noted:

Fig. 4.3   View of the riverside at Twickenham in 1744 by Augustin Heckell, showing Secretary Johnston's house and garden. Courtesy of Orleans House Gallery.

Here is an admirable prospect of the most charming part of the Thames, where the eye is entertained by a Thousand Beauties not to be conceived but from this Situation. The Gardens are extreme curious, the plantations most artfully disposed and everything contributes to express the refined taste and great politeness of the Master.

Johnston's famous garden was terraced down to the river, with espaliered fruit trees to the east. Behind the house, on the entrance side, there was a straight avenue with twin basins, and vines further away. Batty Langley published a plan of it 'improved' in his *New Principals of Gardening* of 1728 which shows these features as well as canals fed by the river, and a mount; Macky mentions these features, as well as a wilderness and a grotto.[13]

James must have been quite well known in Twickenham. Apart from the villa for Secretary Johnston, he rebuilt the parish church to a new design, though on old foundations and retaining the old tower, in 1714–15. It was in plain brick, but with a massive Baroque treatment inside and out and little to suggest anything by Jones. James's contribution to the Twickenham riverside, as shown by Heckell in his engraving of 1744, was quite extensive.

After 1711, James's authenticated domestic work shows a stronger Jonesian influence, while retaining nevertheless evidence of his training in a different style. Wricklemarsh, Blackheath, Kent, of 1723–4 (dismantled from 1787 onwards), for Sir Gregory Page, a wealthy City merchant and brewer, was the most Palladian and fashionable of his designs, and the one which best fits the description of a villa, although a large one (fig. 4.4).[14] The main block was nine bays by five, and was reputed to have been inspired by Houghton Hall, Norfolk. Be that as it may, both Houghton and Wricklemarsh drew inspiration from Jones, or works

Fig. 4.4   The south front of Wricklemarsh, Blackheath, Kent, 1723–4, by John James, as published in Vitruvius Britannicus, *vol. 4, 1767.*

attributed to him – the Queen's House at Greenwich, which James knew well, having prepared it for Sir James Gifford, as Governor of Greenwich Hospital, in 1708, and the garden front of Wilton House.

The buildings of Wricklemarsh had a villa-like arrangement, with the main block linked to two service blocks by low Tuscan colonnades, and they were set in an extensive park, with a formal layout of gravel walks, turf and ponds, possibly also to James's design, although there is no documentary evidence. In fact, James had contacts with gardeners throughout his career, but documents linking him with the design of garden features are rare. This may well be due to the non-survival of the records, and it is very likely that he was involved on such work on a number of occasions.

For the gardens at Herriard, George London and Henry Wise were consulted, and London produced a plan. James may have recommended them, because there was a family connection with the Wises. Henry Wise was married to Patience Banckes, cousin of James's wife, Hannah Banckes. James Johnston apparently designed his riverside garden at Twickenham himself, but James must have been interested in it since he was busy translating Dézallier d'Argenville's *The Theory and Practice of Gardening* in about 1710, and dedicated the translation when it was published in 1712 to Johnston. At Swallowfield in Berkshire there is documentation showing that James was concerned with remodelling the garden and park for Governor Pitt. From 1718 to 1726 he was modifying the interior of the house, adding service and farm buildings and adapting a series of ponds and canals, making new ones, and building cascades, fountains and a bathing room.[15]

A small house called Warbrook, at Eversley, Hampshire, is identified on James's epitaph in Eversley parish church as built by him for his own use (fig. 4.5). With its central tetrastyle block and lower side blocks, it is like a plain, red

Fig. 4.5 Entrance front of Warbrook, Eversley, Hampshire, 1724, by John James.

brick and stone version of yet another design by Inigo Jones – St Paul's Covent Garden. However, where Jones used a recognizable Tuscan order, James's house is astylar, with simple pilaster strips, and as well as recalling Covent Garden church is also reminiscent of Chelsea Hospital. For a small house, it has a grand Baroque presence, and is one of the best illustrations of the way James drew on two different style traditions to produce a personal interpretation. Originally, an approach road lay on the axis to the house, and behind it the central line is continued by a canal bordered with trees, and radiating avenues. The interiors and the garden layout are probably also the work of James.

Standlynch (now known as Trafalgar) House, near Salisbury, Wiltshire, of 1731–4 is firmly documented as a James design by Chancery proceedings brought by James against Sir Peter Vandeput, his client, to recover his money for the building.[16] Vandeput came from Richmond, was created a baronet 'of Twickenham' in 1723, and probably knew James from his work there. The setting of the house here was clearly very important to James. It was at first proposed to build near the river in a 'lawn or grove'. James then found a more convenient place on higher ground on which to build the house, which afforded extensive views. After building had begun, it was decided to raise the chamber floor and have an attic added. The house as originally conceived would have had very different proportions, closer to Wricklemarsh and Palladian and Jonesian examples. However, as built, allusions to Jones are not very marked on the exterior. The house is in plain brick, with window surrounds of blocked rustication in stone and Venetian windows at the centre of each side. It was bought by Henry Dawkins in 1766, and a front porch was added by Nicholas

Revett and the wings by John Wood junior. Some of the interior work appears to be contemporary with the building of the house, including some fashionable plasterwork in the cube-shaped hall and the bust of Inigo Jones in low relief above the chimneypiece. If this interior can be attributed to James, it is another direct allusion to his hero late in his career.

It may seem perverse to include a discussion of these houses by James in a publication devoted to the villa. However, they are considered here as a response to the work of Jones (and by extension of Palladio) by an architect trained in the traditions of the late-seventeenth century London building world of Wren and Banckes, and influenced by close association with Hawksmoor. Of course, James was aware of changes of style and fashion and responded to them, but although he was receptive in principle, he was perhaps not totally at ease with them. His training militated against Lord Burlington's Palladianism, even if it had also nurtured a lifelong admiration for Jones, and the result was intensely personal and interesting work, unlike that of any of his contemporaries.

5 The Transformation of Lord Burlington: From the Palladio and Jones of his Time to the Modern Vitruvius[1]

John Harris

My starting point will be Daniel Defoe, who when evaluating Tottenham Park, Wiltshire (built from 1720), described its architect, Richard Boyle, 3rd Earl of Burlington, as the Modern Vitruvius. Whether this was simply pejorative does not matter. What does matter, I think, is the Earl of Shaftesbury's earlier recommendation that a new architecture, to replace that of the Wren and Baroque establishment (Hampton Court *et al.*), be in the 'Greek taste' – or, as Sir Thomas Hewett would have it in 1725, the 'fine Greek taste'. Of course, Shaftesbury (who died in Naples in 1713) meant not the architecture of ancient Greece, but of ancient Rome.

In fact, from the little we know of Hewett, the architecture he advocated or practised was not remotely 'ancient' in this sense. Hewett was a leading member of an Anglo-Irish–Italian coterie comprising Lord Stanhope, Sir George Markham, John Molesworth and Alexander Galilei. They planned to set up their New Junta in architecture and to effect a better taste. By the early 1720s they appear to have been in opposition to the conventional Palladianism of Colen Campbell, but were dismayed by the growing influence of Lord Burlington from 1720. Whether they recognized that this architect earl was succeeding in the 'Greek taste', where they were ineffectual, is a moot point.

More interesting is our knowledge that Lord Shaftesbury had corresponded with John, Lord Somers (died 1716), to whom he addressed his famous *Letter Concerning the Art and Science of Design* in 1712. Somers is an enigmatic figure in art and architecture. He was one of the 'advisors' appointed by the Countess of Burlington's trustees in 1703 to attend to her young son's upbringing and education until he came of age in 1715. Of course, we have no way of knowing how Somers communicated with Lord Burlington. That must have been a private matter. It is not that Burlington might have immediately taken the advocacy of a 'Greek taste' to heart as part of an educating process, but that the recommendation had sunk into his subconscious. He would revive this dormant idea later. In reviewing the effect of the New Junta upon Palladian architecture in England, it failed dismally. It was Burlington alone in the Europe of his day whose 'fine Greek taste' earned him the title of the Modern Vitruvius.

There is no evidence of any special architectural interests prior to his Grand Tour in 1714. Surprisingly architecture is hardly mentioned. Music is his passion, and a moderate and conventional interest in buying paintings. He returned to London and to his responsibilities, having come of age in 1715. In that year the publication of the first volume of Colen Campbell's *Vitruvius Britannicus* (subscribed to by Lady Burlington) and the first book of Leoni's *Palladio*, passed him by. In 1716 he was still employing James Gibbs, the family's Baroque architect, at Burlington House and Chiswick. But by the end of 1717 Gibbs is out and Campbell in. Campbell makes the first design for the front of Burlington House, and encourages Burlington to make his first solo design: the Bagnio at Chiswick, described by Campbell in the third volume of *Vitruvius Britannicus* (1725) as 'the First Essay of His Lordship's happy invention'. And so it is, but it is so Campbellian that Campbell must have guided Burlington's hand. It is surely significant that the Bagnio is isolated in its time, and no drawn design survives by Burlington before 1719.

We can imagine Burlington reading the text books. Of this there can be no doubt. Then comes a watershed. Burlington decides to see the architecture of Palladio for himself. He leaves for Italy in August 1719 and returns to London in December. From this period we have a scrubby amateur drawing of the front of San Giorgio Maggiore in Venice. But Burlington is seeing enough of Palladio and Scamozzi to recognize the derivative character of Campbell's architecture, the very architecture of his own Burlington House in Piccadilly. And it is my guess that he was listening to Sir Andrew Fountaine, his mentor and *éminence grise* at this time. The library wing (1718) of Fountaine's Narford, and the garden there (fully made by 1724), were influential on Burlington's thinking. It is to Fountaine that he writes from Italy about buying 'some drawings of Palladio at Venice'. Whatever these drawings, and they were probably those for the Roman baths, they were to be an invigorating catalyst for a new style.

The crucial year is 1720, when we must deal with two concurrent buildings designed by Burlington. First the Westminster Dormitory, which is a Campbellian 'Great Master' composition in that it takes the height, proportions and pulvinated frieze of the Jonesian Chevening, alludes to Covent Garden and the piazzas, and knits it all together with Palladio's Ionic measures and mouldings. If anything can be detected as Burlingtonian, it is a certain frozen quality, a bareness, an astylism that he will return to with a vengeance later.

Then come the designs for Tottenham (fig. 5.1), where Flitcroft was first in attendance in July 1720. Although in the initial stages the project can be described as Campbellian, combining elements from the Great Masters, already the architect earl has outstripped the professional Campbell in the intelligence of the composition. Webb's Amesbury and Gunnersbury are under tribute, so are extracts from Palladio's woodcuts, and an innovatory interpretation of the Palladian tower house. Turning to the garden front, the centre is based on Jones's porticoed front of the Queen's House, so again an acknowledgement of a Great Master. Then a traumatic intervention occurs, and this is what I have called the 'stupendous purchase'.

The account books at Chatsworth reveal two purchases: in May 1720 of a 'Book' of the designs of Jones and Webb, and in July 1721 of a 'parcell' of designs by Palladio. We simply do not know if the 'parcell' contained Palladio's drawings of the Roman baths, or if these were the ones that had been bought in Venice in 1719. If the latter, their significance then escaped Burlington. I want to make a distinction between the two purchases. The Jones–Webb ones were immediately

Fig. 5.1 Lord Burlington, Tottenham Park, Wiltshire. Design for entrance front, 1720. Courtesy of the Royal Institute of British Architects.

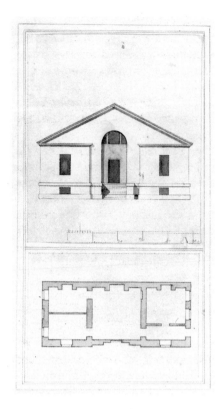

Fig. 5.2   Lord Burlington, Tottenham Park, Wiltshire. Design for kitchen wing, c. 1722, based on a design by Andrea Palladio. Courtesy of the Royal Institute of British Architects.

comprehensible by many clear inscriptions and signatures. Nevertheless, we must remember that in Burlington's time poor John Webb had been forgotten, and nearly all his buildings were given to Jones. In contrast, of the Palladio drawings, only the inscribed baths were comprehensible. So Burlington selects appealing models by Palladio, but knows nothing of them. However, with Jones he ventures on an exciting odyssey. He is discovering the unknown Jones. In sorting through the drawings he finds he has Jones's design for a chimney piece in the St James's Chapel closet, and goes there to see it for himself. It was the same for the chapel at Somerset House, long lost to view. It really was an Aladdin's Cave, and Burlington recognizes he has in his private library the materials for his own personal version of a renovated architecture. It is significant that the borrowing is never acknowedged, and no one in his day observed how every part of Chiswick is founded upon this paper archaeology. The realization came to Burlington right in the middle of building Tottenham.

How Jones and Palladio affected Tottenham can be seen in just two comparisons: for the forecourt pavilions and the entrance doors in the quadrant links, in both the design and the source. Burlington is here feeling his way. The design for the kitchen pavilion (fig. 5.2) may be scrubby and amateur in drafting technique, but its minimalism and monumentality are augurs for the future. It is based upon a design for a small villa by Palladio. The able Flitcroft will progressively improve Burlington's draughtsmanship until by 1730 designs by

Burlington can be indistinguishable from those by Flitcroft. The growing maturity of Burlington can be demonstrated before Tottenham was finished by comparing Campbell's front of Burlington House with Burlington's design for General Wade's house in 1723: a Palladian palazzo that would not look out of place in Vicenza.

Then comes the triumph of Chiswick, where for the first time he is bringing to bear all the hoards in his Cave: designs by Jones and Webb, by Palladio, the engraved authority of Desgodetz, Palladio's *Quattro libri*, and his study of the actual buildings of Jones and Webb, not least the latter's great villa at Gunnersbury, whose estate nearly joined Chiswick's. He is now also recognizing the significance for a new architecture of Palladio's reconstruction drawings of the Roman baths. But there is something else. In discovering the essential Jones through relating design to the building, with Flitcroft at hand to make measured drawings, Burlington made a personal discovery that Jones was alone in his use of Palladio's fourth book of ancient Roman architecture in constructing the trim of his interiors. Of course, this is a simplification of something complex, that involves an assessment of what Jones did as a Modern Vitruvius at old St Paul's Cathedral in 1633, and a view as to whether Burlington had seen some of Hawksmoor's noble designs for Oxford. However, I will only suggest that from 1726 Burlington's obsession with Roman antiquity is an intensely personal achievement that isolated him from most of his colleagues.

If the stupendous purchase was an educational boost, so were the preparations to publish the *Designs of Inigo Jones*, edited by William Kent and published in 1727. There is circumstantial evidence in the survival of some proof engravings that Burlington had plans to do the same for Palladio. But he was at a loss to identify them properly, so about 1729 he concentrates upon sorting out the inscribed bath drawings. Isaac Ware is busy at work as a paid draughtsman, as can be seen in the comparison of an original with the engraved and bistre-washed plate. Alexander Pope was to write the preface (his 'Letter on Taste') and an editor (this might have been Scipio Maffei) sought to provide an archaeological exegesis. In fact, the book was never published properly, and only found a limited distribution in about 1740, even if its title page, inscribed *Fabbriche Antiche*, is dated 1730.

I am going to suggest that a catatonic watershed had been reached in this year. Burlington is now poised to fulfil the prophecy of the Modern Vitruvius. I cannot say if he recollected what Shaftesbury via Somers advocated for a new taste, but the germ of it must always have been lurking in his mind. The influence of Palladio's bath drawings cannot be over-estimated. In 1730 there is an extraordinary coalescing of antique projects: the York Assembly Rooms from May 1730, and in June, not only the Chichester Town Hall project, but that for an addition to the Painted Chamber of the House of Lords. In reviewing these we can observe the transformation in Burlington's style. It is one that sets him quite apart from any other architect in Europe.

At this point I want to refer back to that editing (from about 1724) by William Kent of the *Designs of Inigo Jones*. This task transformed him from painter, decorator and furnisher, to architect and ultimately to landscape gardener. By

1730 the minds of Burlington and Kent were one. This is demonstrated by Kent's advanced designs for the Painted Chamber. On the façade we have the Venetian window set in a relieving arch combined with a Diocletian opening. Inside, the wall system is based upon Palladio's reconstruction drawings of the Roman temple of Serapis, while its Trajanic frieze disrupts all our preconceived notions of when this sort of neo-classical innovation began in the eighteenth century.

The Chichester Council House designs (fig. 5.3) are also exceptional, but for other reasons. Here is an arcuated style of the severest minimality, hinting of Roman amphitheatres, of which Burlington had engravings in his collection, and certainly of the Roman temple of Bacchus in Palladio's fourth book. All were appropriate for a building on the site of a Roman temple. The culmination of this trend to ancient Rome, as Rudolf Wittkower ably demonstrated so many years ago, was York. Here we cannot better his analysis of how Burlington brought many antique Roman sources into play: the bath drawings, Palladio's Egyptian Hall, basilicas, the Roman house in the Barbaro edition of Vitruvius. With the elevation he triumphs, for he needed a façade with a clerestory, and there were no obvious precedents in antiquity. But he noticed the temple of Bacchus, and to prove this was his starting point, his copy of that woodcut from Palladio exists in the Avery Library. Out of it came a novel opening up of the wall, a transparency in architectural elevation. Here we are witness to the birth of a modern Vitruvian style.

Wittkower was right to suggest that after 1733 Burlington, for whatever reason,

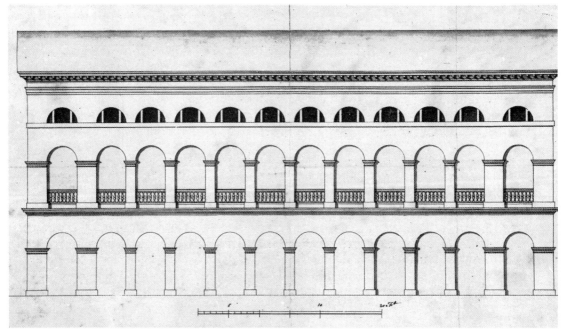

Fig. 5.3   Lord Burlington, Chichester Council House. Design for side elevation, 1733. Courtesy of the Public Record Office.

handed over the torch to Kent. He is no longer the pioneering front man. He can sit back and be the *éminence grise*. It might not have been so if there had been a happy conclusion to the announcement in the *Gentleman's Magazine* in March 1733, that Burlington had the matter of designs for a new Houses of Parliament in hand. For reasons unclear, Hawksmoor too had made designs, but must have been mortified to have had them vetted by Burlington, with obvious consequences! Designing went on sporadically until 1737 and nearly all the drawings are by office draughtsmen (John Vardy, etc.) after Kent's lost sketches, except for one – a single design (fig. 5.4) that must have amazed Kent's staider colleagues in the Office of Works. I am sure this is Burlington's. The front is 427 feet long, the huge pavilion wings are fenestrated in the York manner, the 20-column colonnade is of the scale and height (40 feet) of the Roman temple of Peace, the Pantheon or Jones's St Paul's Cathedral portico, and of a monumentality only exceeded by the temple of Serapis with its 58 foot columns. The dome hints of vast crossings and basilical halls, as in Kent's projects.

What Burlington and Kent achieved with the Parliament project was on a heroic scale that only Hawksmoor, that 'embitter'd Roman' might have matched. The loss of his rejected designs is tantalizing, for they must surely have acted as a spur to Burlington and Kent. However, this is not to say that Hawksmoor rightly deserves the epithet Modern Vitruvius and not Burlington. Hawksmoor's delving into Roman antiquity produced an architecture that lacked the purity of what Burlington was able to produce by his paper archaeology. In contrast, with his volumetrics and elevational modelling, Hawksmoor could never escape his Baroque education. What sets Burlington apart is the rigour of his precedents to produce an architecture wholly neo-classic. The York Assembly Rooms or Parliament would not have looked out of place if built in post-Revolutionary Paris. The few sections that survive might have served for the Assemblée Nationale. For this very reason continental historians have always been uncomfortable when attempting an assessment of Burlington's late works. This only confirms his status as a Modern Vitruvius.

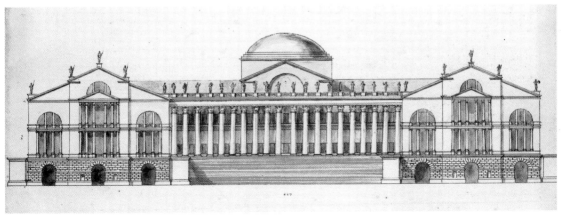

Fig. 5.4 Design for a new Houses of Parliament, 1733–7. Courtesy of the Public Record Office.

6 Poor Palladian or Not? Some Alternative Sources for the Early Georgian Villa in Ireland

Seán O'Reilly

The importance of the villa in the history of architecture is widely recognized.[1] In practical terms its small scale and ornamental inclinations inspire an experimental and often idealistic attitude in both architect and patron. Similarly, in an historical perspective, the villa plays a central role in the development of domestic architecture as it provides the link between the grand country house and the modern suburban home. However, when we assess the villa we may see it too much through the perspective of history, imposing on it a typology and significance that do not necessarily apply. This restrictive adoption of historical values is apparent in the presumption of Palladio as the proper inspiration for the early Georgian villa.

The tendency towards an exclusive emphasis on the Palladian tradition as a source for the development of villa forms in the eighteenth century is associated with a series of interdependent definitions and axioms.[2] The central philosophy evolves as follows: as Palladio defined the mature villa form then the true villa should aspire to the Palladian ideal; consequently a villa that fails to aspire to Palladio equally fails as a villa.

Thus as we assess a villa using principles rooted in those of Palladio, that villa can only fail our aesthetic of the villa the further it moves from Palladian ideals. Yet problems must arise when presumptions about a historical form generate the understanding of its history. Such a limited perspective has an especial impact on the appreciation of architecture in a country such as Ireland which, by its very distance from the Classical world, too easily finds innovative ideas reduced to the convenient compartment of provincial ignorance.

An example of how such preconceptions can obscure an appropriate critical evaluation is apparent in the response to Woodlands in Co. Dublin (fig. 6.1). The house is attributed to an architect recognized as Ireland's finest Palladian master, Sir Edward Lovett Pearce.[3] The traditional interpretation of Woodlands is that in its design Pearce fluffs the Palladian ideal by following the old fashioned example of Coleshill, Berkshire.[4] Pearce's use of this seventeenth-century source – regardless of any association with Jones – is seen to be regressive because of its non-Palladian features. However, this analysis relies on the adoption of Palladian principles that mean much more to the modern historian than to the original architect. As we shall see, a closer examination of Pearce's Woodlands shows him to be more than capable of composing innovative architectural forms, but on his own terms.

Before any examination of the villa in Ireland, the question of defining our subject requires consideration. As a starting point I would like to adopt the most simple and consequently the most broad definition of the villa: a non-urban building with a significant recreational component. The recreational theme may manifest itself exclusively, as in the example of a hunting lodge. Alternatively the building may simply have recreation as a prior concern, as in a rural residence with agrarian needs as a secondary interest.

The advantage of this type of definition is that it incorporates practical rather than formal variables into the equation, allowing a flexibility of reference unhampered by stylistic preconceptions. Thus we may distinguish the villa

Fig. 6.1   Edward Lovett Pearce, Woodlands, Co. Dublin. Courtesy of the Irish Architectural Archive.

proper from the more impressive urban residence that adopts features from the villa – such as the Provost's House in Trinity College Dublin – and from the traditional country seat, in which aspects of farming policy tend to play a dominant role. In this definition formal perspectives are not excluded, and the recreational priorities of the villa may commonly inspire idealized designs that might take the form of a building with four formal elevations.

However, limitations arise in any simple perspective on the definition of the villa. Terms such as 'villa' change their meaning through history, and our concern with the villa, whether as a recreational building or as a Palladian type, is just that: our concern.[5] The use of the term villa in the *Georgian Society Records*, Ireland's standard source for Georgian architecture, illustrates just how narrow such perceptions might be.

The directory of country houses included in the fifth volume of the *Georgian Society Records*, published in 1913, lists 276 entries on houses of all sizes and degrees of formality and extending right across the island.[6] Despite a huge variety of types described there, and a broad range of terms from 'building' to 'country house' being applied, there is only one house in the directory described as a 'villa', Delville in Co. Dublin.[7] Delville, now lost, is best known through its association with Mary Granville, Mrs Delany, a woman remembered for her social correspondence and pretty water-colours. The impression is that the associations of this house inspired the authors to use the term 'villa', allowing its connotations of delicacy and a soft romantic nature to allude to Delville's particular feminine renown.

Today our understanding of the term villa might not stand on such flimsy ground as that of the *Georgian Society Records*, but a century from now who knows how small-minded our social or formal perspectives may appear. Bearing in mind this qualification, a close analysis of the villa in Ireland reveals a surprising variety of forms and sources of inspiration.

Research into the development of the earlier Irish Georgian villa has confirmed the central role played by Palladian inspiration.[8] However, our single-minded exploration of the Palladian phenomenon can disguise the complexity of the situation. Indeed there is a wealth of non-Palladian sources in the development of the Irish villa not all of which may be reduced to reminiscences of a seventeenth-century tradition.

Powerscourt House in Co. Wicklow highlights a variety of problems that may arise in the assessment of the Irish villa, not least being the matter of whether it even qualifies as a villa (fig. 6.2).[9] The house was built from about 1730 for Richard Wingfield, later Viscount Powerscourt, by Ireland's most prolific Palladian architect, the German Richard Castle. Though incorporating fabric from an earlier house – fabric that played no small role in the final appearance of the building – Powerscourt is properly recognized as incorporating some of Ireland's most successful Palladian schemes.

Castle's design for the entrance front adopts a rich and expressive Palladian vocabulary – one that continues inside in the impressive two-storey saloon derived from Palladio's reconstruction of the Egyptian Hall. The absence of any indication of an original system for heating this immense saloon suggests its role as a place for summer entertainment. On this preliminary observation we may propose the house as an occasional residence in the fashion of a villa. Adding weight to this suggestion is that since at least 1717 the Wingfields had maintained a residence in South William Street in Dublin, less than twenty miles distant, perhaps even then an urban seat to the family's villa retreat.[10]

The initial assessment of Powerscourt as a villa might be questioned because of the scale of the building. However, such preconceptions – inspired by Palladio – should be laid aside and Castle's Powerscourt be considered in a broader tradition. No less an authority than the native Italian architect Alessandro Galilei found scale no obstacle to his idea of the villa. He described Castletown House – the huge, thirteen-bay pile with Palladian wings built by William Conolly at Celbridge, Co. Kildare, some twenty miles from Dublin – as a 'palazzo di villa'.[11] Galilei created here a perfect portmanteau of concepts. The term accommodated both the Roman urban palazzo and the rural villa sources for the scheme.[12] It also recognized that, as at Powerscourt and in the fashion of the villa as retreat, Castletown's location was distinguished by its proximity to the family's town house in the capital. Dublin, of course, was the seat of Conolly's first duty, Speaker to the Irish House of Commons.

Powerscourt's status as a villa need not be justified simply by location and Palladian form alone. While in much of Powerscourt its architect uses a formal vocabulary that is ostensibly Palladian, this interpretation does not apply to the building as a whole. The central saloon of Powerscourt, if considered as a domestic interior rather than as a Palladian derivation, is suggestive more of the grand architectural forms of the large Roman villa – the *androne* as described by Professor Alistair Rowan in chapter 8 below. It is significant that the other great design of this date following Palladio's Egyptian Hall – Lord Burlington's Assembly Rooms at York – is a scheme for a public building rather than for a private room.

Fig. 6.2 Richard Castle, Powerscourt House, Co. Wicklow, c. 1730. Courtesy of the Irish Architectural Archive.

The garden front of Powerscourt provides confirmation of Castle's interest in sources other than those defined by the confines of the Palladian tradition. The garden front is an intriguing if not especially appealing thirteen-bay composition rusticated throughout the three storeys and with terminal bows of three bays. The general form is, in part at least, a consequence of the incorporation of earlier fabric – hence the asymmetry. This front has not been assessed seriously, a phenomenon due in part, no doubt, to the fact that the form is alien to the Palladian tradition. If we leave that tradition aside this design may gain a new meaning.

One obstacle to the assessment of the garden front at Powerscourt has been the uncertainty over the extent of the impact of the pre-existing structure on the early Georgian design. In addition the degree to which the present scheme represents the original intentions of Castle and Wingfield has been obscured by later work and lack of information. Consequently the incongruity of the detail of the garden front – of rustication, tower-like bows, irregular elevation and asymmetrical features – has resulted in its critical neglect.

The destruction of the interior in a fire in 1974 uncovered much of the internal fabric, allowing Castle's original scheme to be determined in more detail. This, in conjunction with a reassessment of the documentary evidence, confirmed a broad agreement between the modern appearance and the architect's original intentions.[13] Most notable was the confirmation that the unusual rustication of this front was an original feature, for in October 1734 William Spence was paid for carrying out more than 2,000 feet of 'rustick work at the back front'.[14]

Only one major alteration to the garden elevation has occurred since Castle's day, the addition of the third floor in the later eighteenth century.[15] In 1787 Lord Powerscourt recorded: 'I am taking down the cornice at [the] top of the house at Powerscourt in order to raise an attic storey on the back front, which will bring it just to the height of the top of the saloon, and make a uniform appearance to the country on that side.'[16] Evidently Powerscourt intended this addition to hide the discrepancy, then prominent, between the three-storey entrance block and what was then a two-storey garden front. The different axes of the entrance front and garden exacerbated the lack of co-ordination between the two. Thus from the 1740s to the 1780s – before the raising of the top floor – Powerscourt's garden front presented itself as a two-storey irregular rusticated elevation flanked by heavy rusticated bows at each end and, rising one storey higher behind, an asymmetrical attic corresponding to the upper storey of the saloon. Such a scheme would have been not only disconcerting to a strict Palladian mind, but unacceptable.[17] When Castle developed this scheme he must have had in mind a quite different conception of architectural form.

The complex history of the gardens at Powerscourt has also caused some confusion, again obscuring the original intentions of the early Georgian scheme. The details of the present formal layout date largely to the nineteenth century.[18] However, the present character of the scheme as a formal symmetrical garden rising up in terraces to the house is consistent with Castle's work for Wingfield. Rocque's map of Co. Dublin records the pattern of the terrace gardens before 1762, while more recently the discovery of an original estate map of 1740 by

Thomas Reading documents the formal arrangement as a feature present in the early Georgian development.[19] The gardens recorded by Reading may well pre-date Castle's work, but these records confirm Castle's purposeful conception of the garden front of Powerscourt as an architectural extrapolation of the stylized landscape.

Despite the irregularity and grandeur of Powerscourt's un-Palladian garden front this does not necessarily impugn either the quality of the architecture or the status of the building as a villa. The view from the garden does not evoke the idealized domestic tradition of the Venetian villa, but the more sturdy and pragmatic villa of the non-Venetian Italian Renaissance, notably the Roman. A complex such as the Villa d'Este, for example, with its sturdy rectangular mass and end towers, acting as a monumental climax to a formal terraced garden setting, conveys a mood consistent with Powerscourt's garden composition.[20] It is clear too that the mood of this Roman villa derives from more than just the frame of the garden – a feature which in itself has extensive precedent in the English Baroque – but pervades the very architecture itself.

If a non-Venetian Renaissance theme in Irish Georgian villas seems at first surprising, there are strong arguments for the enlightened Irish patron turning to Rome or Florence for inspiration over Venice. Such arguments are apparent in the historical, cultural and social parallels uniting Georgian Ireland and non-Venetian Renaissance Italy.

Concerning the Renaissance villas of the Veneto, Ackerman points out how they tend to be new works involving expansion into undeveloped districts.[21] In such cases the matter of pre-existing structures is of little concern. In contrast both Roman and Florentine Renaissance villa architecture, and the villa architecture of Georgian Ireland, vies for space with centuries of earlier construction and with more recent rapid urban expansion. This situation often leads to a pragmatic incorporation of pre-existing structures in the buildings and, consequently, a necessary irregularity in finished schemes that might undermine the idealistic aspirations of the more typical villa form.[22] In Powerscourt, alongside numerous other Irish early Georgian houses, pre-Georgian buildings are adapted to new purposes and life-styles, as in the villas of Renaissance Rome.[23] In these cases a realistic response to an earlier fabric requires the subordination of the idealism more often associated with the Renaissance.

In addition, personal security in villa residences had a particular relevance to both the Irish and the Roman and Florentine aristocracy. In Renaissance Rome and Florence, for example, potential threats to the security of the villa lay in brigands, the rising of a dissatisfied underclass or an over-ambitious peer. In these situations a significant degree of security could be a factor in determining the villa's form, as may be observed in the early villas of the Medici. In contrast, the Veneto enjoyed a more established social order. For the residents of the Venetian villa the only real danger was invasion from an outside force. In this event no villa could provide adequate protection and the matter was ignored, allowing for the more open compositions typical of the Palladian manner.

For the Irish early Georgian villa-builders dangers existed on a scale similar to those in Renaissance Rome and Florence. Even after the turn of the eighteenth century the security of the Irish gentry could not be assured despite the comparative peace of the Irish countryside, and the danger of an uprising could not be wholly ignored. Thus the immediate security of the villa might be a real consideration. Matters relating to this question may be seen to have had an impact on early Irish villa forms.[24]

The garden front at Powerscourt captures a self-conscious security. Located in the Wicklow mountains, some distance from the capital and adjacent to centres of potential native disorder, Powerscourt might happily present an especially robust façade. The monumental scale, extravagant rustication and tower-like bows of the garden front all encapsulate this distinctive mood. Even the irregular massing added to its imposing nature.

On a less theoretical note, the mutual interest in hunting in the society of both Georgian Ireland and the Roman Renaissance also inspired a common perspective in architecture. Though in Roman society, as it evolved from the sixteenth century to the seventeenth, hunting became less important,[25] the architecture of the hunt appears to have drawn the Irish architects to Roman explorations of the theme. This is a matter to which we will return towards the end of this chapter. What does seem apparent is that the parallels between Powerscourt and the form of the Roman villa enhance the case for regarding Powerscourt as a villa.

If Powerscourt's status as a villa is accepted then the degree of non-Venetian influence may be questioned with validity. The combination of what might be described as imperfect Classical architecture and formal symmetrical garden may be seen to have a significant precedent in the architecture of an outdated English Baroque. However, it seems harsh to reduce Powerscourt's garden front to an ill-sorted provincial scheme after acknowledging the superiority of the Palladian entrance front. Considering the building in the broader perspective of the Irish villa form, such a judgement appears obtuse.

Castle's Belvedere House, in Co. Westmeath, exemplifies the more obvious features of the early Georgian villa in Ireland, with private recreation and perfected architecture as the concerns of both architect and patron.[26] This elegant and intriguing building was constructed about 1740 for Lord Rochfort as a villa-retreat to serve his nearby country seat at Gaulston. The title of the house clearly expresses its status as a pure villa, while the seldom-noted fact that it has four formal façades – with dummy windows giving symmetry to the rear elevation – manifests Belvedere's idealistic pretensions.

The architectural sources for Belvedere are as complex as those at Powerscourt. The plan of Belvedere consists of an apparently simple arrangement. It has a connecting corridor at the rear of a range of reception rooms. This layout ensures optimum views across the descending gardens and towards the lake below. Beyond the appropriation of motifs such as Venetian and Diocletian windows, the scheme owes little to Palladio's concept of the villa.[27] However, the presence of such formal links should not lead exclusively to the identification of an uninspired mind or a reactionary tradition. Powerscourt has indicated how such an assessment may detract from our understanding rather than enhance our appreciation.

Castle's composition of spaces in Belvedere derives not from the Palladian tradition but from a logical response to the requirements of the building – with rooms laid out to take in the landscape. Similarly the projecting end bays of the façade, flanking a short recessed centre, again explore a less Palladian villa tradition. This layout has more in common with the original form of the Villa Belvedere in Rome – a linear composition with projecting ends – than with any by Palladio.[28] Castle need not have been aware of such a Roman parallel. The point is that his design is an inventive response to the peculiar requirements of the commission, unfettered by Palladian dogma. Though the plan is akin to a half of a double-pile plan, the building is not English Baroque; though its elevation uses Palladian details it is not Palladian; and though it evokes some Roman precedents, it is not Roman. It is, instead, Irish early Georgian.

If Castle's German origins suggest the possibility of continental sources, the work of the Sardinian architect Davis Ducart – the most idiosyncratic architect working in Ireland in the mid-century – has an even more impressive potential for non-Palladian associations.[29] Richard Hewlings, in his assessment of the importance of James Leoni's Italian background, notes how little of his native Italian experience this architect brought to England.[30] In a similar fashion Ducart's documented work shows little novelty either in spatial organization or in the composition of masses.

Ducart's name has been linked with Castlecor in Co. Longford – admittedly with little foundation beyond the scarcity of possible authors.[31] Though later extended, it consists of an octagonal block with squared projections along its diagonal axes and with a single vaulted reception room inside. The original form of the house is unique in Ireland and suggests the possibility of a non-Palladian pedigree.[32]

Castlecor attests to its status as a villa first in its role as a subordinate building. The Very Reverend Cutts Harman, who inherited the estate, appears to have developed Castlecor as a lodge to serve his nearby house of Newcastle. Castlecor's original arrangement also indicates its status as a villa for occasional use. This consists of the two-storey octagonal block containing kitchens below a raised *piano nobile*. Here a central pier carries the vault in a marble-floored saloon. Such a large space would be difficult to heat, as in Powerscourt's saloon, though the fireplaces in the central pier might take some chill out of the air on a cold hunting day.

The peculiar design of Castlecor has inspired extensive speculation concerning its sources, including unlikely early suggestions that Windsor Castle might have inspired its form.[33] More feasible, though still not necessarily even plausible, has been the observation that some familiarity with Stupinigi might have inspired its form, perhaps leading to the introduction of Ducart's name. Such a scenario is not impossible, but whatever the source Palladio's villas have played little role in the conception of Castlecor.[34]

If Ducart provides perspective here as curiosity, the work of Sir Edward Lovett Pearce presents a coherent assimilation of non-Palladian features. Pearce, both as a student of Vanbrugh and as the leading Irish exponent of the Palladian style, is often viewed as a provincial Palladian unable to relinquish his Baroque heritage.[35] At present this assessment is undergoing a radical reappraisal.[36] Rejecting the presumption of his localized perspective, and viewing him as a talented architect acquainted with Italy over a stay of up to two years, his work gains a new significance. Pearce's interest lies not in initiating an Irish tradition of Burlington-inspired Palladian architecture – in which terms he may be seen to have failed – but in a personal reformulation of a broader and richer Classical tradition – a task at which he triumphed most ingeniously.

As with many of the more idealistic villa designs, Woodlands, formerly Clinshogh, in north Co. Dublin, also has four formal fronts. Set in a walled park, it is this building that gives a real sense of the breadth of Pearce's inspiration. Woodlands was built sometime before 1735 as the home of the Reverend John Jackson, Vicar of Santry and a friend of Jonathan Swift.[37] The house remains today as an especially coherent and intact example – though lacking its original doorcase – of an Irish early eighteenth-century residential villa. At present no documentation confirms Pearce as the architect of Woodlands, but his is the only hand in Ireland at this time known to be able to produce a design with such a subtle variety of overtones.

As noted at the outset of this chapter, if we assess this building solely in Palladian terms it has many lapses. Pearce seems to take his inspiration from what may be seen today as a less sophisticated English building tradition, notably in the use of Coleshill as a source for the elevations.[38] While perhaps an acceptable source in the eighteenth century because of its association with Inigo Jones, the 'artisan' mood of Pearce's source suggests a more reactionary attitude. Similarly the arched belvedere or gazebo rising over the centre of the roof might be interpreted – for want of more appropriate sources – as an English Baroque belvedere in the manner of Coleshill, or even as an echo of the arcaded chimney stacks of Pearce's mentor Vanbrugh, neither of which does especial justice to Pearce's composition.[39]

The form of the belvedere lies outside the tradition of the Palladian villa but it is not simple *retardataire* in its association with the English Baroque. The Roman Renaissance villa frequently incorporates the belvedere, and even a cursory review of Vignola's Villa Lante at Bagnaia provides a clear if rather ornate parallel for Woodlands.[40] Not only the belvedere, but the square mass, sharp vertical contours, fenestration and restrained articulation all suggest the Villa Lante as a source for Woodlands before any Venetian villa or English Baroque composition.

Pearce's interests ranged more widely than a highlight of Roman Renaissance architecture. The plan of Woodlands (fig. 6.3) is an interesting example of an arrangement that is unfamiliar in both Palladian and English traditions. It is distinguished by a central axial corridor piercing the depth of the house from the entrance, giving access to a broadly symmetrical array of rooms and to the staircase at the rear.[41] Again the architecture of the Roman Renaissance provides Pearce with his real inspiration.

A comparison of Woodlands with a little-regarded hunting lodge by Vignola at Caprarola (fig. 6.4) confirms that the formal coincidences between Dublin and Rome are not a product of chance but the consquence of mature and creative adaptation by the Irish architect. The hunting lodge to the Barco or hunting park which Cardinal Alessandro Farnese established near Caprarola provides a

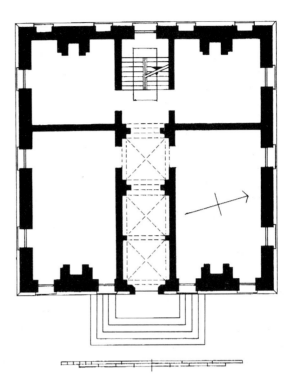

Fig. 6.3 ?Edward Lovett Pearce,
Woodlands, Co. Dublin,
c. 1730–5. Groundplan. Courtesy
of John O'Connell.

consistent source for the distinctive features at Woodlands. The lodge is known to have been under way by 1574 and, as with the Villa Lante, it was built to the designs of Vignola.

The illustration of Vignola's lodge by Lebas and Debret in the early nineteenth century indicates a building remarkably similar to Woodlands, though at some sixty feet square it is slightly larger.[42] The proportions, the square arched belvedere, the reticent eaves, the corner fenestration, the sheer contours and the unmodulated wall surface all suggest a direct link between the two buildings. Confirming the derivation is the internal arrangement which anticipates the essential features of Woodlands. A corridor – here barrel-vaulted – cuts a central axis through the house, while symmetrical doors give access to rooms leading off. A separate staircase on the first floor leads to the belvedere, again an arrangement repeated at Woodlands.

Though Pearce does not sacrifice any of the Vignolesque logic, Woodlands is a more dramatic articulation of the composition, outside with its steep roof and tall chimneys and inside with piers defining bays in a division of the central corridor reminiscent of Vanbrugh. Such features give Pearce's building a stronger formal distinction and a striking northern European edge, evoking Coleshill and the English Baroque. Such a response is wholly acceptable as Pearce clearly recognized a need expressed by Isaac Ware some quarter of a century later: 'we are not to take the *Italians* as our perfect model . . . because they adapted their edifices to their country and so must we'.[43]

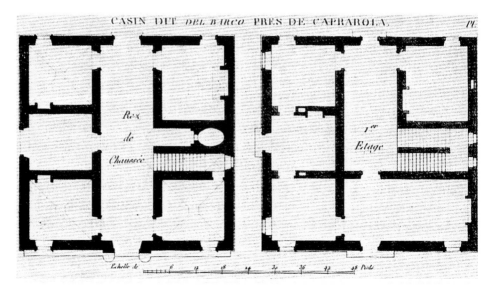

Fig. 6.4   Vignola, hunting lodge to the Barco at Caprarola, 1574.

Pearce's familiarity with the lodge at Caprarola seems likely, though at present the documentary record is not clear. There is some suggestive material. On the one hand the Vanbrugh–Pearce drawings of the Elton Hall collection confirm Pearce's interest in the work of Vignola.[44] Adding weight to Pearce's interest in the architect's work is the survival of a drawing of the cornice and wall at Caprarola.[45]

However, while Pearce is known to have toured northern Italy – notably Venice, Turin and Florence – in 1723–4, there is no documented confirmation of his having visited Rome. Certainly he was energetic in developing links between Italy and Ireland, providing sculptures for Irish patrons and even delivering drawings between Galilei and Conolly. Considering him to be an enlightened and enthusiastic supporter of Italy, it seems unlikely that during his time there he would have failed to familiarize himself with Rome. A deeper examination of his work further suggests Pearce's general concern with the Roman villa tradition, particularly in the use of a central corridor for access.

Pearce's interest in the use of the corridor-access brings together a rather tidy set of schemes linking sixteenth-century Rome and eighteenth-century Ireland. The plan of the Cardinal of Ferrara's hunting loodge at his Barco at Bagni di Tivoli adopts that of Vignola's earlier and more sophisticated lodge at Caprarola, including the use of the central corridor.[46] Here staircases – taking the form of two half-spirals – lie to the rear of the building in a fashion loosely reminiscent of both Woodlands and Belvedere.[47]

Pearce's own concern with the corridor-access bore particular fruit in a variety of different fashions. The corridor-style entrance appears in a selection of the drawings associated with Pearce or his school in the Elton Hall collection. Designs by Pearce, recently identified as being for the Deanery at Christchurch, imaginatively exploit a corridor to provide simultaneous access to three houses under peculiar and difficult circumstances.[48] Similarly in drawings for villas in the same collection associated with Richard Castle the corridor was used successfully and, despite the echoes of an English Baroque style, these preserved a close relationship with Pearce's Roman interests.[49]

If we accept a specific inspiration from the Roman Renaissance in Pearce's Woodlands, then the principle may be applied to other examples of his domestic work.[50] Pearce is seen to be at his most ardently Palladian in the villa designed for Thomas Coote at Bellamont Forest in Co. Cavan, of *c.* 1730.[51] The roundels in the entrance hall typically are viewed as an adaptation of the roundels appearing in the hall at Coleshill in Berkshire. Yet the salon of the Palazzo Farnese in Rome has an array of roundels that is quite as impressive as that at Coleshill. Considering the type of interior, the Roman source provides a more appropriate inspiration than Coleshill's stair-filled hall. Certainly the Palazzo Farnese inspires other aspects of Pearce's work. For example he adapts the columnar entrance vestibule of the Palazzo Farnese to create a similar feature in his designs for Richmond Palace.[52]

Exploring Pearce's Roman interests further we can turn to another Dublin villa – in this case a genuine hunting lodge – which seems to capture a peculiar admixture of Renaissance Roman and northern European traditions. Through later associations the building is now commonly referred to as the Hell-Fire Club (fig. 6.5).[53] Its history has been chequered. As early as 1779 Austin Cooper noted the building's disrepair, while it has been in ruins since at least the mid-nineteenth century when it formed the platform to a bonfire in honour of Queen Victoria's visit.[54]

The building is situated on a hilltope site, Montpelier Hill, convenient to both Castletown and Dublin, and dates to the early eighteenth century when it appears to have been erected as a hunting lodge for Speaker Conolly. It sits in the middle of what seems to have been a walled hunting park extending over the entire mountain of Montpelier and the surrounding hills.[55] There is no documented link with Pearce known at present, but the persistent association of patron and

Fig. 6.5   Edward Lovett Pearce, The Hell-Fire Club, Co. Dublin, c. 1730.

architect suggests the probability of Pearce's involvement. Stylistic links with Pearce's Roman manner tend to enhance the case.

The Hell-Fire Club takes the simple but solid form of a stone vaulted single-storey over basement gabled block, with a gabled porch to the front and a corresponding square return to the rear.[56] Flanking this central composition are loosely co-ordinated lean-to extensions that boast the suggestion of a mezzanine level.[57] The architectural pretensions of the lodge are evident in the strong articulation of a *piano nobile*, and in the formally disposed niches inside. This informal formality is wholly appropriate to the rural milieu of a hunting lodge.

Again it is the rustic mood of Roman hunting lodges such as that at Bagni di Tivoli, already mentioned, where a congruence of mood and mass may be observed despite the differences in detail. The plan of the Irish lodge consists of a central corridor leading to the return, flanked by larger reception rooms. Though with parallels in later Irish architecture the plan of the Hell-Fire Club may also be interpreted as a simple contraction of the Roman corridor-arrangement noted above. Here the space is abbreviated, as the building is only one room deep. While we may not be dealing with a specific adaptation of the Roman lodge we may well see in the Hell-Fire Club a reminiscence of that manner.[58]

If in the early eighteenth century Ireland's *rapprochement* with the architecture of Rome was tentative, by the 1750s – under the patronage of Lord Charlemont – the impact of Rome became explicit. In north county Dublin Charlemont developed a suburban villa and demesne in the Roman style. Charlemont's main interest lay in the elaboration of the estate which he renamed Marino. It was developed in the fashion of a Roman suburban villa with the demesne laid out in the contemporary informal fashion. Here Charlemont recreated the Claudian idyll, as the architecture provided a formal counterpoint to the relaxed composition of nature. The effect was perfectly encapsulated in the Casino – his villa's belvedere – as designed by the arch-Roman William Chambers.

The Casino is the first and perhaps the finest major example of Chambers's early Franco-Roman compositions to be executed, and marks a high-point in the development of the villa in Ireland. Its antique, almost monolithic appearance belies its real nature – a three-storey block hollowed out to provide appropriate rooms for a man of sophisticated taste to escape from the hustle of public life and seclude himself among his various collections.

In conclusion, given the emphasis of non-Palladian work on the traditional Palladian villas discussed here, it is perhaps fitting to note a role possibly played by Palladio's architecture in this Roman-inspired structure. As early as 1754, when Charlemont was touring Palladio's villas, his admiration for the Villa Rotonda inspired thoughts of what would turn out to be quite a different building. In a note recently discovered by Sir Howard Colvin, Matthew Brettingham writes of Charlemont's interest in Palladio's Villa Rotonda, recording that Charlemont had 'a mind to build it again in Ireland'.[59] Perhaps, as a formal four-square composition, the Casino is Charlemont's response to this desire. If so then, as in both Powerscourt and Woodlands, the strength of the Irish version lies less in the exclusive adoption of specific prototype than in the inspired reformulation of a more general Classical ideal.[60]

7 'Heretical and Presumptuous': British Architects Visiting Palladio's Villas in the Later Georgian Period

Frank Salmon

In 1825 the British architectural student George Wightwick visited Vicenza. In his memoir of the trip Wightwick wrote: 'Palladio's fame is connected in some degree with British patronage, and his genius was no doubt greatly influential as the guiding star to a superior condition of British taste . . . but his greatness as an architect is apart from the *present* worth of his designs, many of which exhibit as much for our careful avoidance as for our grateful acceptation.'[1] Wightwick thus recognized the importance of Palladio as a source of Stuart and early Georgian architectural design, but for him this was a matter of history, not a matter of contemporary relevance. In the same year of 1825, however, another young British architect, Sydney Smirke, wrote home from Vicenza: 'It would be heretical and presumptuous to doubt [Palladio's] excellence.'[2] Smirke's use here of the language of religion expressed the exceptionally high regard in which Palladio could still be held by travelling British students. In fact the sole book specifically dedicated to Palladio's buildings to be published by a Georgian architect, Francis Arundale's *The Edifices of Andrea Palladio*, dates not from the eighteenth century but from the year 1832. The illustrations in Arundale's work are no more than simple measured outline engravings of four Vicentine buildings, including the Villa Almerico or Capra, better known as the Villa Rotonda. A far greater significance attaches to the preface. There Arundale wrote:

it is with regret that we see Greek forms introduced in situations wholly at variance with the purpose for which they were originally intended. . . . Although Palladio studied, he did not strictly imitate, the remains of antiquity; he adapted its forms and designs to the age in which he lived . . . none have better appreciated his peculiar excellencies than the leading architects of Great Britain, as shewn in the works of Jones, Wren, and Chambers, where we find examples of the Palladian style, which reflect credit on their taste and discrimination, in adapting to our English wants and feelings the results of his well applied study of the antique.[3]

In censuring the predominant Greek Revival of the 1820s, then, Arundale was concerned to establish the continuing suitability of neo-Palladianism in British design. So towards the end of the reign of George IV we are faced with a clear dichotomy. Did later eighteenth- and early nineteenth-century British architects who visited Italy discard Palladio, as they pursued eclectic neo-Classical and Picturesque ideals? Or had the neo-Palladian mentality of the early eighteenth century permeated the British architectural mind so thoroughly that later Georgian visitors to Italy were unable or unwilling to cast it off?

In this chapter I shall address these questions by studying visits to Palladio's villas made by British architects between about 1750 and 1830, a time span which, for present purposes, I shall refer to as the later Georgian period.[4] In the first half of the eighteenth century, when the influence of Palladio was at its strongest in Britain, the fact of the matter is that we have virtually no information about first-hand visits made to Vicenza or to Palladio's villas by the key figures.[5] We do not actually know, for example, whether Colen Campbell went to Italy at all. No villas are mentioned in William Kent's brief notes on a visit to Vicenza in 1714, although Kent must have passed the Villa Foscari at Malcontenta as he travelled on the Brenta Canal from Venice to Padua in the company of Thomas Coke. We only know for certain that Lord Herbert was in Venice in 1712, although his architect-protégé Roger Morris was studying palaces in Vicenza in 1733. This shortage of information increases the value of the documentation for Lord Burlington's second visit to Italy, made in 1719. Although we cannot be certain that Burlington's observations on six of Palladio's buildings, recorded in the famous interleaved 1601 copy of the *Quattro libri* at Chatsworth, were written *in situ*, the comments themselves leave no room for doubt that he had seen and studied the Villas Rotonda and Malcontenta.[6] We also know that Burlington visited a third villa, the Villa Barbaro at Maser, and that his plans to visit other villas were curtailed by serious flooding in the Vicentine countryside.[7] At Malcontenta Burlington's comments focused on the portico, its high podium with central door, four windows and lateral steps later providing a key source for the principal front of Chiswick. (Even closer formal correspondences with Chiswick suggest that Burlington might have visited Vincenzo Scamozzi's Villa Rocca Pisani at Lonigo, perhaps also in 1719.[8]) These visits and the cursory notes Burlington made on compositional features thus provide a bench-mark for later first-hand Georgian study of Palladio's villas.

Although the current scholarship of John Harris and others is leading to a reappraisal of Burlingtonian and British neo-Palladianism, it can surely still be asserted that in the 1720s Burlington wished to see a national architectural taste established on broadly Palladian principles. Given this context, it is striking to note that the Earl is not known to have sent any of his architect-protégés to study in Italy. (The men I have in mind here are John Vardy, Isaac Ware, Henry Flitcroft and Daniel Garrett.) I should stress that I have no evidence to suggest that any conscious obstruction of travel took place. According to James Ackerman in his book *The Villa*, these men simply couldn't be bothered to go to Italy because Burlington had imported the principal collections of Palladio's drawings to London.[9] An alternative and perhaps more plausible explanation might be that Burlington's demands or their official appointments in the Office of Works kept them so busy they could not be spared for a visit to the fountainhead itself. But the fact that so many of the key figures in English architecture during the neo-Palladian phase learned their architecture from drawings and books under the careful guidance of Burlington himself, does suggest that the inculcation of a particular style of architecture depended to an extent on a control of architects quite contrary to the individual nature and exploratory spirit of travel. It was not, in fact, until the second half of the eighteenth century, when an independent profession was beginning to emerge, that travel to Italy became commonplace for young students of architecture on completion of their apprenticeships.

Now by the 1750s, when British architects began to travel to Italy effectively as a final part of their education, the concept of the villa in England had already begun to develop away from strictly Palladian models, and this must have preconditioned their responses to Palladio's villas themselves. The evolution of the English villa can be seen microcosmically in the comparison of two Thames-side houses in Richmond: Roger Morris's archetypally neo-Palladian Marble Hill of 1724–9 and Robert Taylor's Asgill House of the early 1760s. Both would have been widely known through their inclusion in *Vitruvius Britannicus*: Marble Hill in vol. III, 1725, Asgill in vol. IV, 1767. As Ackerman has pointed out, neither Palladio nor Burlington would have introduced a bow to a façade wall as Taylor did at Asgill, because the perspective effects distort the perception of proportional relations.[10] Yet it was precisely the use of a projecting ellipse, circle or polygon that John Soane later recommended to students for villa plans in his seventh Royal Academy lecture, given from 1815: 'This projection, altho' it may in some degree destroy the architectural effect, increases the variety of outline, adds to the richness of the perspective, and at the same time occasions the light to be more equally diffused into every part of the room.' Soane further commented that for his villas Palladio had 'adopted a needless and studied Uniformity, injurious to convenience and monotonous in effect'. In this he had been followed by Inigo Jones and by Burlington, 'forgetting that it is not necessary that in the two equal divisions of a Plan, each half shall exactly correspond'.[11] In this lecture Soane simply put into words what he had already demonstrated in print in his 1793 book *Sketches in Architecture, Containing Plans and Elevations of Cottages, Villas, and other Useful Buildings*. In Soane's hands villas had become country retreats 'calculated for the real uses and comforts of life, and such as are within the reach of moderate fortunes'.[12] It was a short step from here to the wholly Picturesque concept of the villa. Among the many early nineteenth-century books illustrating such villas, Robert Wetten's *Designs for Villas in the Italian Style of*

Architecture, which the architect actually prefaced while at Rome in June 1830, may stand as a testimony to the conversion of late Georgian taste to highly informal plans and central Italian models far removed from those of Palladio's villas.[13] An underpinning factor for the British architects who travelled to Italy in the later Georgian period, then, must have been their knowledge that close study of Palladio's villas would not serve them in practice as it might have done their predecessors in the first half of the eighteenth century.

In the later Georgian period we know that more than a hundred British architectural students travelled to Italy: over forty in the years from 1740 to 1805 and over sixty in the years between 1815 and 1830. Of these, there is written or drawn evidence of visits to Palladio's villas by some thirty architects. The general itinerary of the British architectural students who went to study in Italy remained fairly consistent. Rome was the primary goal and most reached it by travelling down the west side of the Apennines or by sailing to a west coast port. In a few cases architects made expeditions to the Veneto from Rome or passed through Venice *en route* further east: James 'Athenian' Stuart's sketches of the Villa Malcontenta (fig. 7.1) and other Palladian buildings, for example, were made in

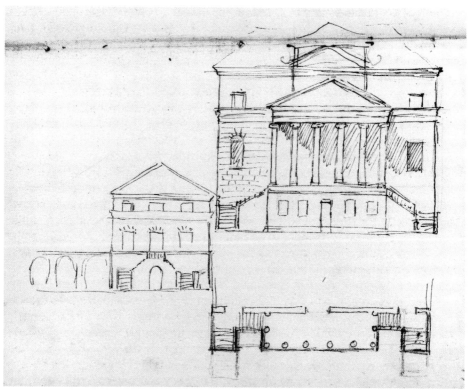

Fig. 7.1 James 'Athenian' Stuart, sketchbook elevation of Palladio's Villa Foscari, Malcontenta, 1750. Courtesy of the Royal Institute of British Architects.

1750 while Stuart was waiting at Venice for a passage to Athens.[14] But visits to the Veneto more usually took place when the students left Rome for the return journey north, taking a route to the east of the Apennines. Often they had exhausted their meagre allowances by then, yet the lengths to which some were prepared to go in order to gain this part of the Italian experience can be seen from the case of Charles Heathcote Tatham. Compelled by the occupying French army to avoid travelling north through Florence in July 1796, at which Tatham said his regret exceeded 'all bounds', the young Englishman none the less decided to risk journeying home by the eastern Italian route and Austria in order to fulfil his longstanding desire to visit 'the birth place of Palladio' and study 'the works as they exist from the designs of that celebrated master'. Avoiding the French at Ravenna, Tatham managed to reach Vicenza for 'four days well spent' sketching and admiring, beyond all else, the Villa Rotonda.[15]

It should be recalled that British architects visiting Italy in the later eighteenth century found Vicenza a city of the Venetian Republic. However, after Napoleon abolished that republic in 1797 its territories were ceded to Austria in compensation for the loss of Lombardy. Despite a brief period as part of the Kingdom of Italy from 1810, the Veneto was reassigned to Austria by the Congress of Vienna in 1814. Thus almost all the British architects who reached the region in the early nineteenth century found it effectively a land under foreign occupation: 'Poor fallen Venice where exists now its freedom', lamented George Basevi in 1817.[16] This political situation was not without its implications for travelling students. In the summer of 1804 Robert Smirke found that Verona was on the border between Austrian and Cisalpine territory. The Roman amphitheatre was on the Austrian side and consequently inaccessible to an Englishman.[17] Vicenza was also in 'German territory', and it is clear that this political situation affected early nineteenth-century British architects trying to visit Palladio's villas. In 1820 Charles Barry and John Lewis Wolfe had the nightmarish experience of a nocturnal visit from the police at Bassano. Barry noted in his diary:

> The police very curious to know who we were. Had a visit from the Commissary and others after I had been in bed an hour who having examined our passports & not finding them signed at Vicenza for visiting this neighbourhood said we must return to Vicenza the following day for the requisite signatures. What seemed to surprise them most was in finding our passports signed at Venice 10 days ago for Verona and our being at this time wandering so much out of our direct course.[18]

In this day and age it is also easy to forget how much more problematic travel was in an age before motorized transport and metalled roads. The physical difficulties inherent in attempting to visit Palladio's villas in the later Georgian period should not be underestimated. We have already seen that in 1719 Burlington's villa itinerary had been curtailed by the inundated countryside. A century later Barry and Wolfe's journey to Lonedo to see the Villas Godi and Piovene obviously came close to disaster for similar reasons, their 'chaise sometimes up to the axles in mud and other times nearly overturned by great stones and the insufficiency of width of road, which in great part was covered with water'. And this was a trip made in the usually clement month of June! Given that when they finally arrived at Lonedo Barry pronounced the Villa Godi to be 'an unarchitectural pile', it is small wonder that the students returned to Bassano 'quite fatigued and annoyed by the unprofitableness of our journey'.[19] Palladio's villas nearly all lie within an arc of about forty miles radius from the north-east to the south-west of Vicenza. In 1817 a disillusioned Basevi wrote from Vicenza: 'most of the great works by Palladio are villas at great distance from one another'.[20] Although he stayed in the city for the unusually long period of a month, there is no evidence to suggest that Basevi undertook the arduous excursions necessary to see the villas.[21]

In fact the great majority of British architects who made documented visits to the Veneto in the later Georgian period seem only to have seen two villas. One was the revered Rotonda, of course, situated so close to Vicenza that it was often called a *fabbrica suburbana* rather than a villa. The Rotonda had added significance as the acknowledged source for Chiswick, a point repeatedly commented on down to Arundale in 1832, who rather blindly thought Burlington had been 'so impressed with the beauty of this edifice, that . . . he caused Chiswick House to be erected, in exact imitation of the beautiful original'.[22] The second frequently visited villa was the Malcontenta, which students saw while *en route* between Padua and Venice. At Malcontenta Wolfe had the perspicacity to note: 'Lord Burlington had doubtless in view when he designed Chiswick house both this villa and that of the Rotunda at Vicenza.'[23] In the later Georgian period we have documentation for visits by at least fifteen British architects to the Rotonda, and eight to Malcontenta. Aside from these two villas, there is drawn evidence to show that William Chambers and Thomas Hardwick visited the Villa Caldogno in 1755 and 1779 respectively, that Chambers had also seen the Villa Forni at Montecchio, and that Henry Parke went to the Villa Chiericati at Vancimuglio in 1822. It might be noted that both the Villas Caldogno, Forni and Chiericati are all in the immediate vicinity of Vicenza. In only two cases do we have documentary proof of British architects making more extensive circuits of the villas. In the autumn of 1757 William Mylne stayed at Vicenza for two months. During that time he made a journey to the south to study the Villa Pisani at Bagnolo, the Villa Poiana and the Villa Saraceno at Finale. Mylne certainly visited the Villa Malcontenta from Venice and might also have seen the villas north of Vicenza, since he went to Bassano, Castelfranco and Treviso.[24] The second instance in which we know such comprehensiveness was attempted came in 1820 when Barry and Wolfe visited Vicenza. They saw the Villas Malcontenta and Rotonda. They too went south to the Villa Pisani at Bagnolo. They also travelled north to reach the Villa Valmarana at Lisiera, the Villas Godi and Piovene at Lonedo, Barbaro at Masér and Emo at Fanzolo.[25]

So what, then, was the nature of the first-hand studies of Palladio's villas made by these British architects in the later Georgian period? This question cannot be answered unless we understand the nature of the studies they could make of Palladio's villas *without* seeing them. Their knowledge of the villas derived principally, of course, from the *Quattro libri*, readily available in Italian and in English editions. That the students engaged with the published work is clear, not least from the fact that several purchased copies while in Italy itself. At Vicenza in 1819 George Ledwell Taylor noted: 'Took a glimpse at Palladio's palaces in passing, and bought the book.'[26] In 1817, in an uncanny reflection of Lord Burlington a century earlier, Basevi reported: 'I purchased a common small edition of Palladio at Venice and had it interleaved. I find this to be an excellent method, it prevents my papers multiplying and being inconvenient.'[27] A substantial amount of information could be gleaned from the *Quattro libri*. In Book 2, Palladio described and illustrated twenty-three villas he had designed. These villas were placed in a single sequence, except for the Rotonda (which Palladio included with Vicentine palaces because of its close proximity to the city), and the famous scheme for a Villa Mocenigo on the Brenta (which appeared right at the end of Book 2 in a section of unbuilt designs), source for the plans of Holkham, Nostell and Kedleston. Each villa design was shown in plan and elevation (half elevation, half section in the case of the Rotonda), an indication being given of the cardinal measurements. However, this information immediately presented British architects with a number of difficulties, and these certainly affected the nature of the studies they made when visiting the actual buildings. In the first place visitors would find that fewer than half of the villas had been built in anything like the form in which they appeared in the *Quattro libri*. Some, indeed, had been either destroyed or never built at all. A second respect in which the villas given in the *Quattro libri* did not correspond with reality lay in the measurements indicated. These were of limited use to British architects because they were made according to the Vicentine foot, which is 5.2 cm longer than the English foot. More importantly, the figures given by Palladio represented the ideal proportions he sought to create rather than the actual measurements. A third difficulty lay in the fact that in graphic form only the plan and a single elevation of a villa were shown. At the Villa Pisani, Bagnolo, Wolfe's and Barry's studies focused on the entrance (east) façade (fig. 7.2), no doubt because in the *Quattro libri* Palladio had chosen to show the west (rear courtyard) side of the complex.[28]

In the eighteenth century two other major publications showed the villa buildings of Palladio. The first volume of Francesco Muttoni's *Architettura di Andrea Palladio Vicentino*, published in 1740, included ten plates showing villas as they existed in the mid-eighteenth century rather than as given in the *Quattro libri*. Muttoni's illustrations included the Villa Repeta at Campiglia, rebuilt after a fire of 1672, and the Villa Angarano, where a Baroque house had been added to the *barchesse*, the only part of Palladio's design to have been erected. However, while a Vicentine scale was given, Muttoni provided no actual measurements.[29] The second major eighteenth-century publication on Palladio's buildings was Ottavio Bertotti Scamozzi's *Le fabbriche e i disegni di Andrea Palladio*, a liberally illustrated four-volume work first published at Vicenza between 1776 and 1783 (see fig. 7.5 below).[30] Where possible Bertotti gave the real rather than the ideal measurements, still in Vicentine feet of course. These showed, for example, that the four corner rooms of the Villa Rotonda actually had dimensions of 24 ft 4 in by 15 ft 6 in, that is shorter and wider than the ideal 26 ft by 15 ft given by Palladio in the *Quattro libri*.[31] Muttoni and, particularly, Bertotti also engaged in

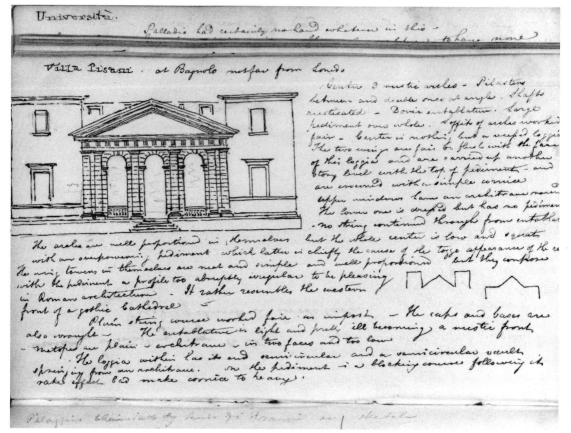

Fig. 7.2 *John Lewis Wolfe, sketchbook elevation and notes on Palladio's Villa Pisani,
Bagnolo, 1820. Courtesy of the Royal Institute of British Architects.*

their texts with questions of the chronology and authorship of the villas. Some care
needs to be exercised, however, in determining the extent to which British architects
were influenced by the works of Muttoni and Bertotti. As far as I have been able to
establish, only the libraries of George Dance the Younger and of John Soane
contained copies of Bertotti, although there was a copy in the Royal Academy library
by 1802 and Wolfe certainly made use of one prior to his departure for Italy in 1819.
But Chambers did not have a personal copy, neither did Robert Adam, nor Robert
Smirke. And it might be added that I know of no British architect or institution
possessing a copy of Muttoni's work in the later Georgian period.[32] Nevertheless, it
can be assumed that the debates these two Italians had stimulated in the later
eighteenth century must have been current among the *ciceroni* and antiquarians of
Vicenza whom travelling British architects met (Bertotti himself had met Matthew
Brettingham the Younger, Chambers and Adam).

  It was, then, questions of actual appearance, measurement and attribution
which tended to preoccupy the British architects who visited Palladio's villas in

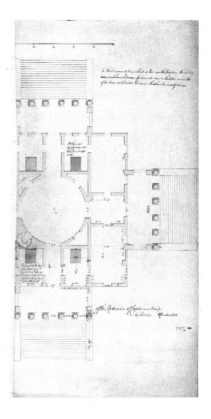

Fig. 7.3 William Chambers, measured part plan of Palladio's Villa Rotonda, Vicenza, 1755. Courtesy of the Board of Trustees of the Victoria & Albert Museum.

the later Georgian period. In 1757 William Mylne was something of a pioneering British explorer of Palladio's villas, so much so that he made a special trip to Marocco, between Venice and Treviso, in search of a Villa Mocenigo given by Palladio in the *Quattro libri* of which only one-third of the main body had been built.[33] During his two-month stay in and around Vicenza Mylne probably visited at least eight villas by Palladio, possibly several more. His letters to his brother Robert in Rome show that his concern at these villas was to obtain accurate measured drawings of them. No such drawings survive from Mylne's surveys, but we do have some made at the Rotonda by William Chambers in 1755. Among these are a three-quarter (cut down) plan of the villa's *piano nobile*, measured in French feet, the choice of this unit of measurement being consistent with Chambers's training at Jacques-François Blondel's Ecole des Arts in Paris (fig. 7.3). When both are converted to metric, Chambers's measurements of the four corner rooms differ from Bertotti's by as much as 9 cm, showing the significant degree to which such figures could vary.[34] In July 1779 Chambers's pupil Thomas Hardwick visited Vicenza, producing a sketchbook part elevation of the Rotonda which, perhaps not coincidentally, corresponds with the portion of the villa shown in Chambers's part plan (fig. 7.4, below).[35] Hardwick drew out a plan of the Rotonda as well: he recorded the measurements in English feet and, when converted to metric, his figures are very close to Chambers's measurement on one axis and to Bertotti's on the other![36] The respective plans of Chambers and Hardwick also make an important

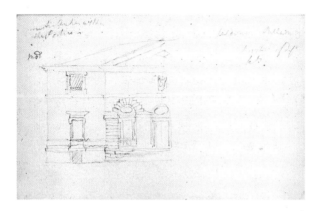

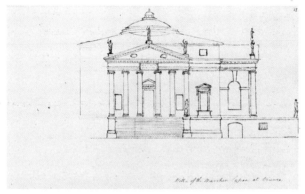

*Fig. 7.4 Thomas Hardwick,
sketchbook elevations of
Palladio's Villas Caldogno and
Rotonda, Vicenza, 1779.
Courtesy of the Royal Institute
of British Architects.*

contribution to our understanding of the history of the four staircases situated around the central *sala* within the villa. Taken together with the plans published by Bertotti, the work of the two Englishmen enables us to establish that the conversion of the south stair from a triangular timber to an oval stone form (mirroring that already carried out on the west stair) was undertaken between 1761 and 1779.[37]

Chambers and Hardwick also both visited and sketched the Villa Caldogno (fig. 7.4, above), a Palladio attribution first illustrated by Bertotti (fig. 7.5) and now confirmed as his design. The choice of this particular building perhaps indicates that master and pupil were interested in the new attribution to Palladio of a villa not shown in the *Quattro libri*.[38] Support for this interpretation of the evidence can perhaps be found in another architect's sketch of a villa not in the *Quattro libri* but illustrated by Bertotti and said by him to be from the school of Palladio: Henry Parke's hand-held pencil plan of the Villa Chiericati at Vancimuglio was made at the site in 1822.[39] Parke's interest (and this is the only Palladio villa he sketched in passing through the Veneto) thus lay in a building of questionable authorship. The rough nature of his drawing also serves to remind us of a likely reason for the relative shortage of measured plans of Palladio's villas by travelling students: namely difficulty of access. During the eighteenth and nineteenth centuries the buildings remained in private hands, of course, and the rarity of recorded comment on interior disposition or décor suggests that entry was by no means always permitted.

The later Georgian architect who engaged most systematically with the literature on Palladio's villas was John Lewis Wolfe. Even before leaving England Wolfe prepared for his visit to Vicenza by trying to sort out attributions and locations. In *Notitia architectonica italiana*, an architectural guide to Italy written for students and published in 1818 by Wolfe's master Joseph Gwilt, a list of eight villas had been given.[40] Wolfe broke up a copy of Gwilt's book and pasted its pages into his own travelling sketchbooks. Gwilt's itinerary was then combined with information gathered from Bertotti to identify a further twelve villas.[41] The list of twenty villas thus produced contained, however, the destroyed Villa Repeta at Campiglia and two buildings not designed by Palladio. These were the Villa Trissino at Cricoli ('I believe by Palladio', wrote Wolfe) and the Villa Francesco Tornieri outside Vicenza.[42] The design of the Villa Tornieri had been attributed to Palladio by Bertotti (though he knew it had been erected after Palladio's death), an attribution of which Wolfe was wary when visiting it later but which Barry

Fig. 7.5 Ottavio Bertotti Scamozzi, measured elevation and details of Palladio's Villa Caldogno, Vicenza, from Le fabbriche e i disegni di Andrea Palladio, *vol. 2 (Vicenza, 1778), plate 44. Courtesy of the Trustees of Sir John Soane's Museum.*

readily accepted, saying: 'Evidently a work of Palladio and a very creditable one'.[43] On the other hand Barry was reluctant to accept Palladio's indubitable authorship of the mutant Villa Valmarana at Lisiera, noting that it 'could not be believed if it were'nt [sic] in his own book'.[44]

A number of later Georgian architects, then, concerned themselves with obtaining measurements and assessing attributions when they visited Palladio's villas, attempting to put the published information together with their own first-hand observations. What remains to be discussed are the formal and aesthetic judgements passed on the villas by these and indeed by other later Georgian architects. In a letter of 1774, Chambers told his pupil Edward Stevens to travel round the Veneto studying buildings by Palladio and Vincenzo Scamozzi. Now Chambers's *Treatise on Civil Architecture* shows him to have been a great admirer of Palladio, but even Chambers 'improved' certain villas when drawing them and described Palladio's style to Stevens with qualification as being in a 'Simple chaste but rather tame manner'.[45] It is striking how these same words were to reappear in Soane's Royal Academy lectures, where Palladio's villas were criticized for 'excess of Simplicity, or rather tameness'.[46] In fact, as more and more British architects visited Palladio's villas, criticism of them became less and less reserved. Passing the Villa Malcontenta and visiting Vicenza in 1757, Robert Adam spoke superciliously of 'the *Celeberrimo ed Illustre Palladio* . . . that so much adored master', while at the Villa Rotonda James Adam found 'the fronts, the round room within and indeed all the particular parts . . . very poorly adjusted'.[47] Theodosius Keene, who visited Italy in 1775, effectively 'neo-Classicized' some of Palladio's buildings. Drawing the Tempietto adjacent to the Villa Barbaro at Maser, for example, Keene removed the lantern so as to make the dome more like that of the Pantheon. His elevation of Il Redentore simply ignored the rather medieval-looking twin round *campanili* which flanked the dome.[48]

When Robert Smirke reached Vicenza in 1804 he wrote that 'Palladio, the boast of the country, has sunk low in my estimation.' Of Palladio's buildings only the Villa Rotonda, which Smirke drew in perspective within the landscape, met with approbation: 'scarcely any [building] appeared to me as having any particular merit except the villa of which that in the Duke of Devonshire's Gardens at Chiswick is a feeble incorrect imitation. I was surprized how Palladio who designed this building could have been the architect of so many wretched ones that are to be seen.'[49] Charles Robert Cockerell, at Vicenza in 1816, described Palladio as 'not the sublime & inimitable genius one imagines him at a distance'.[50] With Wolfe's and Barry's visits to eight villas in 1820, Palladio's reputation came under the most sustained attack. At the Villa Emo, Fanzolo, their criticisms of the *barchesse* show the extent to which the later Georgians had lost sight of Palladio's concept of the villa as fundamentally an agricultural establishment. Wolfe noted that the 'Body of [the] building is perfectly plain without any ornament whatever – it is quite a farmhouse excepting this loggia [Doric portico]', while Barry said that the portico 'is all that is remarkable – its accessories mean and farm like', the pediment 'disgraced by arms and supporters in tympanum'.[51] Of the Villa Barbaro at Maser Wolfe had noted prior to leaving England: 'see this if possible'. Once there, however, his attitude changed completely: 'It is given in Palladio's book and therefore his character must bear the stigma which every man of taste will attach to the architect of this façade worthy almost of Borromini'![52] According to Barry, the villa's façade was 'Palladian but very frightful . . . Austrian eagles & allegorical figures – wretched'.[53]

Finally, at the Villa Rotonda (fig. 7.6) the two students began deferentially enough, Wolfe describing it as 'certainly Palladio's chef d'oeuvre in this class of architecture'. But then the criticisms began. The arch at the side of the portico, said Wolfe, has been 'blamed as an unpardonable defect and certainly so it is'. Barry criticized the steps – 'too many', overpowering the portico; he criticized the frieze for being convex rather than flat, the placement of the statues, the two 'eye windows' within the pediment and the way the inscription tablet interrupts the entablature. Then the students turned on the features of the building said by Bertotti to have been completed by Vincenzo Scamozzi: the projecting stylobates flanking the steps, and the cupola.[54] The stylobates, according to Wolfe, were 'very offensive to the eye', and 'very injudicious upon the building in a lofty situation' according to Barry. Ultimately Barry's eye fell on the cupola: 'The apple pie dome is a vile invention of the enemy Scamozzi who has done much to mar this beautiful edifice.'[55]

Clearly, then, some of the British students who visited Palladio's villas in the later Georgian period were indeed prepared to be 'heretical and presumptuous' in

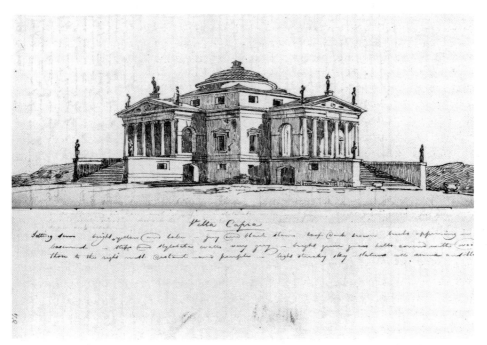

Fig. 7.6 Charles Barry, sketchbook perspective view of Palladio's Villa Rotonda, Vicenza, 1820. Courtesy of the Royal Institute of British Architects.

their assessment of an architect granted almost divine status in Britain during the first half of the eighteenth century. It is also striking, though perhaps hardly surprising, to note that those who made the most unequivocal criticisms – the Adams, Soane, Smirke and Barry – proved to be, successively, the individuals most instrumental in developing Georgian Classical architecture further and further beyond the confines of the Palladian tradition. But it would be wrong to infer from this that Palladio had been entirely discarded by later Georgian architects. Given that the English villa was developing steadily away from Palladian prototypes, it is in itself noteworthy that at least one-third of those who reached Italy between 1750 and 1830 still ensured they included one or more Palladio villas in their itineraries.[56] Moreover, as I have suggested, failure to reach the outlying villas can certainly be put down in part to the financial, political and practical difficulties students encountered when travelling in the Veneto. A number, notably including Chambers and Hardwick, made measured drawings of villas, while others investigated the relationship between the villas as shown in the *Quattro libri* and those actually built by or attributed to Palladio. These investigations belong with the quest for personal verification so typical of Enlightenment thought, but they also represent a great advance on Lord Burlington's brief comments of 1719 and on the absence of any first-hand observations on the villas among Burlington's protégés. Furthermore, Chambers utilized his studies of the villas in the *Treatise on Civil Architecture*, a work which remained the standard English handbook on Classical architecture throughout the later Georgian period.[57]

In fact even those who most disparaged Palladio's villas felt the compunction to exonerate the architect from some of the blame for what they saw as his own shortcomings. Robert Smirke conceded that 'when one considers the prevalent style at his time, for him to have done so much better shows an extraordinary superiority', and despite his criticisms Cockerell considered Palladio as still 'the first arch[itec]t'.[58] Moreover, among Smirke's and Cockerell's contemporaries were many who felt less constrained by the supposed obsolescence of the master. In 1817, for example, Basevi's anticipation of reaching Vicenza was couched in rhetoric of almost Keatsian intensity: 'I admire [Palladio] more than I can express . . . I die to arrive at Vicenza to be surrounded by his immortal works.'[59] (Basevi later had his second son christened James Palladio!) Joseph Gwilt, in his 1818 architectural guide to Italy, instructed students that Palladio was 'the father of modern architecture, and has never been equalled by his successors'.[60] And it seems appropriate to end as I began with George Wightwick, an architect who clearly understood both the past history of British neo-Palladianism and, from the perspective of 1825, its unlikeliness as a source for contemporary design. Having expounded these views, Wightwick none the less went on to add that the poorer quality buildings associated with Palladio's name had no doubt been erroneously attributed to him, and that: 'We are scarcely at liberty to express anything less than a very lofty opinion of Palladio's general merits.'[61] Indeed. We have scarcely been at liberty to do so ever since.[62]

PART IV

SOURCES AND INFLUENCES FOR THE LATER GEORGIAN VILLA

8 Villa Variants

Alistair Rowan

The Georgian villa, by about 1760, had adopted a wide variety of forms. This was the moment in British architecture when Robert Adam had just begun to make his way as a fashionable architect in London, and we might begin with the observation that the Adam brothers were to build or to design a great many houses of this type. Some, though by no means all, are unequivocally identified as villas by whoever put the inscriptions into the volumes of Adam drawings in the Soane Museum.[1] Usually, however, they are simply called houses, but they are small or smallish houses by the standards of the day that saw them built. Two neat examples are Brasted Place, in Kent, built in 1784 for Adam's own medical adviser, Dr John Turton, and Newliston House, in West Lothian, outside Edinburgh, built from 1789 for Thomas Hogg, whose father had earlier employed William Adam to design a large Palladian house which remained unbuilt. The trim rectangular massing of these two houses, with their shallow pediments and understated eaves, seems perfectly expressive of the taste of the 1780s, with Brasted, as it suppresses the basement storey to a mere third of its height, appearing as the more up-to-date. These are elegant smaller houses or Georgian villas whose style and appearance might prompt us to put ourselves imaginatively into the position of Robert and James Adam and to ask what were the models that presented themselves to the brothers when approaching the villa theme, and what earlier work would have been familiar to them? What was the commonality of experience for these two brothers who, born in Scotland no more than a generation after the Union of the two kingdoms in 1707, were to dominate fashionable architectural taste in London for the first two decades of George III's reign?

The combination of inspired patronage and dedicated professionalism, so characteristic of innovative design in many different parts of eighteenth-century Britain, is a marked feature of the Adam brothers' early experience. Here the patron dilettante is John Erskine, 11th Earl of Mar, whose interest in the formal qualities of architecture was communicated to an influential circle of people in the building world in Scotland, including the brothers' father William Adam, who published one of his schemes – semi-anonymously, since Lord Mar was then living in exile as a Jacobite – as a design 'Invented by a Person of Quality'.[2] Lord Mar exhibits a mind fascinated by the perfection of ideal schemes: the plan which William Adam reproduces, though its elevation is bizarre, seems to be a derivative of J.H. Mansard's main block at Marly as it makes notable use of a central octagonal space rising through the height of the building and contained within a square, with the main rooms radiating out in a cruciform plan between suites of apartments in the outer corners. Though William Adam calls this 'A Royal Palace' the geometrically dominant central hall has more the character of a place of retreat or princely villa, and that such notions were not unfamiliar to Lord Mar is demonstrated by a number of schemes which are recorded in the volumes of drawings made either for or by Lord Mar, now in the Scottish Record Office. One of these is an intriguing scheme for a small house, laid out on a plan like a bow tie with a circular domed hall at the centre of the bow, fronted by segmental colonnades and flanked by dart-shaped suites of rooms on either side. The building is described as a 'Design of a House by way of a Villa for a Hunthall' and was drawn at Geneva in 1718 and copied in Paris four years later in 1722.[3] The inscription on the curving entablature, ICI FAY QUE VOUDRAS, suggests that Lord Mar thought of this villa as a Trianon more than as anything else.

Now this sort of formal complexity, the playful juxtaposition and interpenetration of the domed central hall and its flanking suites of rooms, is also a marked feature in the work of the leading architect in Scotland around 1700, James Smith. Smith's drawings of house designs in the RIBA collection[4] often include ideal schemes which give prominence to a central hall: five of these are circular, three are cruciform and two are square, while at least two designs seem to offer adaptations of Palladio's Villa Rotonda form. Among these designs is a wonderfully skilful octagonal villa in which a domed central hall contains the principal staircase, with the main rooms accommodated, with a good deal of ingenuity, around it to provide a saloon with two apses at either end, a rectangular dining-room and a suite of four bedrooms each with its bed recess and dressing-room.[5] Smith provides a section of this design which seems to bear an almost direct relationship to the Adam brothers' own work in the staircase at Home House in Portman Square, and indeed in the magnificent colonnaded and oval staircase which Robert was to add to Culzean Castle, in Ayrshire, in 1787.

Lord Mar and James Smith's quest for the ideal may have remained on paper but it is worth noting that an early example of a smaller Classical house with a central staircase was produced by Smith's associate Colen Campbell at Shawfield Park outside Glasgow in 1711. The plan and elevation were published by Campbell in *Vitruvius Britannicus* and it seems clear that the façade is an adaptation of a Smith formula regularized and tidied up (fig. 8.1).[6] Interestingly Campbell notes in his commentary on Shawfield that 'the principal apartment is in the first storey and the staircase is so placed, in the middle, as to serve four good apartments in the second storey'. So something of the Lord Mar/Smith

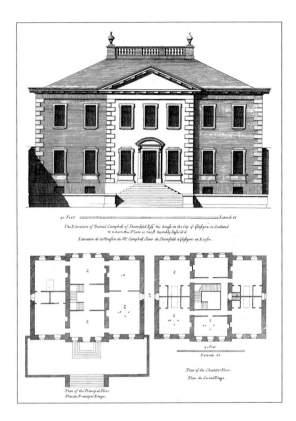

Fig. 8.1 Colen Campbell,
Shawfield Park, Glasgow, 1711.

villa ideal survives here, and we may also observe how one man's ideas impact upon another's, and bring these early references back to the Adam family, if we note that the façade of Shawfield, long since demolished, was adapted by John and James Adam for the garden front of Paxton House in Berwickshire, a villa type house built from 1758 to which we will return later.

Campbell's design of Mereworth in Kent is, inevitably, the house that links most closely to Lord Mar and Smith's domed designs (fig. 8.2). Its dome and indeed most of its design is clearly a direct tribute to the Villa Rotonda at Vicenza built for the Papal Secretary Paolo Almerico and perhaps for that reason employing the dome for the first time in domestic architecture, a motif which had previously been reserved for sacred architecture (fig. 8.3). We do not need to point to Mar or Smith to establish a precedent for Mereworth, yet it is worth pondering whether Campbell would have admired this particular Palladian villa so much if he had not shared their enthusiasms for ideal and geometrical plans.

The ideal, and a desire for centrality, is very much in evidence in Campbell's other great villa, Stourhead in Wiltshire (fig. 8.4). In *Vitruvius Britannicus* Campbell publishes two plans of the house, what was built and, on the left-hand side, his preferred solution which was to have arranged the main rooms in a cruciform shape about a central staircase set within a space which was to be twenty foot square (fig. 8.5).[7] Both Mereworth and Stourhead have always featured

Fig. 8.2   Colen Campbell, Mereworth Castle, Kent, 1722–5.

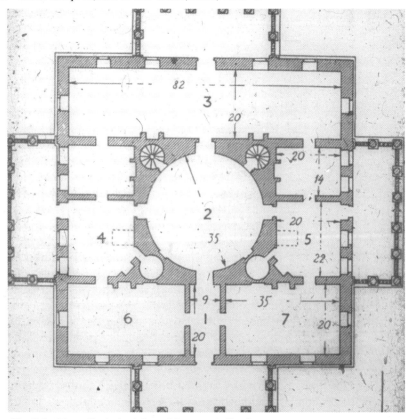

Fig. 8.3   Plan of principal floor, Mereworth Castle.

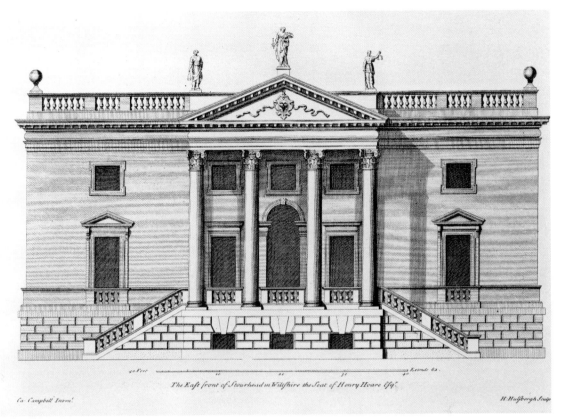

The East front of Stourhead in Wiltshire the Seat of Henry Hoare Esq.

Ca: Campbell Inven.   *H: Hulsbergh Sculp*

Fig. 8.4   Colen Campbell, Stourhead, 1720–4, Wiltshire.

prominently in the history of the dissemination of Palladian taste in the British Isles and their influence is well known. It is perhaps worth noting that Campbell calls both of these houses 'Castles', which distinguishes them by name from all his other designs, and it is also clear that, in these Palladian castles, the setting is an aspect of the design which is of importance to the architect. Of Stourhead Campbell writes 'the front gives a very beautiful and extensive prospect over the rich vale of Dorsetshire, east and south, and is protected from the north by high mountains covered with downs' and it was of course the peculiar beauty of the site of the Villa Rotonda, on its saucer-shaped hill south of Vicenza, which had encouraged Palladio to make use of the famous quadripartite plan on that occasion.

A reported concern with the setting of a property appears in at least two further designs by Campbell for little houses. In the case of the charmingly Raphaelesque 'House for John Hedworth at Chester-le-Street, Co. Durham', which remained unbuilt, Campbell tells us that, as the north prospect was not very favourable, he 'made no windows on this side but to the two staircases',[8] whereas at the diminutive Ebberston Lodge, which was built in 1718 for William Thompson of Humbleton, the reader is told that the building is 'about three miles from his principal seat' and that it 'stands in a fine park well planted, with a river which

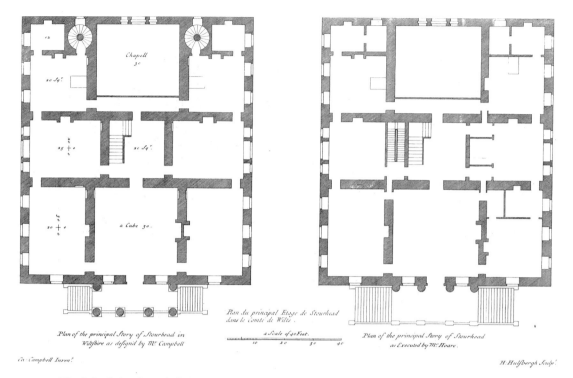

Plan of the principal Story of Stourhead in Wiltshire as design'd by Mr Campbell

Plan du principal Etage de Stourhead dans le Comte de Wilts.

a Scale of 40 Feet.

Plan of the principal Story of Stourhead as Executed by Mr Hoare.

Co: Campbell Inven.t

H: Hulsbergh Sculp.t

Fig. 8.5   Colen Campbell, Stourhead, Wiltshire.

forms a cascade and canal 1200 foot long, and [which] runs under the loggio in the back front' (fig. 8.6).[9] So whether a villa is on a grand scale, like Mereworth and Stourhead Castles, or a miniature structure built as a place of retreat like Ebberston Lodge, its setting according to Colen Campbell's views is always of significance.

Obviously the Adam brothers were very well acquainted with Campbell's publications; another Scottish architect whose work they knew well was James Gibbs. Gibbs came from Aberdeenshire and at his death in 1754 left a substantial part of his personal fortune to Lord Erskine 'in gratitude for favours received from his father the late Earl of Mar', so with James Gibbs we retain a strong connection to the circle in which the Adam brothers formed their views. Gibbs enjoyed one great advantage which Robert and James Adam will certainly have known of and ultimately were to copy: he had studied abroad. In 1703 Gibbs had travelled to Rome where he was inscribed as a clerical student in the Scots College. Within a year he had transferred his interests to architecture and from 1704 to 1709 had studied in the studio of Carlo Fontana, Bernini's favourite architectural pupil and the leading architect in the Rome of his day.

Gibbs's contribution to the variety of models for villa designs is aristocratic and Italianate. It is emphatically not Palladian – or not immediately so – and is based on the idea of the *villa suburbana*, or residential retreat outside the capital for a great

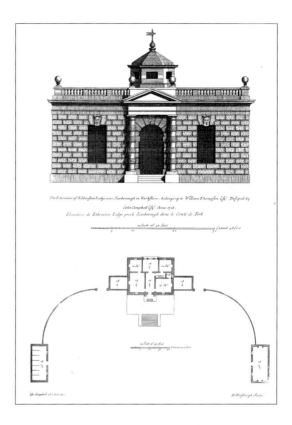

Fig. 8.6 Colen Campbell, Ebberston Lodge, Yorkshire, 1718.

political magnate whose power base and whose family estates are elsewhere. Two designs which well demonstrate these preferences are Sudbrook, near Petersham in Surrey, built from 1715 for just such a magnate, the 2nd Duke of Argyll (fig. 8.7), and Down Hall in Essex (fig. 8.8), a house planned for the court poet Matthew Prior but never carried into execution on account of Prior's early death.[10]

Both Sudbrook for the Duke and Down Hall for the poet present a formula which is familiar in Italy but uncommon in England. In each Gibbs proposes an ample central hall – a veritable *sala di festa* at Sudbrook – which runs from the front to the back of the building, like the deep *androne* of the traditional Italian country house. Gibbs screens this deep hall in both designs by a colonnaded loggia at Sudbrook and a lower arcade and upper loggia at Down Hall. The effect of such a plan is to chop the house in two so that it requires two staircases and two suites of apartments on either side of the central space. There is here some parallel with Lord Mar's Geneva Villa which also proposes two suites of apartments on either side of a central hall and in a sense this type of plan exhibits, in its very impracticality, the temporary nature of the villa ideal as Gibbs understands it.

Gibbs's debt to the Italian *androne* as the generating idea for a small country house is very evident in the design illustrated as plate 62 in his *Book of Architecture* of 1728, which rather intriguingly seems to take as its starting point an uncharacteristic Palladian source in the Villa Pisani at Bagnolo. This small country house of 1542 has a similar deep hall running front to back, a similar arrangement

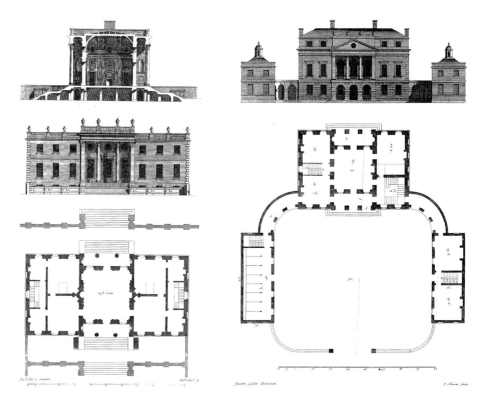

Fig. 8.7   James Gibbs, Sudbrook,
Surrey, 1715–19.

Fig. 8.8   James Gibbs, Down Hall, Essex, 1720,
unexecuted.

of double staircases and the same over-scaled Diocletian window to light the upper part of the central hall as the most conspicuous element of its elevation. The Duke of Argyll's successor, as Earl of Islay, also employed Gibbs to produce designs for a suburban villa for his estate at Whitton in Middlesex. In the largest of these[11] the *androne* appears again as a huge central hall rising through two storeys and with two suites of apartments given separate staircases on either side, such as we have already seen Gibbs propose elsewhere. The entrance front which Gibbs illustrates for this design seems almost canonical and deceptively like many an English Palladian country house by Isaac Ware, John Adam or John Carr of York, but its plan is nonetheless distinctly different and remains continental in its origin.

When your client will not build a large house you may have more luck with a smaller design. The Adam brothers were certainly to discover this, and Gibbs's smallest proposal for Whitton is described disarmingly as 'a little house for Lord Islay'.[12] This little building seems to me to anticipate, rather like Campbell's Ebberston Lodge, many of the later developments in polite rural architecture of the 1760s and 1770s. It is miniature in scale; a principal room is entered directly from the outside with the main apartment over it. Its offices are either in the basement of the buildings or are sunk and placed out of sight behind shallow flanking walls; and finally – a crucial consideration in many later villa designs – the architect has contrived a clever juxtaposition of usable small spaces and handsome rooms by the use of a split-level arrangement so that there are more storeys at the back of the house than there are at the front. In this little house the staircase has come into the middle of the house, where Campbell and Smith both liked to place it in a villa.

John Adam may have had the little three-bay, two-storey façade by Gibbs in mind when he designed his small town house in the Canongate in Edinburgh – really a town villa – for Lord Milton in the early 1750s.[13] He certainly made use of architectural pattern books in this way and there is evidence that Isaac Ware's *The Complete Body of Architecture*, published about 1756, provided the Adam family with inspiration for their own work.[14] Ware is a familiar figure in second-generation English Palladianism who, in his published work, had an important part to play in popularizing the idea and the ideals of villa life. One of Ware's most modest designs is for a little house, five bays wide and two storeys high, with the central three bays rising one storey higher than the rest and finished with a pediment (fig. 8.9).[15] The house is not identified as a villa, but as part of the text of *The Complete Body* is taken up with a consideration of the appropriate features for modest residence in the countryside, not for grand houses but for comfortable retirement, and as it seems to have been designed to enjoy a view with all its rooms looking in the one direction, it may be accommodated within our theme.

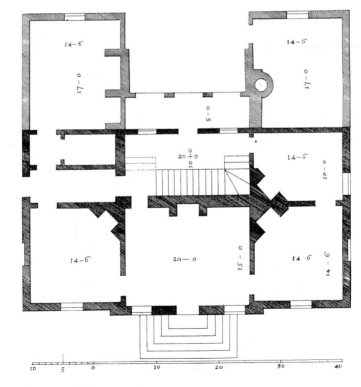

Fig. 8.9 Isaac Ware, a small house, 1756.

Indeed it seems to provide another proto late eighteenth-century villa type, as Ware tells us that, like Gibbs's design, it was to have the offices mostly out of sight as single-storey extensions at the back. Here once again the position of the staircase is immediately behind the entrance hall in the centre of the plan, while the extra height of the middle section of the building anticipates the façade of Sir Robert Taylor's celebrated Richmond Villa for Sir Charles Asgill. Both features were to become common in later eighteenth-century villa design.

John Summerson long ago identified Ware's designs as marking a characteristic shift from the great house in the villa.[16] The two schemes in *The Complete Body* illustrate this change: neither is very large and both are limited to a plan which provides for one staircase only. These are houses which were designed not for grand but for moderate living, contrived either for those who wished to make a seasonal retreat into the country or for retirement on a modest competence. One house is described as a 'House for a Gentleman near London', the other as 'built for Alexander Johnston, Esq., in Scotland', though it was apparently never carried out.[17]

Ware is often characterized as Lord Burlington's most faithful acolyte, a man of no very original talent who carried on a routine Palladianism well into the 1760s, but he is also a writer of considerable charm and the text of *The Complete Body* gives us a useful insight into how these villas or smaller country houses came to be planned and how they were to be used. 'Where the proprietor has spirit and the chosen spot allows of due extent,' says Ware, 'the house should have a court before it and a garden behind.'[18] The house near London was evidently intended to be built on a restricted site as it has straight wings, on a line with the main front, whereas the Scottish house was to have more space and has a front court framed by flanking pavilion wings and linked by quadrant walls to the main block of the house. This tidy Palladian formula represents Ware's preferred option. Houses, he states, are:

> edifices in which the distribution of apartments is principally to be considered. . . . Where there is a garden of tolerable extent, some of the principal apartments, supposing the situation proper, may be very conveniently placed in the hinder part of the house. They will be these means be freed from noise and disturbance and they will have a good light; the garden also will be a good prospect. . . . [Rooms to] be suited to the seasons of the year as well as to their purposes. Thus rooms for summer may be placed towards the north, and winter rooms to the south and west, because we seek coolness in summer and in the winter as much sun as we can. Those rooms for summer should also be large, and those for winter small, for the same plain reason that a smaller room is easier warmed and that a large one is always more airy.

Such practical considerations are not, however, Ware's only qualities, and *The Complete Body* also speaks of the pleasures of country life in the extent to which a rural retreat may offer its inhabitants an opportunity to enjoy the changing seasons. Here setting and sensibility are neatly woven together:

The Italians are very exact in the distribution of their houses; they have rooms fronting the east, which are their favourites for spring and autumn; and they always contrive to have them face gardens, or extensive grounds where there are trees. In both these seasons there is a great beauty in this part of nature; the leaves of trees have a fresh and lively green at the time of their first unfolding, which they lose in a few weeks and never after recover; and towards autumn they have a variety that is not found in any other season. All leaves change colour as they fade, and this they do variously according to their kinds, some earlier and some later. This gives the autumn a colouring unknown at any other season. . . .

    There is the same kind of advantage in the western situation of summer rooms, though from another source. They command the setting sun, where they are not blocked up, and this is a source of beauty beyond painting, and beyond all else in nature. The great luminary of the heavens dropping gradually below the horizon is a noble object; and the paintings of the clouds, during the succeeding half hour, are very beautiful and varied every moment.[19]

Perhaps we catch here in Ware's uncharacteristically poetic description something of the meaning of the villa which too great an insistence on plan types, the influence of antiquity or social status can obscure. The eighteenth-century gentleman, or gentlewoman, enjoyed the countryside, the changing seasons, and knew how to interpret the movements of animals and birds to understand the climate, or to predict changes in the weather. They lived much much closer than we do to the natural world.

    One of Ware's larger designs for houses, 'a building designed for James Murray Esq; of Broughton at Kellie' (fig. 8.10),[20] brings us neatly back to the Adam family for it seems to have been used by John and James Adam as the basis for their own design for Patrick Home of Billie for Paxton House in Berwickshire (fig. 8.11), whose garden front we have already examined as a derivative of Campbell's Shawfield Park. Ware's design is for a big house, four windows deep with a sequence of four rooms on the left-hand side and a pair of main stairs and a secondary service stair, both top-lit, in the centre of the plan. When John and James Adam came to build this house it was too large for their client, who was to inherit the estate of Wedderburn Castle near by, and so the big house was cut down to a large villa by the expedient of removing the front set of rooms and turning the central staircase into the entrance hall so that what was originally the secondary stair became the main staircase.[21]

    The building of Paxton House coincides with the years which saw Robert Adam's return from his Grand Tour and the start of his practice in London in January 1758. The master of villa architecture at that time, and a man well integrated within the patronage of the city of London, was Sir Robert Taylor, and it is to Taylor's practice that we must now look for the next development in the up-to-date villa plan. It seems to me that while Campbell, Gibbs and Ware all had something to contribute to the formation of the Adam brothers' ideas of architecture generally, it was Taylor who provided Robert Adam with the definitive examples of how a small house in the countryside might be contrived,

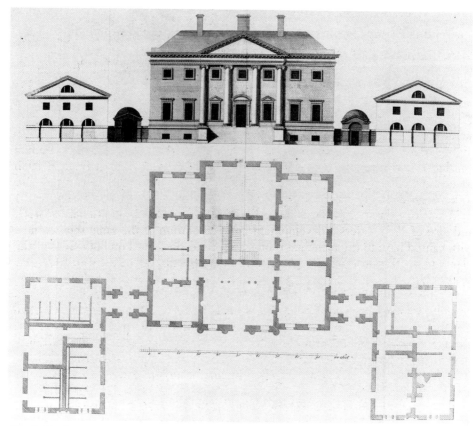

Fig. 8.10   Isaac Ware, design for James Murray of Broughton.

Fig. 8.11   John and James Adam, Paxton House, Berwickshire, 1758.

and how variety in its interior arrangements might best be achieved. Taylor's villas cluster in the mid-1750s and early 1760s: among the first is Harleyford Manor in Buckinghamshire, built for Sir William Clayton in 1755.[22] Taylor, like Ware, thinks of the central top-lit stair as appropriate for a villa, but his planning goes far beyond the tidy sequences of rectangular and square rooms of his predecessors to provide a library with a deeply canted bay window on the left, a drawing-room with an elliptical bow at the back of the house and a complex sequence of apsidal and niched passages to give access to the stair hall and to the dining-room. Robert Adam might later claim it was his brother and he who had carried out the revolution of banishing the rectangular room from British domestic architecture, but if the brothers did espouse this cause effectively – and there is no doubt that they did – Sir Robert Taylor was certainly earlier in the field and dropping beguiling hints. Coptford Hall in Essex, for Richard Holden and also of 1755, offers a development and elaboration of the same themes, now with canted bays to the principal rooms at ground floor level on both sides of the plan and an elliptical bow in the centre to create a three-lobed design which we might characterize as a clover-leaf plan. Barlaston Hall in Staffordshire of one year later is closely similar, and the clover-leaf plan appears again, now in a developed form, at Asgill Lodge, Richmond, in 1761, a design which seems to develop Isaac Ware's little house with its centre one storey higher. Asgill Lodge shrinks the villa now to no more than three main rooms, each of an interesting shape with an apsed ante-room, a vaulted corridor and an oval staircase.

In larger houses by Taylor, Ware's principle of adding consequence by wings and a courtyard seems to apply. These are Danson Hall at Bexley Heath in Kent of 1762 and a later design, Purbrook in Hampshire of 1776. Danson has since lost its wings and Purbrook has been demolished. In these houses it is the shallow, understated treatment of the façades and the pyramid roofs of the Purbrook wings which is the sort of architecture that most appealed to Robert Adam when he returned from Italy, and which he was to lay under tribute in his own designs for country houses. Mersham-le-Hatch in Kent, an early house designed by Adam in 1762–5 for Sir William Knatchbull, has much of the reticence of Taylor's manner. It has two pyramid slated roofs to its pavilions and a deep semi-circular bow in the centre of its garden front.[23] We may notice one novelty however, which Taylor never attempted and which was to become a characteristic of many Adam schemes, in the way the house is tucked into the side of a gently sloping hill so that the entrance front is close to the ground and is, in consequence, only two storeys high, whereas the front to the park sits higher so that the principal rooms can enjoy the view and just those effects of the changing face of nature which Ware so attractively describes.

Mersham-le-Hatch is not one of those opulent, princely houses with which the name of Adam is so readily associated and which marked the launch of Robert's fashionable career: nevertheless it seems to represent a notable moment in his development as a designer of moderate and medium-sized country houses and to mark the outset of his activity as an architect who was to become distinguished in the contrivance of elegant villas. The opulent villa is perhaps best represented by Adam's work at Kenwood for Lord Mansfield in 1767–9. This house is beautifully situated on the edge of Hampstead Heath and gained by Adam's additional wings, portico and a reorganized interior a metropolitan chic which other villas of the period cannot pretend to. Contemporaries certainly refer to Kenwood as a villa but the norm for Adam production in the 1770s and 1780s was for a much smaller sort of house, as seems generally to have been the case in this period.

Two examples of Adam villas of the 1780s are Jerviston in Lanarkshire, a small house built for James Cannison from 1782, and the villa which Adam designed for Captain Matthew Pitts, a scheme of 1783 which remained unbuilt.[24] They represent convention and innovation in Adam's smaller villa designs. The Scottish house offers a subtle reworking of old Palladian themes, with a fairly straightforward plan, while Captain Pitts's villa is smooth and flat in its architecture, with subtle gradations in surface, neat cubic blocks with shallow pyramid roofs at the end of the wings and, a characteristic later Adam motif which we shall meet again, a centrepiece designed to set up a conscious duality, with pylon-like advanced elements flanking an open centre. Indeed it is almost as if Adam had taken the Admiralty screen in Whitehall, his own first public work, and extended it into a villa form.[25]

The straight wings of these two designs seem to be a form which Adam preferred to the more usual Palladian quadrants. Towards the end of his life in 1787 he had great hopes of the wealthy baronet Sir Samuel Hannay of Kirkdale in Creetown, Kirkcudbrightshire, for whom Adam built a new house overlooking Wigton Bay. Sir Samuel died in 1790 so that the house was never finished in the manner which Adam had intended, but the sharp geometrical forms of its main block, shallow straight links and the cubic wings with low pyramid roofs sit well above the bay, and we may note the feature, already remarked at Mersham le Hatch, of tucking the house into the hillside so that the principal rooms are one floor up on the garden front and enjoy spectacular views.[26]

The cubic massing and pyramid roofs of the wings at Kirkdale are elements which were very much a part of the Adam villa idiom. Robert Adam had, throughout his life, an interest in pure geometry and simple solid form. The wings at Mersham-le-Hatch demonstrate this nicely and may be compared with the brothers' first design of 1773 for a villa – it is really a seaside retreat – at Cadland in Hampshire for their banker, Robert Drummond (fig. 8.12). In the event the commission was to go to Henry Holland rather than the Adam brothers. The layout of the rooms in this little house[27] offers an elegant demonstration of economical and resourceful planning with an apsidal entrance hall, the staircase to one side and an oval library on the other, all set across the three-bay front but connecting with a five-bay rear elevation in which the dining-room has a shallow segmental curve against the fireplace wall. And as so often this house was to have had a rear elevation one storey higher than that of the front.

The villa at Cadland may also be compared with a little house in Scotland designed for a Mr Thomson,[28] cubic once again and even more modest in its plan, though of a similar arrangement. Here Adam has had to adjust the window walls of the two principal rooms at the back to accommodate the intervals imposed by the portico on the garden front. It is worth noticing the skill with which he has

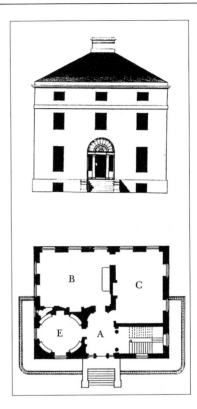

Fig. 8.12 Robert Adam, Cadland, Hampshire, 1773.

managed the lopsided arrangement of the two windows in the dining-room and how, by placing a shallow segmental apse across the end of the room, he has regularized the internal elevation and at the same time provided a connecting door to the study at the front of the house and a china cupboard just where it is needed.

Though neither of these small houses was to be built, the tall square block with pyramid roof does appear at Moreton Hall outside Bury St Edmunds in Suffolk, built for the Cambridge professor John Symonds between 1773 and 1776.[29] Here the flat site could not accommodate the usual Adam device of tucking the house into a hill, and the segmental side bows of two storeys seems almost to quote Sir Robert Taylor's manner, though the house is a good deal taller than any of Taylor's designs. Unusually the rough plan which Adam prepared to work out the overall floor area has been preserved.[30] This allowed the architect to provide his client with an estimated cost and records the original layout in which it appears that the dining-room was in a triple-apsed room on the ground floor, with the saloon above. These rooms looked south and west while the bow on the east side accommodated utilitarian services. Taylor's villas had a neater balance of public rooms on either side of the central axis, and it may be that this plan resulted from the perceived need to lift the saloon one storey higher to give good views over the Suffolk countryside.

The bay-window motif appears in another villa, Sunnyside at Liberton, on the outskirts of Edinburgh, for which Adam prepared a bewildering series of variant plans before fixing on a final version for Sir Patrick Inglis in 1790 (fig. 8.13). One scheme, which seems to date from about 1785, is based on a type of clover-leaf plan, with segmental bay windows on the two side elevations and at the back of the house, very much as a development of the Taylor ideal though now a good deal later.[31] At this stage the accommodation of the plan to the external shape of the rooms was undoubtedly forced; however, by the time Sunnyside reached its final form[32] the plan had been refined into a scheme of admirable conciseness where the sequence of spaces was perfectly considered and most artfully contrived. From a miniature *porte cochère* the visitor entered a square hall which connected directly with an ample drawing-room behind with free-standing columns in each corner. Beside one of these a short lobby permitted guests to progress directly from the drawing-room to the dining-room, without the need to return to the hall, when servants would be bringing food from the kitchen in the basement below; on the other side of the hall is the staircase with a water closet discreetly accommodated on the landing, and given its own little window hidden within the recess of the centre of the façade. Next to the WC was Sir Patrick's study. The façade, like that of Captain Pitts's villa, presents the late Adam duality with an open and understated centre held between two pedimented blocks.

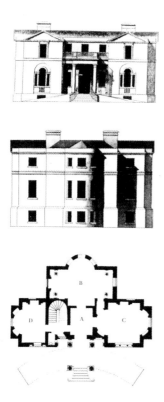

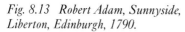

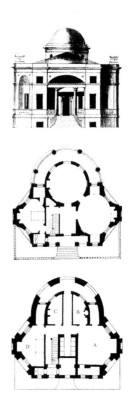

Fig. 8.13 Robert Adam, Sunnyside, Liberton, Edinburgh, 1790.

Fig. 8.14 Robert Adam, House for Mr Wilson, c. 1790.

To return from Sunnyside to the Deputy Ranger's Lodge in the Green Park, whose plan was engraved for publication but never issued in *The Works* during the brothers' lifetime,[33] is to emphasize the subtlety of a late Adam villa against a somewhat routine production of 1768, with just one round room on the garden front and a range of plain rectangular spaces on either side. Here what is most noticeable is the garden façade which offers a fusion of a two-storey domed rotunda – we might almost go back to Lord Mar's hunting lodge – with a regular astylar two-storey façade. Otherwise the Deputy Ranger's Lodge was unremarkable, except perhaps in its early use of the staircase entrance hall, which Sir William Chambers had pioneered at Duddingston House in 1763 and which Adam was to use increasingly in various later designs.[34]

Adam is an architect who always enjoyed playing with an idea, and it seems clear that the domed rotunda of the Deputy Ranger's Lodge finds its apogee and is fused with the Sunnyside plan in an extraordinary little villa which has been identified in the Adam drawings as 'A House for Mr Wilson' (fig. 8.14). Mr Wilson may perhaps be identified as William Wilson of Keythorpe in Leicestershire, a Member of the House of Commons who served in the same Parliament in which Adam represented Kinross, a cultured, intellectual bachelor, sometime member of Clare College, Cambridge, who 'passed the later part of his life at the German Spa and other parts of the Continent and died immensely rich at Pisa' in 1796.[35] For Mr Wilson Adam has devised a villa of the most engaging ingenuity which combines a rectangular entrance hall, a circular saloon and oval dining-room; there is an octagonal bedroom, with a convenient stair and little water closet thoughtfully positioned off the staircase and just beside Mr Wilson's bedroom. The sequence and inter-relationship of the rooms is closely similar to Sunnyside but every room shape is revised and perfectly accommodated to its position in the plan. The rotunda-like front to the gardens and, we must assume, the principal prospect, is a full three storeys, while the entrance façade is tucked into a sloping site and offers a variant of the late Adam open-centre elevation with pylons flanking a colonnaded recess. We must surely regret that William Wilson did not build this ingenious little villa but kept his cash for prodigal self-indulgence in the Grand Dukedom of Tuscany instead.

A younger son who built a late villa by Adam was Dayhort MacDowall, from Castle Semple in Renfrewshire, whose unusual triangular house at Walkinshaw was begun in the autumn of 1791 within six months of the architect's death.[36] It has long been demolished, but the plans survive and exhibit the same facility in the condensation of an idea so that not one piece of space is wasted within the layout of the house. Walkinshaw makes use of a semi-circular entrance-staircase-hall, from which a neat square lobby communicates directly with a breakfast room, in the octagon at the apex of the triangle; the dining-room and drawing-room – both double-apsed spaces lit by tripartite windows – are set at forty-five degree angles on either side. The sequence from octagon to apsed chamber to octagon is indeed not unlike Lord Burlington's famous arrangement of the spaces on the garden front of Chiswick Villa, but here there is absolutely no waste space. The study is in the left-hand octagon near to the servants and to the back stair, and on the other side is a bedroom and dressing-room with once again

– and I think the care of this planning is worth noting – a water closet beside the dressing room and opening directly off the hall. Here Adam's delight in the authority of pure geometry and in the purity of a symmetrical plan contrasts robustly with the subtlety and fluidity of his scheme for William Wilson; in either case, however, we may note how, by the 1790s, the villa has shrunk in size as it increases both in its spatial complexity and ingenious contrivance. James Gibbs's bold and confident blocks for the Duke of Argyll or Lord Islay seem designed to serve the needs of a quite different age, and even Isaac Ware's modest Palladian houses are larger – he recommended a sixty-five foot frontage – and more complete in their provisions.

The Adam legacy should perhaps receive some mention. Of the many books for villas and country houses issued towards the end of the century none is more closely related to the Adam idiom than the publications of George Richardson, their long-serving principal clerk, whose *New Designs in Architecture* of 1792 offers two schemes for what seem to be enormous houses which Richardson nonetheless characterizes as villas.[37] 'These designs of Villas', he writes, 'exhibit buildings of considerable extent, in which convenience, utility and solidity have been studied in the plan and, in the elevations, variety, elegance and beauty. They are contrived to contain all the principal apartments on the same floor and these are of such number and dimensions as may be sufficient for the comfortable habitations of gentlemen possessed of considerable fortunes.'[38] The grandest design was calculated by Richardson to cost £7,100 according to the prices of labour and materials in London in 1791, and the second, more modest scheme was priced at £5,580. Even compared with Sir Samuel Hannay's Kirkdale it is a vast house with a first and second drawing-room, a best dining-room and a common eating parlour, eight main bedrooms with dressing-rooms and separate closets and a large master bedroom.

Richardson also published the two volumes of *The New Vitruvius Britannicus*, in 1802 and 1808, which include the plan and elevation of a vast house at Putney, designed for Beilby Thompson by William Porden.[39] Once again, this very substantial residence is described as a villa and, though its sheer size might leave us in doubt as to its true status, Richardson's accompanying letterpress takes time to establish its setting and stylistic credentials for inclusion in the genre:

> This house is pleasantly situated on the north side of Putney Heath commanding, to the south, a view of the various roads which intersect and enliven that spacious piece of unenclosed country, and to the north [is] an extensive prospect of the fertile meadows of Surrey and Middlesex, through which the river Thames majestically winds in its course from Richmond to Fulham. The salubrity of the air and the beauty of the scenery, unite in making this place a delightful retirement from the smoke and noise of the metropolis; where the quiet of rural amusements may be mingled with the charms of polished society, the adjacent villas being inhabited by families of fashion and distinction.[40]

Richardson includes the fascinating note that the two smaller bows at the side of the plan 'were built about 40 years earlier in a house for Mr John Morris', which prompts the thought that Putney Park may at its core have been an earlier villa, of a more modest scale, by Sir Robert Taylor.

Porden and Richardson emulate the Adam manner on an enlarged scale: the more modest inspiration of their later villas is clearly reflected in David Laing's *Hints for Dwellings* of 1800. Laing had been articled in John Soane's office in 1790 and there is indeed something Soanic about many of the small villas with the large round rooms in the centre of the rear elevation, though this plan type was very standard by the 1790s. Another two-storey villa with a shallow articulation to its façade, which Laing describes as 'for a gentleman at Ballymahon, near Mullingar in Ireland', clearly recalls the open centre and conscious duality of many late Adam designs.[41]

When is a villa not a villa? This discussion of the Georgian villa has tended to avoid architecture which is not patently Classical, yet in a review of Robert Adam's contribution to the genre the small castles which he designed for so many Scottish clients towards the end of his life should not be totally ignored. I must limit myself to one example which is undoubtedly the finest, Seton Castle in East Lothian, designed in 1789 for the lawyer and minor landowner Alexander McKenzie of Portmore.[42] Seton is given unusual consequence by the extent of its wings which form two back-to-back U-shaped service yards and frame an entrance court. However, the plan of the main block offers one of those condensed and succinct statements which is typical of the Adam villa at its best: a staircase entrance hall like the one at Walkinshaw and a tight sequence of drawing-room, dining-room, master bedroom and dressing-rooms arranged round the volume of the stair. But there is more here than is usual in a small villa, for the wings provide accommodation for an entire establishment to support a delightful rural life. The left wing contains two coach houses, a slaughter house, the kitchen and sculleries, the butler's room with a business room and dressing-room for Mr McKenzie and a convenient back door. On the right the dairy and laundry are connected to the house by a quadrant corridor with stables for coach and farm horses, a cow shed, a hen house and, upstairs, accommodation for the dairymaid, hen keeper, the cow man and stable boys.

And Seton Castle, like so many of the Classical villas, exhibits one scale on its entrance front and has another taller and more imposing elevation fronting the gardens and overlooking the view north to the Firth of Forth. The idiom may be unfamiliar but the type of life that could be led within its walls is emphatically that of polite retirement in the later Georgian age.

9 Soane's Concept of the Villa

David Watkin

Sir John Soane spent much time in studying and translating the works of key writers and theorists of the Enlightenment such as Laugier, Winckelmann, Rousseau, d'Hancarville and Milizia, in preparation for the lectures which he delivered at the Royal Academy from 1809. The stress of these writers on the need to return to origins and to first principles was close to his heart. Since antiquity was a principal staging post on this route to first sources, it is to be expected that in his concept of the villa Soane was first of all indebted to ancient Rome. We shall discover that for Soane, as for so many before him, antique and modern Rome tended to merge in his imagination. During his comparatively short but immensely formative stay in Italy in 1778–80, he studied and made drawings at both Pompeii and Hadrian's villa at Tivoli. Though he knew that the latter was far from typical of Roman villas, he interpreted it as a forerunner of Chambers's gardens at Kew which were similarly dotted with imitations of buildings of different times and countries.[1] At Pompeii, he showed himself interested in Roman bathing complexes, making a plan of baths and kitchens labelled 'rooms under the villa near the temple adjoining the soldiers' quarters'.[2]

For knowledge of ancient villas he also relied heavily, like many architects from the early Renaissance onwards, on the younger Pliny's celebrated account of his villas at Laurentinum and Tuscum. In preparation for his Lecture IX, he studied Pliny in the fascinating illustrated edition of his letters by Robert Castell, *Villas of the Ancients Illustrated* (1728), a book of which he acquired as many as four copies, the first in 1780.[3] A member of Lord Burlington's circle, Castell produced a work of imaginative scholarship which was a key document in the development of neo–Palladian ideas about the antique villa and its gardens. What was especially important was the implications of these ideas for modern garden design, as typified by Lord Burlington's garden at Chiswick. Soane made careful notes on what Castell described as the third manner of laying out gardens amongst the ancients: here, the 'Beauty consisted in a close Imitation of Nature; where, tho the Parts are disposed with the greatest Art, the Irregularity is still preserved.' This *imitatio ruris*, as Soane noted, is a parallel to 'Accounts we have of the present Manner of Designing in China'.[4]

Noting that Castell had claimed of garden design that, 'The invention of this art seems to have been owing to the first builders of villas,' Soane noted in the margin, 'Query Gardens of Semiramis'.[5] As often, he was concerned to trace everything back to first sources, here to ancient Babylon. However, he was also interested in the second part of Castell's book in which, unusually, he drew on the accounts of the *villa rustica* as described by Varro and Columella, both of whom wrote books called *De re rustica*. Soane claimed that, 'Of this species of villa, Claremont in Surrey, as designed by Sir John Vanbrugh, with its Palladian farm, was a magnificent example.'[6] Soane, who was always ready to praise Vanbrugh, knew Claremont well. When he became a clerk to Henry Holland in 1772, the principal task in the office was the replacement of Vanbrugh's house at Claremont with a new one by Holland and Capability Brown. Soane, who regarded the new house as inferior to Vanbrugh's more poetic work, owned a plan of the round pond and amphitheatre at Claremont,[7] possibly in the hand of Bridgeman who worked on the gardens in the 1720s before the arrival of William Kent in 1729.[8] Soane criticized both Claremont and Sir Robert Taylor's Danson Hill, Kent (*c.* 1760–5) for the inconvenient underground passages which connected the houses to their offices.[9]

Soane's notes from Castell included the phrase, 'I shall now notice what other buildings they commonly had within their larger parks which were of two sorts . . . [for] hunters [and for] the "master",' in which category he singled out the 'Triclinium, Musaeum, Ornithon'.[10] Soane was intrigued by Varro's 'Ornithon', or aviary, a circular peripteral temple over a pool, housing birds and used as a banqueting house.[11] He made sketches of its reconstruction by Montfaucon, after Pirro Ligorio, in his *L'antiquité expliquée*, where it was included in the course of a section on the 'maisons de campagne et jardins' of the ancient Romans.[12] Soane illustrated Varro's 'Ornithon' in a handsome coloured drawing prepared for use in his lectures, in the course of which he also referred to the reconstructions of Pliny's villa by Scamozzi, Félibien, Fossati and by Chambers's pupil Edward Stevens. Though illustrating Stevens's drawing, he complained that 'it abounds with anachronisms and has but little of the character of the architecture of the age in which the building was erected'.[13]

Soane seems to have used Castell's *Villas of the Ancients Illustrated* principally as a guide to the correct relation of a villa to its setting. While reading Castell, he noted that, 'Columella (lib. 1 cap. 2) gives the description of a most eligible situation', adding in his own words that the 'situation of every building is the first thing to be determined. The architecture that is in its character suited to the quiet scenes of Claude will ill accord with the terrific grand landscape of Salvator Rosa.'[14] In Lecture VII, Soane emphasized that, in villa design, 'the first point to be considered is the situation', arguing that 'a villa should not be placed too near a city or populous town so as to occasion those who occupy it to be eternally annoyed by troublesome visitors'.[15] He suggested that Sir Gregory Page's villa, in Wricklemarsh, Kent (*c.* 1725), had been demolished because of its too great proximity to London.

He stressed the importance of making a villa appropriate to the climate of the country in which it was built. He was therefore hostile to the imitations of Palladio's Villa Capra in England. In one of the few jokes in his lectures, he observed drily that 'a good living room in Egypt might . . . make an excellent wine cellar in England'.[16] In conflict with his own practice was his claim that 'rooms lighted from above . . . [produce] that repose, and as if it were half-tint which in warm climates is peculiarly pleasant . . . but is not calculated for living rooms in a northern climate'.[17] In true Plinyesque fashion, he saw the villa as the setting for 'pleasing and rational reflections, which are necessary to satisfy the mind in philosophical retirement'.[18]

Soon after his arrival in Italy in the spring of 1778, Soane's concept of the villa was to be enlarged, if not shaken, by the sight of two spectacular examples, the Villa Albani in Rome, and the Villa Palagonia at Bagheria, near Palermo, which he visited on his Sicilian tour in April 1779. The Baroque Villa Palagonia, with its convex and concave façades, had been built in 1705 from designs by Tommaso Napoli. However, it had been eccentrically altered for Don Ferdinando Francesco Gravina, Prince of Palagonia (1722–89),[19] who redecorated the interiors and added the grotesque figures lining the approach walls. Speaking in 1817 of the illogicalities of Pompeiian wall decoration, Soane complained: 'But all these instances of bad taste are nothing to the palace at Bagaria near Palermo.'[20] He proceeded to quote at length from the account in Brydone's *A Tour through Sicily and Malta* (1776), a book which he had taken with him on his visit to the villa with Rowland Burdon in 1779. In 1819, preparing his Royal Academy lectures, he wrote to Burdon for further information about the 'monster-making Prince at the Bagaria'.[21]

Soane's lecture audience, hearing accounts of the Villa Palagonia such as, 'The inside is as whimsical and fantastical as the out. The ceilings are composed of large looking glasses joined together. . . . The windows are composed of glass of different colours,'[22] may yet have felt that there were surprising analogies with Soane's own house and museum. Like Goethe, whose reactions on his visit in 1787 were virtually identical to Soane's,[23] Soane had a love–hate relationship with this exotic villa, which has been the most frequently described Baroque building in the whole of Sicily.[24] Soane subsequently explained how,

When I was at Palermo in 1780, this original genius, after having in this strange manner consumed half a million of Scudi, was at last condemned to pass his days in a mad house! Let those, however, who censure (without mercy) the strange taste of a besotted individual recollect that many of our ecclesiastical buildings and castellated mansions are disfigured with frightful monsters and sometimes with obscene representations.[25]

In Rome in 1779–80 Soane was confronted with perhaps the most prestigious modern *villa suburbana* of all, the Villa Albani (now Torlonia) on the Via Salaria, designed by Carlo Marchionni (1702–86) to house the antique marbles and other works of art of Cardinal Alessandro Albani (1692–1779), 'the Hadrian of the eighteenth century'. Piranesi published engravings of it soon after its completion,[26] and may have introduced it to Soane who met him in Rome on the advice of Chambers. The Villa Albani was widely visited in the eighteenth century but, because it has been difficult of access for many years in the twentieth century, its impact has been underestimated by art historians.[27] It was largely built in 1751–62, though work on the interior continued until 1764 and on the terraces and garden buildings until 1767. The later phases were indebted to advice from Winckelmann, Cardinal Albani's librarian, in whose time the villa became one of the principal European centres of Classical research.

The Villa Albani is heavily decorated externally and internally in a somewhat Piranesian style by Marchionni and his son Filippo, as in the overdoors in the saloon. The villa is indebted to a study of sources which ranged from the Golden House of Nero and Hadrian's villa, to the Villa Giulia and Castell's reconstruction of Pliny's Laurentine villa. On his visit, Soane made plans of the villa, including the elaborate complex of Roman baths at the end of the cryptoporticus (fig. 9.1),[28] and also made elevational drawings of the principal first-floor *salone*.[29] He will also have admired the two 'Greek' tempietti which Marchionni added on to the wings of the villa, as well as the Canopus, or coffee house decorated by Clérisseau, and the more dramatic ruined Tempietto.

In the *salone*, as recorded by Soane, antique sculpture and bas-reliefs were set as rich ornaments into the marble-lined walls and partly gilded friezes. Further sculpture was displayed in mirror-lined wall niches: 'Glass behind the figure', as Soane noted on his drawing. Robert Adam, who knew Cardinal Albani and visited his nearly completed villa in 1755, may have echoed this sumptuous interior in his ante-room of 1762–5 at Syon,[30] which has a similarly rich polychromatic floor in variegated scagliola.

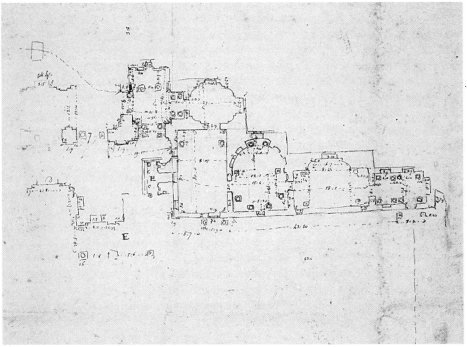

Fig. 9.1   John Soane, sketch plan of Roman Bath complex at Villa Albani, Rome. Courtesy of the Trustees of Sir John Soane's Museum, London.

One of the most memorable features of the Villa Albani was the elaborate recreation of an ancient Roman bath complex at the end of the south wing. This certainly attracted the attention of visiting architects such as Pierre-Adrien Pâris who made a series of drawings of it,[31] and there can be little doubt that Soane was similarly impressed. As early as August 1779, when in Milan, he made a design for a bath house for Thomas Pitt, with apses, niches, a saucer dome and a Doric loggia.[32] This was to be attached to an existing house, probably Pitt's London house off Oxford Street, in a conjunction similar to that of the baths and main house at the Villa Albani. Soane, who already knew the novel bathroom which Henry Holland had provided for Lord Clive in the basement of Claremont,[33] had published a design for a free-standing bath house in his first book of designs.[34] After his return from Italy, Soane designed a bathroom at Malvern Hall, Warwickshire, in 1783 for Henry Greswold Lewis, whom he had met in Italy.[35] The central space, defined by four Corinthian columns, contained the plunge bath, while there was a hot bath in the form of a sarcophagus on one side, and a day bed on the other. Doors in the two apsidal ends were covered with opaque or 'rubbed' glass. The neo-antique splendour, with torchères and statues in niches, recalled the attempts of Cardinal Albani to recapture the spirit of the luxurious thermal establishments of ancient Rome. Not surprisingly, the room remained unexecuted, as did Soane's similar design of 1784 for a bath house at Taverham Hall, Norfolk.[36] The only bathroom he built was the comparatively modest one at Wimpole Hall, Cambridgeshire.

In December 1778 Soane left Rome for a journey to Naples with his new mentor, the Bishop of Derry. By Christmas Day they believed themselves to be at the site of the villa of Lucullus near Terracina. 'This villa', Soane recorded, 'is exceedingly in ruins yet there are many marks of its former grandeur, such as the great extent, the dimensions of many rooms, the marbles of all sorts &c.'[37] Here, as he subsequently recalled, 'after wandering over those monuments of departed greatness, we determined the site of the Apollo and banqueted within the ruins on mullet fresh from the ancient reservoirs'.[38] By 'the Apollo' Soane meant the dining *triclinium* in which Lucullus was supposed to have provided a banquet for Pompey and Cicero. Soane and the Bishop of Derry now conceived the notion of making the proposed summer dining-room at Downhill, the Bishop's house in Ireland, in the form of the Apollo *triclinium*.[39]

Fountains and the provision of water were always vital to the ancient Romans and their architecture. Soane's numerous designs for *un castello d'acqua decorato d'una pubblica fontana* for the prize competition of the Parma Academy also show influence from the Villa Albani (fig. 9.2). The great hemicycles and fountains of Soane's designs, made in 1779–80, with help from Thomas Pitt, bear a close resemblance to the Canopus or coffee house area of the Villa Albani. Indeed, Soane's impressive fountains carried by atlantes are direct echoes of the principal fountain at the Villa Albani which was made the subject of an engraving by Piranesi. Soane subsequently praised this fountain in his Royal Academy lectures as an example of the correct, i.e. load-bearing, use of caryatids: 'If caryatids or Persians are admitted in modern works,' he asserted, 'it must be . . . as Cardinal Albani did at his villa near Rome, where four antique male statues supported a fountain.'[40]

Fig. 9.2 John Soane, Castello d'acqua, 1779–80. Elevation. Courtesy of the Trustees of Sir John Soane's Museum, London.

Provision of water also featured in the fantastic design for stables and kennels which Soane made in Rome as part of a villa, or casino, for the Bishop of Derry. The splendour of these out-buildings evidently recalled features of ancient Roman villas such as Varro's aviary. Soane recounted the story as follows:

it having been noticed that a magnificent hunting casine without an appropriate house for the dogs and their attendants, and stables for the horses, would be incomplete, the lively mind of that elegant classical scholar [the Bishop of Derry] . . . suggested that the exterior of those buildings should partake of the character of ancient structures with columns and basso relievos of every kind. In the house for the dogs, fountains were to be continually playing to refresh the air. . . . The walls and ceilings were to be painted with arabesques, the rooms paved with marble, and the beds for the animals supported by sphinxes, griffons and lions.

Soane evidently considered this as a light-hearted *jeu d'esprit*. Nonetheless, he had learnt a serious lesson from this project, and from his contemporary design for a temple-villa: this was the impossibility of literal copying from the antique in modern villa design, a principle which he believed that architects such as Wilkins, in templar houses like Grange Park, Hampshire (1805–9), had never grasped. We may be able to see his Doric barn at Malvern Hall for Henry Greswold Lewis, the Warwickshire squire whom he had met in Italy, more as an essay in this templar theme than as an example of primitivism.

It seems that this problem had first presented itself to Soane while on his Grand Tour when he first made designs for what he called a 'Roman temple altered into a casina retaining the general character of the exterior of the ancient edifice' (fig. 9.3).[41] He claimed that the idea had been suggested to him by Thomas Pitt, later Lord Camelford,[42] and Henry Bankes of Kingston Lacey, Dorset, who was in Rome in the winter of 1779–80. However, Soane soon came to believe that 'the great effects of light and shadow [of ancient temples] are not obtained'[43] in the kind of templar house which he had been happy enough to adopt as a young man in Rome. His dissatisfaction with this kind of architecture led him to observe that,

> Authorities and examples, however sanctioned, whether by the practice of the ancients or the works of the great modern masters, if they deviate from the first and pure principles on which our art is established, must be rejected. . . . We must never judge of the works of the ancients without referring to their origins. Experience shows how vain it is to attempt, and still more so to expect to see the beauties of ancient temples transposed into modern houses.[44]

Soane had apparently presented a similar design, in the form of a 'hunting casino', to the Florentine Academy as his *morceau de réception* in October 1779.[45] This was doubtless close to the hunting casino which he had published in his *Sketches in Architecture* (1778) as the first appearance in his work of the bombé façade which was frequently to recur in his villa designs. An early example is a design made in Rome, dated 11 November 1779 and inscribed with a reference to the temple of the Sun at Baalbec being the source for the semi-circular bay on the south (fig. 9.4). This plan type, as du Prey has observed, derives from the practice of Sir William Chambers who himself borrowed the form from the French *pavillon*, as typified by Ange-Jacques Gabriel's celebrated Pavillon de Butard of 1750, a *rendez-vous-de-chasse* for Louis XV near Marly. The notion of the central bow goes back to Le Vaux at Vaux-le-Vicomte of 1657.

Soane incorporated the curved projection, or bombé façade, in the design of numerous villas, mainly for minor gentry. He argued in Lecture VII at the Royal Academy that this form 'increases the variety of the outline, adds to the richness of the perspective, and at the same time occasions the light to be more equally diffused into every part of the room.'[46] However, he felt that 'the ellipse and the circle . . . are better suited to public buildings and temples than to habitable rooms'.[47] Despite this, he proposed such rooms, behind bombé façades, in numerous designs, such as those for Burn Hall, Co. Durham (1783),[48] Letton Hall, Norfolk (1783), Saxlingham Rectory, Norfolk, Sydney Lodge, Hampshire, Holwood House, Kent (1786), for William Pitt, and Chilton Lodge, Berkshire. In all these villas he relied on volumetric clarity for external effect, while the austerity was often emphasized by his favourite Suffolk white bricks.

Soane was evidently influenced by the blocky austerity of Palladian domestic architecture in Italy. This he emphasized in the rapid sketches he made of Palladian villas such as the Villas Maldurin and Molin, near Padua, when travelling home from Italy in May 1780. These provided him with inspiration for designs for Castle Eden, Durham, made later in 1780 for Rowland Burdon, who had travelled with him in Italy.[49]

In 1800 Soane decided to create a villa for himself, Pitzhanger Manor at Ealing,

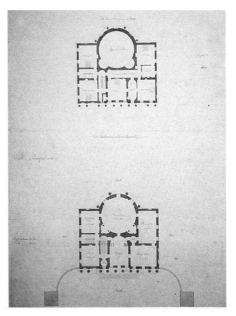

Fig. 9.3 John Soane, design for a Roman temple as a casina: plan and elevation. Courtesy of the Trustees of Sir John Soane's Museum, London.

Fig. 9.4 John Soane, plans for a villa, made in Rome in 1779. Courtesy of the Trustees of Sir John Soane's Museum, London.

partly to house his growing collections and educate his sons, and partly to act as a showplace with which to impress friends and potential clients.[50] Pitzhanger suggests that the memory of Soane's Italian journey never left him (fig. 9.5). Indeed, it remained the loadstone for his views on architecture for the rest of his life. Certainly, in the field of villa design, which was to occupy so much of his career, he had learnt much and seen much. The Villas Albani and Palagonia had taught what to imitate and what to avoid, while his essay in the design of a casino for the Earl Bishop of Derry, had led him to see the inadequacy of the kind of antique copyism which many of his contemporaries and followers were never fully to outgrow. For him, the designer of the modern villa should principally study the Roman baths, Hadrian's villa and the work of the 'painter architects of the fifteenth and sixteenth centuries'.[51]

The existing house on this site at Pitzhanger had been designed in 1768 by George Dance for his future father-in-law, Thomas Gurnell. Since this was at exactly the moment when Soane joined the office of Dance, who was to become his revered master, Pitzhanger became an expression of Soane's life story. In an early project, Soane had envisaged the addition of bizarre, faintly neo-Jacobean turrets to Dance's building so as to add another layer of resonance to its associations. He explained that, 'The interior of these turrets would form convenient and appropriate recesses, and if the walls were wainscotted with English oak, would bring back the recollection of the old Manor house, formerly the scene of English hospitality.'[52] George Richardson, echoing Soane's language,

Fig. 9.5 John Soane, Pitzhanger Manor, Ealing. Elevation with corner towers, c. *1800. Courtesy of the Trustees of Sir John Soane's Museum, London.*

wrote in 1808 that Soane 'has added to these rooms[53] a small villa, which he has spared no expense to enrich with many valuable pictures, antique marbles, Etruscan vases, and a very large collection of casts from antique subjects'.[54]

To proclaim that Pitzhanger was the home of the architect of the Bank of England, Soane provided it with a striking frontispiece echoing his triumphal arch leading from Lothbury Court to the Bullion Court at the Bank. Designed at the same moment, they formed a kind of commentary on each other. Indeed, in accordance with his belief in the role of expressive character in architecture, he interpreted Pitzhanger as a self-portrait in a manuscript of 1813. Here, he considered showing his pupils at the Royal Academy a 'Drawing of the front of Ealing', and inviting them to guess its function. This, of course, was three years after he had sold the house, so they would not necessarily connect it with him. He mused that it was 'probably intended to give some faint idea of an Italian villa', adding,

> Describe the front. No man will suppose that the architect or owner had attained civic crowns for saving the lives of his fellow citizens, nor that they had followed the Roman eagles from the Danube to the Euphrates, and witnessed their splendid achievements. Nor can it be supposed that the monsters of poetic fiction, half human, half beast . . . were attended to in the nineteenth century.

Arguing that, 'in like manner in the fronts of Italian villas we see an immense quantity of ancient remains of sculpture and architectural fragments', he explained that,

To judge of this species of building we should endeavour to discover the object to be attained: for example, in the building before you, if we suppose the person about to build possessed of a number of detached pieces of ornament, such as eagles and wreaths, demiboys and foliage, columns and statues, pedestals and acroters &c., and that from a desire to preserve them from ruin, or to form a building to give a faint idea of an Italian villa . . . this building may thus be considered as a picture, a sort of portrait.[55]

Soane's son, George, was shortly to suggest that the front of 13 Lincoln's Inn Fields 'seems as if [it] were intended to convey a satire upon himself . . . a mausoleum for the enshrinement of his body'.[56] As originally executed, with the loggias unglazed, it bore a certain resemblance to the design of the Soane Tomb in St Pancras Gardens. Soane himself argued that,

The front of a building is like the prologue of a play, it prepares us for what we are to expect. If the outside promises more than we find in the inside, we are disappointed. The plot opens itself in the first act and is carried on through the remainder, through all the mazes of character, convenience of arrangement, elegance and propriety of ornaments, and lastly produces a complete whole in distribution, decoration and construction.[57]

When Soane said that he intended Pitzhanger 'to give a faint idea of an Italian villa', the home of a collector, it is not improbable that he had in mind the Villa Albani, since it was unquestionably the most impressive example of its type that he had seen. This suggestion is confirmed by his decision to encrust the front of Pitzhanger with casts of antique fragments in Rome, including eagles within wreaths below the windows, from the bas-relief at the church of SS Apostoli, and roundels in the attic after the lion statues at the Villa Medici.[58] Near the garden front of the Villa Albani was a large free-standing version of the Medici lion, of which he also exhibited a cast at 13 Lincoln's Inn Fields. Soane also incorporated ornaments inspired by the pedestals of the candelabra in the so-called temple of Bacchus (Sta Costanza), a building which, according to Pâris in the 1770s, could be seen from the gardens of the Villa Albani.

The four Erechtheion caryatids which surmount the free-standing Ionic columns on the entrance front of Pitzhanger also echoed the caryatid portico on one of the two 'Greek' tempietti at the Villa Albani. The four caryatids on the western tempietto were removed and replaced with columns in the nineteenth century, but were recorded *in situ* by Percier and Fontaine in their account of the villa in *Choix des plus célèbres maisons de plaisance de Rome et de ces environs* (Paris, 1809), a work which Soane owned. Soane's Coade stone caryatids, like those at the Villa Albani and, incidentally, at Hadrian's villa, had their arms restored.

The pediment of the western tempietto at the Villa Albani is crowned with a statue of the many-breasted Diana of Ephesus, while another version of this bizarre but celebrated statue was housed within the portico of the eastern tempietto in Soane's time. In 1801 Soane himself bought an important ancient Roman marble version of this statue which, illustrated in Montfaucon's *Antiquité expliquée* (1719), was probably the one recorded in the grounds of the Villa Giulia, Rome, in the sixteenth century.[59]

The echo of the Arch of Constantine in the columnar façade of Pitzhanger was originally to have been emphasized by roundels of the chariots of the Sun and Moon, after Thomas Banks's terracottas of the famous medallions on the short sides of the arch. In the executed design Soane transferred them to the entrance vestibule. In their original position, they may also have been intended as a souvenir of Dance's façade at Cranbury Park, Hampshire (*c.* 1780), which also featured Banks's medallions.

In the breakfast room Soane supported the corners of the shallow dome with four Coade stone caryatids and pedestals in an Egyptianizing style. This device echoed the decorative use of caryatids which was a dominating feature in both the interiors and the gardens of the Villa Albani. Soane ordered the caryatids in 1802 from Coade and Sealy who had intended them for more conventional use as jambs on chimney-pieces.[60] In the library at Pitzhanger, as in the dining-room at 13 Lincoln's Inn Fields, Soane adopted from the villa Albani the use of mirror-lined niches for urns and vases, while the room also contains a cast of the Aldobrandini Marriage inset over the door.

A final parallel with the Villa Albani is Soane's creation of elaborate Roman ruins in the garden on the north side of the house. These are similar in conception and even in detail to the artificial ruin at the Villa Albani, modelled on the temple at Clitumnus. Incorporating antique architectural remains, this served, improbably, as an aviary, even more elaborate than that described by Varro. Soane, who had visited Clitumnus in August 1779, had made a beautiful drawing[61] of the celebrated temple which was, in fact, not Roman but remade from antique fragments in the fourth or fifth century. Shortly after, he sent a copy of his drawing to Lady Miller in the hope of persuading her to erect a copy of the temple in England. She had admired the building in her *Letters from Italy*[62] which Soane had used constantly as a guide book on his Grand Tour. 'Accept my best thanks for the sketch of the Temple', Lady Miller wrote to Soane from Bath in July 1780, 'and your ingenious criticism on Architecture; if I ever put it into execution I shall adhere strictly to your advice.'[63] But she died in the following year, leaving it to Soane to fulfil belatedly at Pitzhanger, over twenty years later, an ambition long since realized in the gardens of the Villa Albani.

10 A Family Affair: Decimus Burton's Designs for the Regent's Park Villas

Dana Arnold

On 26 September 1818 James Burton and his family moved from Burton Crescent in Bloomsbury to The Holme, one of the first villas to be built in Regent's Park (fig. 10.1). The move represented in bricks and mortar the family's rise in social status and increased wealth. James Burton was a speculative developer made good. In only a few years he had grown from carrying out small-scale developments on the south side of the Thames to being one of the most important builder/speculators in London. His developing association with the Prince Regent's architect John Nash was important not only for James's career but also his son Decimus's. James was perhaps one of the first master builders, whereas Decimus started out on a very different social rung. He enjoyed the privilege of private drawing lessons and the Royal Academy schools – part of the training of a gentleman architect. But he left this world of gentlemanly pursuits and went to work in his father's office to produce designs for the Regent's Park project. This afforded him a great opportunity to develop his professional skills but denied him the luxury of the Grand Tour. The mixture of academic training and practical building experience established Decimus Burton as one of the leading practitioners of the day.[1]

James's and Decimus's work together was undoubtedly a family affair. But my theme also shows how the villas in Regent's Park were an important stage in the development of the villa in terms of its relationship to the city and response to the democratizing principles of nineteenth-century society. These villas also raise important questions about the nature of architectural practice in London at that time. Could, for instance, James Burton, even as a master builder, produce or be accepted as being able to produce designs suitable for a gentleman's villa?[2] The designs of his Bloomsbury terraces are, after all, based on the many builders' books available to speculative developers at that time.[3] Did he in fact rely on his son to use his architectural education to provide the correct stylistic dressing for this kind of housing? The benefit of Decimus's Royal Academy training is seen in

Fig. 10.1 Decimus Burton, The Holme, 1818.

the references to Greek and Roman antiquity and the work of established architects such as Robert Adam and Sir John Soane. This gave these villas the gloss and authority of a secondary residence designed by an enthusiastic gentleman amateur. Alongside this, the important role the Burtons played in the development of the Regent's Park project is firmly established.[4] Furthermore, the contribution made by both father and son to the genre of the villa, which has not perhaps received enough attention, is here brought to the fore.[5]

The Regent's Park project played a significant role in the urban development of London and in the evolution of a new form of villa: half in the country, half in the city; small in scale and lived in by a wide range of occupants. It is important, first of all, to remind ourselves of the background to the Regent's Park project as this begins to reveal why it is significant in the context of the villa.[6] In the opening years of the nineteenth century open land to the north of the city in the parish of Marylebone reverted to the Crown. After several years of planning, work began on the park in 1811 when the river Tyburn was channelled to create a decorative lake. The plan, produced by John Nash, was ambitious and included an inner and outer circle which were laid out almost immediately. There was also to be a peripheral ring of terraces, a small royal palace facing a formal basin of water, a magnificent church to serve as a valhalla to the nation's heroes, a barracks, a service area and fifty-six villas, each sited so as to be invisible to its neighbours and thus to appear to be in sole enjoyment of the whole estate. Like the Regent Street project the venture was to be financed by private individuals taking leases from the Crown and building under the watchful eye of John Nash who had the right of veto on all plans.[7]

The Napoleonic Wars hampered the development of the park as speculators were unwilling to risk their capital. Things picked up by 1818 and the 5th Report of the Commissioners of Woods in 1826 pronounced the work almost complete. There had, however, been sacrifices. The inner double ring of terraces, the two northernmost terraces, the royal palace and the handsome church had all been abandoned. The barracks were resited and the number of villas drastically reduced first by over one-half to twenty-six and then to a meagre eight.

The production of town housing by speculative developers was not new. The terraces of West London, Bath and Edinburgh were a common feature of the eighteenth-century city and had done much to form the urban streetscape, but the Regent's Park project introduced a new type of housing into London: the urban villa. This is quite distinctive from both the free-standing, usually aristocratic, townhouse of which there were many scattered across London, and its rural namesake. Up to the end of the eighteenth century the villa had provided a balanced contrast between the city and retreat. Here the villa was brought into the city, albeit on the perimeter, providing retreat, fresh air and a barrier between the Georgian streetplan and the fields beyond. What is more, these villas were not aristocratic playthings which remained in the family even long after the novelty had worn off. They were instead saleable commodities which frequently changed hands. Unlike their predecessors the villas were leasehold. Like their predecessors the Regent's Park villas were set in landscape, but this was part private garden and part public park.[8] These elements and the relationship between the country and the city were also commented upon by contemporaries:

Mr Nash is a better layer out of grounds than architect, and the public have reason to thank him for what he has done for Regent's Park. Our gratitude on that point induces us to say as little as we can of the houses there, with their topolling statues, and other ornamental efforts to escape from the barrack style. . . . We have reason to be thankful that the Regent's Park has saved us from worse places in the same quarter; for it is at all events a park, and has trees and grass, and is breathtaking space between town and country. It has prevented Harley and Wimpole Streets from going further; has checked, in the last quarter at least, the monstrous brick cancer that was extending its arms in every direction.[9]

James Elmes in his *Metropolitan Improvements* (1827) rebuked some of the architectural impurities but made the observation that

Trim gardens, lawns and shrubs; towering spires, ample domes, banks clothed with flowers, all elegancies of the town, and all the beauties of the country are co-mingled with happy art and blissful union. They surely must all be the abodes of nobles and princes! No, the majority are the retreats of the happy, free-born sons of commerce, of the wealthy commonality who thus enrich and bedeck the heart of their great empire.

The creation of a landscaped site on the edge of the city providing upmarket housing of varying categories was an important part of the urban development of London. But its existence also reinforced the notions of social order and control which underpinned many of the Prince Regent's plans for the capital.[10] Moreover, the relationship of Regent's Park to the planning of London cannot be ignored. The development was linked to the then heart of the city, Carlton House, the residence of the Prince Regent, by Regent Street. Carlton House was the focal point of this new axial road. The impact of this was lost when Carlton House was vacated in favour of the more distinguished accommodation at Buckingham Palace, so changing the orientation of London towards a new royal focus.[11] The development of both these royal residences not only had a significant impact on the planning of London but also precipitated large landscaping projects around them. The area surrounding Buckingham Palace was landscaped at the Crown's expense; by contrast Regent's Park was laid out partly by the Crown and partly through the activities of speculative developers and the residents. The alignment of private residences to a royal palace is an unusual choice of urban plan. Originally the Regent's Park villas were to be sited around a small royal palace as well as being linked to Carlton House. This raises the important question of who lived in the park. And what, if anything, did they have in common which made Regent's Park an attractive proposition for a house?[12] Most noticeably some of those who first took up the leases were cronies of the Prince Regent. Did they see themselves as patrons of the monarch's grand vision for the capital?

But the first resident in the park was James Burton, who moved into The Holme in 1818, designed by Decimus with perhaps some parental guidance. If the fact that a speculative developer was the first to occupy one of the villas caused no controversy the design of the residence he built certainly did. The Commissioners of Woods remarked to Nash:

> In your observation that 'it is to be lamented, for the beauty of the Park, that Mr Burton was *allowed* to build the sort of House he has built', the Board (having recently inspected the Park and the Villa in question) command me to state to you that they entirely concur; but they cannot record this concurrence, without unequivocally stating to you, at the same time, that in their judgement the whole blame of having suffered such a building to be erected, as well as the considerable expense to which it is their further mortification to find, by your Letter, the Crown has been put in planting out the deformities of this building, rest entirely with yourself. The Board consider it to be your special Duty to take care that any Building to be erected in Marylebone Park should be so constructed as not only to deform but to constitute a real ornament and a substantial and profitable improvement . . . of the Crown's Estate.[13]

Nash, as overseer of the whole project, took much of the blame for The Holme and James Burton continued to work in Regent's Park. This was not the first time there had been friction between Nash and James Burton. In 1817, Burton had tried to claim compensation of £700 from Nash for a villa he had been forced to demolish opposite the top of Harley Street on the perimeter of the park.[14] Moreover, their outrage did not stop the commissioners employing Decimus Burton only a few years later to carry out improvements in Hyde, St James's and Green Parks.

The Burtons stayed in the park until 1831 when they moved to a villa in their own speculative development of a small town in Sussex, St Leonards.[16] Little is known except the names of the subsequent residents of The Holme.

The lease on one of the few villas not to be designed by Decimus Burton was taken up by Charles Augustus Tulk MP, a philosopher and philanthropist of independent means. He moved into St John's Lodge, designed for him by John Raffield, also on the inner circle, shortly after the Burtons took up residence in the park. Tulk stayed only three years and his villa stood empty for a further five until 1826 when it was taken by John Maberley MP. In 1829 Maberley let it to an aristocratic tenant, the Marquis of Wellesley, the brother of the Duke of Wellington, who employed Decimus Burton to enlarge the villa. In 1833 when Wellesley began his second term as Lord Lieutenant of Ireland, Isaac Lyon Goldsmid moved in and he also enlarged the villa.[17]

The Burtons were building South Villa by 1819 (fig. 10.2). The lease was bought by David Lance of 40 Nottingham Place, only a short distance from the park, but within one year Lance had sold his lease to William Henry Cooper who remained there until 1836 when he moved to Painshill, where Decimus Burton carried out alterations.

Fig. 10.2 Decimus Burton, South Villa, 1819.

Fig. 10.3 Decimus Burton, Albany Cottage, 1826.

Albany Cottage, later known as North Villa, had been built by 1824 for the diarist Thomas Raikes, with some participation on the part of Decimus Burton.[18] Hanover Lodge, designed by Burton for Sir Robert Arbuthnot, was occupied in 1827 (fig. 10.3). Five years later the villa became the home of Thomas Cochrane, 10th Earl of Dundonald.

Three of the villas stand out through their design and occupants. Grove House was one of the most spectacular and well-positioned villas designed and built between 1822 and 1824 by Decimus Burton for George Bellas Greenough, an eminent natural scientist who lived there until his death in 1856. St Dunstan's was designed by Burton in 1825 for the Marquess of Hertford, who held on to the villa until his death in 1842. Holford House, the last of the eight, was owned by the wealthy city merchant James Holford, who applied to the commissioners in 1833 for land in the north-west of the park for a house where he lived until his death in 1854. This too was designed by Burton. The two latter villas were much larger and more flamboyant than the others and used for lavish entertaining. The more personal nature of the planning of these villas perhaps partly explains why these were occupied by single tenants for substantial periods of time.

The leasehold nature of the villas, the rapid turnaround and variety of occupants, and their semi-urban location show the departure the Regent's Park dwellings made from the established villa tradition. But at the same time they offered the idea of a landscaped villa through the fusion of private and common grounds: a kind of English Picturesque in miniature. The intention had always been that each villa would be sited so that it appeared to stand alone in the whole park. The sense of commonality with the landscape is an important part of the ethos of the planning of London at this time, as many of the royal parks were opened up to the public in the 1810s and early 1820s.[19] The villas were not necessarily seen as long-term residences or any kind of permanent base; instead they were sold on for profit or convenience. In many ways they served as glorified townhouses on the edge of the city with a link via the new Regent Street to the centre.[20] It is interesting to note that in 1826, shortly after the decision to move to Buckingham Palace was finalized, the much reduced Regent's Park project was pronounced almost complete. Perhaps the cachet of the dwellings had been adversely affected by this re-orienting of London.

The role played by the Burtons in the whole project is significant, and there is no doubt that the villas played an important part in Decimus's development as an architect. Just as Decimus Burton made an important stylistic contribution to the park, James was an important enabler of the whole Regent's Park and Regent Street project. He was one of the first to take up leases. These give us some idea of the mechanics of the building procedure.

Nash's grand scheme had languished after the initial landscaping works until Burton took up his first lease on 23 November 1816 for a plot of land, on which he built The Holme, of just over two acres including the ditch on the outside of the sunken fence around the premises.[21] The lease was for ninety-nine years; the first year's rent was £14 13s 6d, the second year's £64 13s 9d, rising to £129 7s 6d from the third year onwards, and it was backdated to 10 October 1815. The staggering of ground rent was not unusual and shows that the villas were to be built as rapidly as the terraces which were springing up all over London. The building had to be kept the colour of Bath stone – this effect being achieved by painted stucco. Burton agreed to spend the substantial sum of £5,000 on the construction of the villa and design was, as all buildings in the Park and Regent Street were, subject to the approval of John Nash.[22]

Burton's second lease was taken out two years later on 30 December 1818; this was backdated to 1 October 1817.[23] The rent payable for the first and second years was £15 13s, from the third year onwards £107 10s per annum. The site was smaller than that of The Holme – just over one acre in the south-west of the park – and the same building conditions applied as those for The Holme. The Burtons built South Villa (demolished in 1930) on this plot.[24] The addition of a portico to the original design was carried out at the behest of the leaseholder, David Lance.[25] This would have made the villa more impressive and helped avoid the criticism made of The Holme by Nash and the Office of Woods. The Holme and South Villa demonstrate the discrepancy between the different plots in the park in terms of their final ground rents. The larger plots were not necessarily more expensive in real terms. This was perhaps due to their more remote location. But, even so, the larger the plot the more substantial the contribution of the building and the gardens around it to the overall landscaping of the park.

At this early stage in the development of the park James Burton expressed concern about the distance between the villas and the consequent restricted views. Burton even goes as far to request the Crown not to build any more houses than those specified.[26] His attitude to landscape is, however, contradictory as he originally proposed the building of two villas on the site of The Grove.

James Burton's involvement continued with the purchase of leases on up to two villas in the north-west angle – the most remote part – of Marylebone Park. A letter from the Office of Woods dated 11 April 1822 grants a lease from midsummer 1823 to James Burton for a villa. Burton was to build one villa and if appropriate a second, with the 'rents conditions &tc' (i.e. the design) to be approved of by Nash.

The houses were to be finished according to an approved plan. A letter from John Nash to the Commissioners of Woods reveals much:

> The Drawing of the appearance of the villa accompanying your said letter I return and having seen Mr Burton on the subject I have annexed elevations of the lawn front and entrance front fitted to the plan he shewed me and which I hope he will consent *faithfully* to execute, as in the two villas already executed by him, he has made several deviations injurious to the effect of those buildings and it will be necessary also to stipulate the *precise spots* on which the buildings are to stand and a strict covenant entered into that no other should be erected. [I]t will now be necessary that Mr B should send a plan of the detached offices he proposes to erect and a Design of the entrance with or without lodges that those may be approved of and also a map of the proposed plantations.[27]

These conditions were also to apply to the second villa if built. Nash's extreme caution may result in part from the criticism and blame he received for the design of The Holme. Moreover, the comments on the grounds of this villa show the influence the Burtons had on the development of Regent's Park as a whole. James Burton sold the lease for a villa in the north-west of the park to Mr Lennard of Park Lane.[28] The design had been produced by C.R. Cockerell, who noted in his diary on 10 November 1821, '[I] went to see Mr Leonard [sic], found that Ker & Burton had arranged and managed the plan & considerably altered it for the worse, suggested various improvements: to young Burton.'[29] Cockerell noted in March 1826, 'Mr Lennard sends me a kind note enclosing £100 for past services done at his house in 1821. Acknowledged telling him my regret that I could not control Burtons proceedings.'[30]

The leasehold nature of the villas and the building controls imposed on their designers and builders are new elements in the history of the villa. The mechanics of the leasehold and building process are distinct from the design problems faced by Decimus Burton. In considering these my concern here is not to offer new ideas about the authorship of individual houses, especially as the documentary evidence is so scant. Nor do I wish merely to outline the stylistic precedents of Burton's designs. Instead, I wish to examine what these examples tell us about the development of the villa.

The first question to be raised with reference to Regent's Park is the use of the term villa, as Burton's houses were distinct from their eighteenth-century predecessors.[31] Decimus Burton certainly drew on the neo-Classical adaptations of Palladian formulae seen in the work of Adam, Holland and Soane. In addition,

Robert Adam's studies of the Pantheon, Roman *tholoi* and *thermae* introduced planning ideas which were readily adapted to small villa design, giving the grandeur of antiquity to an otherwise modest dwelling in a way which was different to that used by Palladio. This is seen chiefly in the imaginative treatment of space as well as the applied antiquity of elements like the Palladian temple portico entrance. But Burton's villas are not merely derivative, as he introduced into the designs many new and influential ideas. Burton commented on his work when providing material for John Britton and A. Pugin's *Public Buildings of London* (1825–8), '[I have] aimed only at imbibing the spirit of [my] great models, and have fearlessly deviated from them when rigid adherence would have been incompatible with [my]design.'

The description of Albany Cottage in Elmes's *Metropolitan Improvements* introduces the wider question of the relationship of the villa to the cottage *ornée* at this time:[32] 'As a specimen of the English cottage *ornée*, it is scarcely to be surpassed, even in this region of architectural and picturesque beauty.' But the design is as dignified as the others in Regent's Park, despite the Burtons' interference with Cockerell's plans. A single-storey three-bay central block punctuated by four Doric pilasters was flanked by a pair of slightly higher two-storey wings. A terrace with a metal awning fronted the central block with curved steps leading to the grounds. A very plausible suggestion for this terminology is that Elmes 'was simply desperate to use a different word'.[33] And it would be unlikely that a leading architect such as C.R. Cockerell would design a cottage *ornée* for such a project as this. Certainly Cockerell had been aiming for noble effect when he noted in his diary on 23 August 1823:[34] 'My room looked well proportioned, gentlemanly. The gilt paper had extraordinary effect and its cheapness is worthy remark.'[35]

Decimus Burton's villas in the Regent's Park are varied in design. The larger houses, usually with a flamboyant owner, used principally for entertaining, contrast with the small, compact but prestigious residences which perhaps had more in common with the casinos which had proved so popular at the end of the eighteenth century. The Holme, The Grove and St Dunstan's provide ideal case studies.

The Holme (see fig. 10.1) shows the influence of Decimus's training at the Royal Academy schools. It also contains many features that were to recur throughout Burton's work in the park. Geometry is the dominant design principle. The house is a rectangular block surmounted by a triangular roof, intersected on the garden side by a semi-cylindrical bay topped by a hemispherical dome. The transverse axis is established further by the portico on the entrance front. This type of small-scale house had been popular in England and France since about 1750. Well-known precedents of which Burton was aware include Robert Adam's Deputy Ranger's Lodge (1768) in Green Park and the river front of Rousseau's Hôtel de Salm, Paris (1782–6). Sir John Soane, Burton's mentor at the Royal Academy schools, had occasionally used the semi-cylindrical form of the bay, as seen at his Letton Hall plans (1785–8). Nash had also used these ideas in his casino at Dulwich, Kent, for R. Shawe (1797) and at Rockingham, Co. Roscommon (*c.* 1810). A spinal corridor ran through The

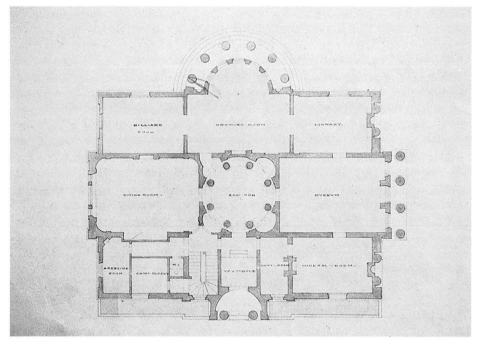

Fig. 10.4 Decimus Burton, The Grove, plan of principal floor.

Holme creating an enfilade effect, terminating with a polygonal conservatory on the eating room side of the house. This transition between interior space, conservatory and landscape was frequently used by Burton in many of his country house and villa designs. The loggia or portico was not well suited for the English climate. The conservatory, of which Burton was a pioneer designer, offered landscape views with the option of central heating!

The Grove (see introduction, p. xi) was one of Decimus Burton's first major buildings and the occupant, George Bellas Greenough, became a close associate who did much to further Burton's career. The designs were exhibited at the Royal Academy in 1822 along with his view of Cornwall Terrace.[36] The plan (fig. 10.4) and exterior are derived from Greek architecture: the influence of the Erechtheion is seen in the transverse axes and subtle variation of different elevations. The south elevation is the principal feature of the house and is based on the north porch of the Erechtheion. This terminates in the library block. The east façade is a semi-circular bay defined by thick Greek Doric columns, this order being appropriate for a male occupant. This was the height of Greek Revival fashion and the variations of level and elevation allowed more freedom in the use of a Greek model than William Wilkins had experienced at The Grange in 1812. This demonstrates Decimus's successful grafting of Greek religious architecture on to a building whose sources are essentially Roman, Italianate and domestic.

Certain architectural features recur in Burton's villa and terrace designs. Most noticeable is the central rotunda used in the plan of The Grove and Clarence

Terrace. There are many possible sources for this including Adam's Luton Hoo and his much grander but unexecuted plan for Syon House. Soane had also used it, and many of Durand's plans for a variety of buildings incorporated this practical circulation device.

Greenough was a natural scientist and his collection was already housed in mahogany cabinets which were built into the library, where Burton carried out a decorative scheme based on the Erechtheion in natural wood. The ceilings were plain except for elliptical mouldings and an anthemion centre rosette. Over the bookcases dividing this room from the smaller library was a plaster frieze cast of the Panathenaic procession from the Parthenon, which appears on several of Burton's buildings.[37] As in The Holme these three rooms on the garden front were enfilade. The offices were situated in the basement. The arrangement of the chamber floor shows a marked departure from The Holme. The floor area is smaller and the chambers in a cruciform plan affording terraces on each of the flat roof areas of the rooms beneath, giving a delightful sense of privacy and providing views across the park.

The grounds were some of the most splendid not only in terms of their location within the park but also through Greenough's enthusiasm for gardening. A screen brick wall cut off the view to the north of the house, confining all vistas to within the park. Near the end of the screen wall facing south was a small glass and iron conservatory, also by Burton, semi-elliptical in plan and elevation and a quarter elliptical in section.

The Grove became one of the most famous of the Regent's Park villas and images of it were widely published in Europe and America. The American

Fig. 10.5 Decimus Burton, St Dunstan's Lodge, south façade, 1825–6.

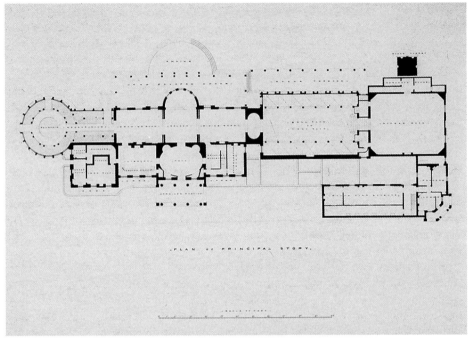

Fig. 10.6   Decimus Burton, St Dunstan's Lodge, plan of principal floor.

architect Itheil Town built a close copy of the villa in New Haven in 1830. In common with many architects he had seen The Grove on a visit to Europe which had included a visit to Regent's Park.

Designs for the Marquess of Hertford's villa were exhibited at the Royal Academy in 1822 and the villa completed by 1825 (figs. 10.5, 10.6).[38] It was known as St Dunstan's Lodge, as the clock of Old St Dunstan's in the West was purchased by the Marquess and sat in the grounds from 1832 onwards. The villa was situated in the north-west corner of the park with the garden façade overlooking the Serpentine Lake, rather like The Grove and The Holme. The occupant was a colourful figure who was the basis of the Marquess of Steyne in Thackeray's *Vanity Fair* and Disraeli's Marquess of Monmouth in *Coningsby*.

The design was more complicated than Burton's previous villas but still shows a synthesis of his favourite elements. The plan of the main block was two-thirds that of The Grove. The entrance comprised a single-storey porch with a double row of columns in the same order as the Tower of the Winds. This led directly into the elliptical saloon. There were three rooms on the garden front, the central one having a semi-cylindrical bay. These adjoined large spaces for parties on one side and a circular conservatory on the other. The irregular composition was drawn together by a strong horizontal axis created by the enfilade of the rooms. The interior was expensively decorated, especially the splendid 'tent room' whose architectural conceit extended to the treatment of the roof line.

These buildings helped to establish Decimus Burton's career as an architect through the quality of their design. But are they villas? To call The Holme and The Grove small houses would certainly rob them of status. But there were precedents for small-scale domestic architecture on a grand scale, if that is not too much of a contradiction in terms. The casino – literally a small house, though not usually a permanent residence – was popular in the late eighteenth century. This featured in the work of Adam and Soane, both of whom influenced Burton.[39]

Decimus Burton's contribution to the development of the villa was his absorption of past precedents and his reconstitution of them, adding his own ideas to meet modern needs. His work in Regent's Park covered the whole range of what could be termed a villa. The relationship between his designs was not in the form or the function. In this regard there is little to connect The Holme to St Dunstan's. The villas were more a state of mind as they offered their occupants a retreat from the rigours of life in the metropolis.

The Burtons learnt much from their work in Regent's Park. They went on to produce designs for large-scale developments of small villas and terraces set in landscaped grounds at St Leonards,[40] Calverley[41] and Cobh.[42] The villa designs for these were microcosms of their larger predecessors in Regent's Park. The layout of the estates made them saleable, offering the middle class a sense of grandeur and the all-important feeling of communality with the landscape.

PART V

INTERPRETATIONS OF THE VILLA

11 The Marine Villa

Lindsay Boynton

The notion of the marine villa seems self-evident: a villa by the sea. And so it was in the time of Pliny the younger, whose Laurentine villa was an exemplar of the *villa marittima*, a type frequently found along the shores of the Bay of Naples and the Mediterranean Sea.[1] However, the concept was less clear-cut in Georgian England, where the national genius for casting a romantic cloak over picturesque scenes confused the villa and the ornamented cottage.[2] The ornamented cottage was a misnomer, of course: it was understood that it was a gentleman's residence; a thatched roof was about all that it had in common with a labourer's cottage. Parsonages sometimes fell between the two. 'The Reverend's residence is literally a cottage,' wrote Mrs Lybbe Powys about Binstead in the Isle of Wight, but it passed muster after all, for it was 'in the most romantic style possible, standing in a sweet garden commanding a view of the sea, the thatched cottage surrounded by tall firs and other trees'.[3] The marine villa only reappeared in the early nineteenth century when the comfortable Georgian muddle was superseded by an increasingly pedantic typology.

Although the relevant literature has been admirably surveyed,[4] less attention has been paid to case histories. It is not clear whether there was a time-gap between the one and the other: did the buildings follow the pattern books, or did the designers exploit a fashion that already existed? This chapter will concentrate on selected cottages and villas in the Isle of Wight – a crucial area for the study of the Picturesque – and especially on the unique section of its southern coast known as the Undercliff (see fig. 11.1). To the late eighteenth-century imagination the site was pre-eminently Picturesque: hills and vales, trees and shrubs, streams and waterfalls, villages and sea. Yet at the same time the towering cliffs above, and the fear of further landslides,[5] were sufficiently awesome to rank as Sublime. Who could be a more appropriate guide than the author of *The Mysteries of Udolpho*? Mrs Radcliffe's standing as a Gothic novelist justifies quotation at length from her journal for 6 October 1801, particularly as it is almost unknown in this context:

Fig. 11.1   The southern coast of the Isle of Wight. Engraving by G. Brannon, 1843.

Set off for the Undercliffe, a tract of shore formed by fallen cliffs, and closely barricadoed by a wall of rock of vast height. Entered upon it about a mile from Kniton [Niton], and found ourselves in such a scene of ruin, as we never saw before. The road is, for the most part, close to the wall of rock, which seems to lie in loose horizontal strata, with frequent perpendicular fissures, which threaten the traveller with destruction, as he passes sometimes beneath enormous masses, that lean forward. This is the boundary on one side of the road; on the other side is an extremely irregular and rugged descent of half a mile towards the sea: on this side, there are sometimes what may be called amphitheatres of rock, where all the area is filled with ruins, which are, however, frequently covered with verdure and underwood, that stretch up the sides, with the wildest pomp, and shelter here a cottage, there a villa among the rocky hillocks. We were two hours and a half in going from Kniton to the inn at Steephill, five miles, W. [presumably her husband William] leading the horse almost the whole way: a Druid scene of wildness and ruin. Sometimes the road led us into vast semicircular bays of rock, filled up entirely to the eye with wild wood and broken hillocks; the sea below appearing to stretch so from point to point, that it seemed impossible to make our way out, till the road led us under projecting crags of the promontory into other recesses, and, winding under those threatening walls, again led near the sea, on which I looked down, not without terror. Descended upon the romantic and sweet village of St. Lawrence, among thickets on a hill, near the shore. Beautiful cottages, with each its garden, and some with little orchards hung with golden fruit; clear, gushing rills passing under the shades to the sea. A mile beyond, the beautiful village of Steephill, in the same style. Went to the New Inn, standing on a hill, with a wide sea view in front, half a mile off, and at the foot of St. Boniface Downs, whose steep green sides rise to a tremendous height behind it, having below them, on the other hand, the little woody village of St. Boniface [Bonchurch], with its beautiful cottages and villas.[7]

Cottages and villas, it will be noted, were planted side by side in Ann Radcliffe's semi-wilderness next to the sea. But were they marine villas?

The marine villa was a hybrid, born out of the passion for the Picturesque crossed with the newly discovered attractions of the sea, both as seascape and as therapy which, along with the rise of the seaside resort, began in the late eighteenth century and gathered pace in the early 1800s. The Isle of Wight was a favourite hunting-ground for seekers after the Picturesque, along with the Lakes, Wales, the Wye Valley and the Derbyshire Peaks. All these were duly furnished with their complement of ornamented cottages. Only the Island – as it will be referred to from now on in deference to Fanny Price's well-established usage[8] – and comparable places by the sea were eligible to develop the marine villa.

The Island's favoured southern coast was peppered with so-called Cottages, which will be distinguished from now on by a capital C. For H.P. Wyndham, in 1794, the three original Cottages of the Undercliff were Knowles (presumably the house usually called Puckaster Cottage),[9] Steephill and St Boniface. The first and third may be dispatched quickly. Knowles, a small house, stood at the beginning of the Undercliff near Niton, and was rarely visited. 'This sequestered and unsociable spot, late the residence of Mr Bradshaw, whose melancholy, perhaps, was encouraged and increased by the horrible scenery around it [crags and precipices, with no vegetation worth mentioning], seems calculated only for solitude and contemplation.' His melancholy led to suicide, a fate shared by the owners of the other two Cottages – Hans Stanley cut his throat while staying at Althorp and Colonel Hill shot himself in the porch of Shanklin Church.[10] This was decidedly against the ethos of a 'retired life', about which we usually hear nothing but eulogies. Yet the Cottages themselves cannot be blamed. St Boniface, dating probably from the 1770s and with considerable additions by 1781, was 'a comfortable house' surrounded by a garden 'laid out with taste' and enjoying partial sea views. It was a summer residence of the Hill family and 'so retired it might almost be styled a hermitage'.[11] Perhaps that was part of the problem: there was not enough happening to pass the time. Colonel Hill had nothing better to do than grumble about Sir Richard Worsley's smoking his Greek tobacco (he had just returned from his epic journey in Greece, with a Greek servant in tow) and poisoning the air of St Boniface. However, he also had serious financial difficulties.[12]

The anguish that drove the owner of Steephill Cottage to suicide was hardly caused by financial worries; he was a bachelor, which may or may not have been a problem. The Rt Hon. Hans Stanley, MP, Governor of the Island from 1764 to 1766, and from 1770 until his death in 1780, built Steephill about 1770[13] in the 'neat' or 'true Cottage Stile'. The outside walls were covered with white composition; there were several distinct roofs of thatch. The main room had a bow window, covered with thatch, which looked west across a lawn. Several descriptions of the inside refer to sea-pieces by van der Velde. But the most singular feature was at the top of the house: a large room with eight beds in different niches. Alcove-beds as such were fashionable, but eight of them in one room is, as far as I know, unique. Facing the door of the dining-parlour outside was a large stone basin, carved in the form of a scallop-shell: this was not only ornamental but also practical, for it was perpetually filled with water from a spring and used to cool wine.[14] One pundit, the Rev. William Gilpin, took exception: 'We everywhere see the appendages of junket and good living. . . . The thing is beautiful, but out of place.'[15] No one criticized the grounds, though, and it was these that 'made' Steephill. The earliest account called Stanley's creation

the admiration of strangers and foreigners. Here he has had the honor to entertain, at different times, several foreign ambassadors, and other persons of rank, who unite in praising this wildly romantic spot, where art conspires with nature to make every thing appear awfully grand, and irregularly beautiful . . . the plantations consist of American and other exotic plants, watered by a cascade falling from a supereminent rock.[16]

As the visitor approached, he passed two contrasting examples of late eighteenth-century garden ornament: on his left, a 'large, noble vase upon a pedestal, after the antique' made of Coade stone; on his right, 'a chair formed of the rough branches of trees, which, though simple, was curious'.[17] More to some tastes, perhaps, was the large conservatory standing on a winding lawn, backed by a fine beech grove.[18] A later account also mentions 'the garden, on a broad terrace, sheltered by a rocky rampart, amongst whose detached fragments is a hermitage lined with moss'.[19] Steephill was eventually inherited by the Hon. Wilbraham Tollemache, later 6th Earl of Dysart. He sold the estate in 1829 to John Hambrough who, in the early 1830s, built a large and ugly Gothic castle designed by James Sanderson (see fig. 11.1).[20] Hambrough had no scruples about sweeping away an inn and several cottages in the cause of privacy, and the public were henceforth excluded from the pleasure grounds.[21] The destruction of the original Cottage is regrettable, for as an early example of the Picturesque put into practice, and of a Rousseauesque return to Nature – duly tamed and civilized, of course – Steephill was significant. But it was not called a marine villa.

For the moment this survey leaves the Undercliff for a site a few miles to the north-east. John Wilkes had loved 'this beautiful island' for many years before he leased Sandham Cottage in 1788.[22] Both house and situation were very different from the Cottages of the Undercliff: Wilkes was not guilty of false modesty when he referred to it as 'very humble' in style,[23] for it was neither thatched nor pretty; and it stood on an open heath, abundantly supplied with adders but bereft of shelter. Wilkes soon improved the place: the house was fitted up more comfortably, and stocked with tea, coffee, chocolate, wines and spirits from London.[24] The garden was more difficult – in a windswept situation his trees failed to flourish as he hoped, but his shrubs did, and in 1792 Mrs Lybbe Powys pronounced the garden 'very fine'.

There was a menagerie, of sorts, although only Chinese pigs, peacocks and guinea-fowl (the latter destined in any case for the pot) were specified.[25] The strong point was the magnificent view over the bay with the Channel beyond. A grass walk 455 feet in length bordered the low cliff; 'Miss Wilkes's seat' measured 14 feet long by 4½ feet deep; and the 'large seat near the sea' was 21½ feet by 16½ feet. This was a shelter-cum-lookout: 'a grand covered bench, formed within the bank, and which opens, from the bottom of the slope, upon a level with the bay and the ocean'.[26] The most prominent feature in the grounds was a monument to the poet Charles Churchill, who had attached himself to Wilkes and satirized his political enemies. It was planned on an ambitious scale to contain an ice-house below and a library above.[27] In the event it was drastically modified. 'It is of oak, in the form of a broken fluted pillar, painted white, about 8 feet high, and 14 inches diameter, near the center of which is a tablet with this inscription:

> Carolo Churchill
> Divino Poetae
> Amico Iucundo
> Civi Optime De Patria Merito.'[28]

Wilkes loved entertaining families. He made up for the deficiency of accommodation by commissioning a series of the fashionable canvas 'rooms' from the Knightsbridge Floor-Cloth Manufactory. These were large, and fitted up in different styles – one was called the Pavilion, another was Miss Wilkes's Dressing-room, others were bedrooms 'all very elegantly furnish'd, and very clever for summer'. Several were decorated with prints and fine 'china', but outstanding for its elegance was the Tuscan or Etruscan Room which Wilkes filled with his Etruscan vases and decorated with a number of engravings given by Sir Richard Worsley.[29] Wilkes evidently added others of his own, for the room eventually contained 1,312 prints.[30] He christened Sandham Cottage his 'Villakin', not without a hint of self-mockery, perhaps, for the house itself was far from being a villa in the conventional sense. Yet the ensemble undeniably had the attributes of a villa and by 1793 it was so called.[31] Above all it was close to the sea and focused on the sea – the essential characteristic of the marine villa.

Among the many guests who dined and often stayed at the Cottage was Sir Richard Worsley.[32] He and Wilkes were in some respects kindred spirits and, apart from their being two old roués, they were both exceptionally interesting characters. It is quite possible that Sandham Cottage inspired Sir Richard's own Sea Cottage. Wilkes wrote on 8 August 1791: 'He is building, as I am told, a cottage on the brink of the ocean in the parish of St Laurence, and every morning visits his workmen and no one else.'[33] Wilkes went to inspect the newly finished Cottage on 5 June 1792 but, as usual, made no comment[34] (fig. 11.2). The Buckler painting (fig. 11.3) corresponds nearly with the extant house,[35] 'a neat and elegant building, which though the roof be slated and the windows sashed, the fashion of the Isle of Wight requires to be called a cottage'.[36] In other words it was *not* in the Cottage style but a conventional late eighteenth-century house: it was almost a scaled-down mansion. The plan and elevations were straightforward and hardly needed an architect: a builder named William Lambert sufficed, though he was capable of drawing plans when required.[37] The interior conformed to the mansion-in-miniature theme.[38] The furniture comprised a mixture of relatively cheap but fashionable painted chairs and expensive inlaid tables and bookcases. Some inlay was described only as 'rich', implying various types of exotic woods; other was of 'burnished gold', which must mean gilt brass of the most up-to-date kind.[39] The grounds likewise were an estate-in-miniature. On 29 January 1792 Sir Richard wrote that he would be 'much obliged to Mr Wilkes for a few Scarlet or Carolina Strawberry Plants, & a few white Rasperry Do. for a new Garden and Vineyard he is making at his Sea Cottage'.[40]

Vineyards had obvious classical connotations, and this one was Sir Richard's special care. He claimed that, having noted the account of wine-making in Britain in Suetonius's *Life of Domitian*, he was putting it to the test on the Cottage's south-facing slopes.[41] In November 1791 he obtained instructions from 'a celebrated French vigneron';[42] in January 1792 he told Wilkes that he expected the vignerons, with stock from the Loire and Burgundy, in a week's time 'if they are not drowned in the passage by the violence of the storms'.[43] They survived, and duly planted two varieties, white muscadine and 'plant verd', in March on a site of rather more than an acre. A second planting on an acre and a half to the east followed in February 1793. To make doubly sure of results, Sir Richard also

Fig. 11.2 The Sea Cottage at St Lawrence. Engraving by G. Brannon, 1835.

Fig. 11.3   The Sea Cottage or Marine Villa. Oil painting by Buckler.

had a terrace made on a south-facing bank in seven stages: these were formed of rough stones, with trellises fixed on the perpendicular faces so the vines might be trained as espaliers. One of these vineyards was said to contain 10,000 vines: it was estimated in 1806 that it would yield twenty-five hogsheads in two years' time. The other two were planted with a more delicate variety and might produce three to four hogsheads.[44] This optimism proved unfounded. The small quantity of wine that was made was barely drinkable and was said to need fortifying with brandy to make it at all palatable. However, the vineyards as such were a novelty – supposed to be unique in England at that time[45] – that drew many visitors. Indeed, there were too many for Sir Richard: although it had been possible to visit the Cottage, a notice went up in 1793 'The Sea Cottage is not shew'd'.[46]

The vineyard was far from being the only attraction in the grounds. A guidebook published a generation after Sir Richard's death described its features thus:

The late Sir Richard Worsley fitted up this villa in a style worthy of his refined taste, and adorned it with a gateway by Inigo Jones, brought from Hampton Court; a pavilion designed from the Temple of Minerva at Athens, a little temple called the seat of Virgil, ornamented with a bust of that poet; and a Grecian greenhouse, copied from the temple of Neptune at Corinth. Of these, the pavilion and greenhouse only remain.[47]

There are problems with this account. It does not mention the highly individual mimic fort with its ordnance which undoubtedly remained. When HRH Prince

Frederick, Duke of York – George III's second son who was bred up to the army – visited the Island he was entertained at the Sea Cottage. This was almost certainly the occasion of the firing of the battery which went down in local folklore. Folklore also recounted that the six cannon were a present from the King; they were supposed to have been cast from the church bells of Nantes, and captured by an English privateer, etc., etc.[48] There may have been something in these tales, but more probably it suited Sir Richard to encourage them, for he had 'borrowed' several of the Island's parish guns in 1777 while carrying out research for his *History of the Isle of Wight*, and these seem never to have been returned.[49]

The other significant omission from Barber's description was the marble model of a Roman warship. This was an outstanding example of eighteenth-century restoration of the antique, and it was probably commissioned by Piranesi himself, for he illustrated it in *Vasi e candelabri* (1778) as in his own possession;[50] presumably Sir Richard acquired it during his residence in Rome, either in 1784–5 or in 1787–8. It was a very suitable object for the collection of such a noted connoisseur of antique sculpture, and especially appropriate for the grounds of the Sea Cottage.

The other problems with Barber's account are that Corinth's principal Doric temple was dedicated not to Neptune but to Apollo, and the Pavilion can be seen (fig. 11.2, left) to have borne no resemblance to the temple of Minerva (i.e. the Parthenon) at Athens, or indeed to any Greek temple. Its curving roof suggested a building in the oriental taste. It has since disappeared from the scene. Its contents suggest a large and handsome interior, and it seems probable that Sir Richard was emulating John Wilkes's wood-and-canvas garden rooms. It was furnished with an 'elegant' carpet measuring thirty-six by eighteen and a half feet; two tables inlaid with rosewood, with 'antique' slabs of imitation marble; two Greek [Grecian?] sofas with 'ears', covered in green leather; six painted stools with cane seats 'richly inlaid with burnished gold'; two large china jars; a copper fire pan, poker and tongs; and a copper fender. The Doric temple, or temple greenhouse, alone remains (fig. 11.2, right). In Sir Richard's time it contained fifteen orange and lemon trees. If there are echoes here of grander landscape gardens, there are undertones also of the *ferme ornée* in the Egyptian cows and sheep which grazed the grounds. There was a Spanish ram also: Lord Cavan's request for its loan met with the comment 'it will be doing a favour to his Lordship & no injury to the animal'.[51] Sir Henry Englefield was almost alone in his less than total enthusiasm:

> Two fine springs water this very singular spot, and their streams run through the grounds belonging to Sir Richard Worsley's cottage in a series of little falls. This is one of the places where improvement has in a great degree destroyed natural beauty; yet the shady little groves, and the views of the ocean through their boughs, with the bubbling streams that wind round the roots of the trees, give a fairy character to the whole place, which it would require uncommon ingenuity totally to destroy.[52]

It will by now be apparent that the Sea Cottage was eminently qualified to rank as a villa in the full sense. When Sir Richard built it, he had only recently returned from four years' incessant travel through Spain, Italy, Greece, Turkey and Russia. His celebrated collection of Greek sculptures, antique gems, etc. had been worked up for publication in the *Museum Worsleyanum* of which the first volume appeared in 1794. The collection itself, along with his many pictures, was housed in the mansion at Appuldurcombe Park, itself resembling a museum and one which attracted many visitors. Although Sir Richard and his housekeeper, i.e. mistress, still used Appuldurcombe, the Sea Cottage tended to become 'home'.[53] The notion of the villa as a retreat from the cares of public life was especially poignant in Sir Richard's case, given the notoriety of his lawsuit against his wife's lover, and his consequent resignation from his Comptrollership of the Royal Household and the Governorship of the Island. Among a little collection of inscriptions proposed for the Sea Cottage was one headed 'Preference of a Country Life', beginning 'Sweet are the uses of adversity'.[54]

Although the Sea Cottage was never actually called either villa or marine villa in Sir Richard's lifetime, there are indications that 'villa' was gaining currency. In 1791 Steephill was called 'a delightful villa . . . in the genteel cottage taste', and in 1793 Cottage and villa were synonymous in the case of St Boniface.[55] Immediately after Sir Richard's death in 1805 his Cottage was styled Marine Cottage[56] which I take to be an early example of the genteel affectation of the new century. By 1807 it had completed its mutation to Marine Villa.[57] Despite the aberration 'St Lawrence Cottage' in the title of fig. 11.2, it has retained the name to this day.

Marine Villa's neighbours in the Undercliff were increasingly designated villas but without the 'marine'. Mirables was 'another charming villa', although the house was in 'the plain cottage style', the grounds were 'not surpassed for rock and sylvan beauty by any seat on the coast'.[58] Puckaster Cottage, shown in an 1825 engraving as a thatched house, with French windows and Tudorish chimney-stacks, was praised for its 'chaste and *appropriate* design, *as a residence seated amidst colossal rocks, precipices, and wild tufted knolls*'; it, too, was called a villa.[59] Brannon also alludes to a gentleman's villa, Westcliff, at Niton. Even Beauchamp, 'an unpretending residence in the simple cottage style', was also classed as a villa along with Puckaster Cottage and The Orchard.[60] Evidently 'villa' had become a vogue word, scattered so liberally as to risk devaluing the currency. The Orchard, however, was outstanding (fig. 11.4). Its owner, General Sir James Willoughby Gordon, Bt, was a prominent officer during the Napoleonic Wars: from 1804 he served as military secretary to the Commander-in-Chief, the Duke of York; he held every staff appointment it was possible for him to hold; and from 1812 until his death in 1851 he was Quartermaster-General at the Horse Guards.[61] The Orchard was called an 'elegant villa' by 1821, and described as 'a spacious villa in the embellished style'.[62]

Orchard [is] in the style denominated Italian: its orange-walks of considerable extent, its terraces and richly-sculptured vases, its fountains and various other embellishments, give it an air that would seem to say, the luxuriant in art shall blend with the grand in nature. The building is irregular and though perfectly a whole, bears the stamp of continual additions. The entrance is a pleasing vestibule, which communicates with the hall, breakfast room, and library, pleasingly fitted up with rich carved furniture. The dining-room is in the same taste, and of fine proportions: connected with the latter are several small apartments, containing

Fig. 11.4   The Orchard, Niton. From Ackermann's Repository of Art, *1826.*

cabinets of rare shells, &c. A circular stone staircase leads to a very elegant small room, containing richly inlaid cabinets and rare birds, and which room forms a vestibule to the drawing-room. Over against this entrance, a corresponding entrance-room or vestibule, fitted up in a similar manner to that just mentioned, has a pleasing effect. The drawing-room is richly furnished, and contains some rare and fine pieces of china, with alabaster figures after Canova. Three French windows, of large dimensions, open into a verandah, which, being furnished with glass, forms a sitting-room, commanding beautiful views of nearly the whole of the Undercliff. The roof, projecting considerably over this verandah, throws a bold shadow, which, in the summer season, renders it truly delightful . . . We ought not to omit mentioning the very pleasing bathing-house constructed by Sir Willoughby on the shore: it is composed of immense stones piled on each other, their rough ends forming dressings to the deep windows and doors. It is most pleasing in its general appearance, and so happily blends with the rude fragments which surround it, that, were it not for the very complete internal arrangements, we should have supposed it to have been merely designed to harmonize with the picturesque and wild scene around it.[63]

The house, however, was set well back from the sea and on a much higher level. This is the only reason, it seems, why it was a villa on the coast but not a marine villa.

After the end of the Napoleonic Wars the Island enjoyed increasing popularity as a summer resort and consequently a spate of villas appeared. Ryde saw 'many tasty villas continually rising in its vicinity'. Among these were, to the west of the pier, the marine villas of Earl Spencer and the Marquess of Buckingham: both had fine sites but were not of architectural distinction.[64] East of the pier, Appley was 'a most lovely marine villa. . . . The mansion is a very neat stone erection of a square form.' E.V. Utterson's newly built villa called St Clare, which soon after became the marine villa of Lord Vernon, displayed 'the elegant variety and lightness of the Gothic taste'.[65]

The Gothic taste was, of course, the zenith of fashion at this time. The grandest mansions now built in the Island – Norris Castle, East Cowes Castle and Steephill Castle – were all Gothic. So, too, was the last of the houses here illustrated, Marine Villa at West Cowes (fig. 11.5). Cowes was fast becoming the premier sailing resort and therefore many villas were built. The hill leading from East Cowes to Osborne was almost lined with villas.[66] Near West Cowes was Westhill, 'a very charming villa in the Swiss taste' which belonged to Sir George William Leeds, Bt.[67] In West Cowes, near the castle, was Lord Grantham's handsome villa. Another villa was notable because the King (George IV) was thought to have intended to fit it up for his own use.[68] He did visit Cowes, both as Regent and as King. In 1821 he dined with Sir John Coxe Hippisley at his Marine Villa.[69] There is surprisingly little information about this house, which was 'remarkable for its exquisite Gothic design' and 'peculiarly light and elegant, though small in size; still, from its architectural character, it partakes of the splendid'.[70] However, it is clear that Sir John was an unusually interesting individual. His career included three highlights: in India he held 'offices of trust and importance' during the war with Hyder Ali and Tippoo; he negotiated the marriage of the Duke of Würtemberg with the Princess Royal, for which he was made a baronet; and he brought the financial hardships of Cardinal York to the notice of George III with good effect. Sir John appears to have had no family links with the Island, but he was a founder-member of the Royal Yacht squadron. He chose as architect of his Marine Villa a man already well-established locally: John Nash.[71]

Fig. 11.5   Marine Villa, West Cowes. From Ackermann's Repository of Art, *1827.*

The reader may by now suspect that there was little consistency in the use of the term 'marine villa'. The villa concept was inherent in those Cottages built or owned by the more interesting individuals, but in the Island, at least, these were not right on the sea, with the important exceptions of those belonging to John Wilkes and Sir Richard Worsley. It was Sir Richard's successor, or rather his representative, who first called the Sea Cottage 'Marine Villa'. When Lord Yarborough's brother, the Hon. Dudley Anderson-Pelham, a captain in the Royal Navy, built his 'picturesque Elizabethan cottage' on adjacent ground, a distinction had to be made, so the original Cottage remained emphatically Marine Villa, and its sibling, which might in other circumstances have been called a marine villa, the Cottage.[72] However, the Cottage was also termed a villa.[73]

To leave the Island for a moment: Sidmouth may have witnessed the apogee of the Cottage when, in 1810, Lord Le Despenser built 'a large thatched building, forming nearly a quadrangle. It contains about forty rooms, many of which are large, and fitted up in a style of simple elegance.' However, Despenser sold 'this fanciful mansion' before it was completed.[74] About a decade later it, too, was styled a marine villa.[75] Also in Sidmouth a thatched cottage, with Gothic french, dormer and other windows, was described about 1825 as 'Mr Fish's Truly Elegant Marine Villa Ornée'.[76] Mr Fish's name suggests that he came from a social background different from that of most proprietors of marine villas. In any case his 'Marine Villa Ornée' nicely demonstrates the overlap between Cottage and marine villa.

One factor in the proliferation of marine villas was the general improvement in communications. As early as 1810 it was written of the Undercliff:

A few rich citizens have built their marine villas and planted their groves, removed the littery *debris*, spread their green carpets among the rocks, and made them accessible by convenient paths. Yet the pleasure of improving once over, they are become indifferent about the improvements themselves, and most of the masters of these beautiful places are absent at this season [July], either in London, or spending their time at public places, or travelling . . .[77]

Thus, the growing ease, and soon the speed, of travel encouraged the building of more and more houses which were now commonly called marine villas. The criteria tended to be implicit: the house must be of a certain size and distinction; it must be situated very near the sea; and its grounds must be 'delightful' but not so large as to compete with parks. Gentlemen's seats of modern erection on the southern part of the Island's coast, wrote Sir Henry Englefield, 'scarcely rise above the character of villas; none being seated in anything like a park'.[78] Almost any house that came within these broad categories could be termed a marine villa. Osborne, in respect of its extensive grounds, and of its having been a main residence not situated right by the sea, had not hitherto qualified. However, after it became a royal retreat it was styled 'the Queen's Marine Villa', both before and after its palatial enlargement.[79] Osborne, though, was a special case and one, moreover, that belonged to the Victorian and not the Georgian era.

12 The Villas of Scotland's Western Seaboard

Michael Davis

For too long our understanding of the Georgian villa has been coloured by a tendency to concentrate on a specific villa type, style or set of attributes. The extent to which a wider understanding is assumed but rarely explored is revealed by questioning one of the most unclear areas of villa culture: the relationship with town and with country. Is the Georgian villa the product of an urban or an urbane culture? Does the villa, by virtue of usually being understood to be a retreat from the town or city, require such a relationship to provide its rationale; or can the villa be considered to exist within a framework of cultural reference which does not actually require a precisely defined symbiosis with an urban centre? Can, for example, a country house far from a town or city be validly described as a villa? On the other side of the coin, can a genteel town residence be a villa?

Precisely this dilemma is revealed by comparison of two extremes. Auchinleck, an Ayrshire country house of the 1750s, was built near no large centre of population at the heart of a landed estate which had been in the possession of its owners for generations. On the other hand, Provost Murdoch's mansion of 1757 in Glasgow was one of a number built cheek by jowl to form the initial development of Argyll Street as it issued from Glasgow into a still largely verdant campagna. Unlike that of the laird of Auchinleck, who surveyed acres of arcadian parkland to front and rear, the outlook of Provost Murdoch was more varied. Despite their differing locations and functions, both houses share considerable similarity in their use of the Scottish Classical style popularized by William Adam which, with pediments 'terribly loaded with ornaments of trumpets and maces and the deuce knows what',[1] was to prove too rich for more chaste Palladian tastes.

In asking which, if either, of these houses can be considered a Georgian villa, I mean to draw attention to several of the many seemingly valid but often contradictory criteria and assumptions which have been and are currently used when defining 'the Georgian villa'. The murky confusion today is simply caused by failure to realize that meaning alters both within the Georgian period and in respect of the different contexts which we ourselves choose to explore. 'The Georgian villa', I would contend, cannot be exclusively defined (if it can be readily defined at all) in terms either of a specific function or, indeed, of a particular architectural style; it is a large grouping of many related types, each with its own individual characteristics which sometimes overlap and sometimes separate one another.

In this chapter I intend to describe a number of the types of villa which made their appearance in the West of Scotland. That some of these are villas at all may be open to question, but I am heartened by the extent to which other writers have at different times thought them – or others like them – to be so! Appropriately for a chapter dealing with an area of social and geographical extremes (from lowland Ayrshire to North Argyll and the Hebridean fringe of Europe) and not simply with concentric rings around a single urban centre, I shall begin by considering, in turn, the more extreme manifestations of the country villa and the town villa.

THE COUNTRY VILLA?

Despite its great distance from an urban centre, Auchinleck actually accords very well with the concept of the villa as a retreat (fig. 12.1). Far removed from Edinburgh though it may have been, Lord Auchinleck's fondness for it brought him there whenever his duties as a law lord permitted. Upon the entablature he had inscribed, in Latin, the telling quotation from Horace – 'What you seek is here in Ulubrae, if you can be content' – which was very much the stuff of eighteenth-century villa philosophy. Ulubrae was intended both as a refuge from travel – appropriate for a circuit judge[2] – and, since the original Ulubrae was not particularly attractive and the lands of Auchinleck were manifestly agreeable,

Fig. 12.1 Auchinleck, Ayrshire. Courtesy of RCAHMS.

there was also the typical homely understatement by which palatial villas were sometimes described as cottages!

Although classicism had been tardy in coming into common usage in the West of Scotland, the instances in which it had made a very early appearance provided a dramatic contrast with an existing tradition which was a long time fading away. A number of precocious examples pre-dated the Georgian age itself and, while there is no reason to suggest that these houses were ever known by the epithet 'villa', their cultural heritage certainly made them analogous to such a description. They were introduced in the West of Scotland before the concept of the villa had been overlaid by any developing local assumptions or subtext of meaning.

Strathleven House of *c.* 1690 in Dunbartonshire is a prodigiously early example of Palladian restraint which must have been the work of James Smith. A 'popish architect',[3] Smith had seemingly spent some years in Italy. This direct experience of Italian architecture has been suggested as a reason for Smith's employment of the Scottish practice of harling at Strathleven.[4] The same might also be said of the remodelling of an old palace wing at Ardmillan in Ayrshire.[5] This is a visually convincing argument, especially when one sees an even plainer harled house such as Monkwook in Ayrshire – the window pediments and so on are later wooden additions! – of unknown date and architect. But the restraint and harl of these houses might well be simply attributable to economy and tradition alone. One finds restraint and harl, and possibly also economy, at Craigie, perhaps of *c.* 1730, with a similarly elevated pediment to Strathleven, set down in an extensive park outside eighteenth-century Ayr.

Rather incongruous Mannerist flourishes on the rear elevation of Fullarton House of *c.* 1745, outside Troon, can simply be discounted as the consequence of thumbing through an unknown volume for something to fill the blank space on the elevation caused by the rise of the staircase. Though more 'correct', Castle Semple in Renfrewshire (1735–40) has been neatly and accurately assessed as 'provincially Palladian',[6] an obvious disappointment considering the precocity of Strathleven so long before. However, the real significance of such houses lies within their cultural context, for these were still among the first few Palladian-derived houses to be built on Scotland's western seaboard.

The sudden appearance in the late 1730s of three further Palladian country houses – of admittedly quite modest scale – in the wilds of Lorn in Argyll seems so striking as to deserve our interest. One can but wonder if the idea of raising neat country houses in the style of Italian (or Twickenham?) villas in such a place struck the lairds of these properties with the daring novelty of the concept. Certainly something made an impression on John Johnstone, the mason at Lochnell, who wrote to Sir John Clerk of Penicuik, expressing his disgust with 'ye highlands'.[7]

Of the three houses, Airds (fig. 12.2) and Lochnell have most in common. The RCAHMS Inventory for Lorn has very neatly observed that 'the elevational treatment of Airds may be derived from that of the south front of Marble Hill House, Twickenham (1724–9). Although lacking the horizontal articulation of that design, the principal façade of Lochnell House displays a certain gaucherie in

Fig. 12.2 Airds, Argyll.

the handling of similar elements, such as the lack of relationship between the cornices of the side bays and that of the frontispiece.'[8]

Relatively near to both houses, by the standards of Argyll, was also Ardmaddy Castle (fig. 12.3), rebuilt in the same years as Airds and Lochnell upon the vaulted basement of a former castle. As James Macaulay has pointed out, 'clearly somebody, thumbing through a copy of Palladio, hit upon reproducing the plan and front of the Villa Emo although the balustrade in the side intercolumniations hint at the Villa Chiericati-Porto'.[9]

Such houses may be explained with the aid of an anecdotal aside. Several years ago, a screenplay by John Byrne, giving a satirical version of Boswell and Johnson's tour to the Hebrides, appeared on television. At one point (as I remember it), approaching a remote island and seeing a welcoming party in full highland kit drawn up on the beach, Boswell triumphantly exclaimed to Johnson, 'At last! The Noble Savage.' On landing, however, the ranks of bagpiping henchmen parted to reveal the Chief, dressed in modishly elaborate highland garb, who announced in the alien tones of south-east England that, as soon as he and his wife had learned that Boswell and Johnson were to visit their island, nothing would do other than that they leave their house in Kensington to travel north to greet them!

Although Byrne perhaps intended his comedy to appeal in the light of more contemporary issues, it has its point for the houses we are considering. The mainland properties of Airds, Lochnell and Ardmaddy were built for men who, as

Fig. 12.3   The Palladian Villa, Ardmaddy, Argyll.

Campbell gentlemen, would have been familiar through their clan connections with the wider world of architectural fashion and taste.

Should this explanation not seem convincing, an examination of the backgrounds of the three lairds involved is more thoroughly revealing. Donald Campbell of Airds, for example, factored Morvern for the 2nd Duke of Argyll for whom Gibbs built Sudbrook House at Petersham in Surrey in 1715–19, and to whom Gibbs dedicated *A Book of Architecture*. It was the Duke's brother for whom Roger Morris in 1724 agreed to build 'the naked Carcass of a house for . . . Lord Ilay at Twickenham'.[10] This was Marble Hill House with which Lord Ilay, later the 3rd Duke, was involved as a trustee. Also in the 1720s, Coombe Bank in Kent, a further Palladian House, was designed by Roger Morris for Colonel John Campbell, the future 4th Duke of Argyll.

Colin Campbell of Carwhin (who built Ardmaddy) was Chamberlain to the Earl of Breadalbane, was great-grandson of the 4th Laird of Glenorchy, married a daughter of Campbell of Stonefield, and his eldest son succeeded to the earldom of Breadalbane.[11] In effect, he too belonged not merely to the wider world of taste and fashion but also to those very circles which had formed the mould of British

Hanoverian Palladianism. Indeed, his father-in-law was owner of Strathleven, which often acted as a stopover point for Campbell gentry travelling to and from their estates in Argyll.

Although Sir Duncan Campbell of Lochnell (to complete the three) could trace his descent from the house of Argyll, his marriage to the daughter of Daniel Campbell of Shawfield[12] may have been more significant, since his father-in-law – a Glasgow merchant – had employed Colen Campbell to build the Palladian Shawfield mansion in Glasgow in 1711. Andor Gomme and David Walker have enthused that 'only one English example of the 18th century Palladian revival is known to be earlier – William Benson's Wilbury Park of 1710. Since Campbell became (after Palladio himself, that is) the greatest single influence on Burlington, English Palladianism may almost be said to have begun in Glasgow.'[13]

Small wonder, then, that sponsorship of Palladianism should have ultimately resulted in the employment of Palladian logic and of Roger Morris at the Duke of Argyll's own Inveraray Castle which, with its symmetrical plan and battlemented Gothick lantern, can surely be none other than a bizarre tribute to Palladio's Villa Rotonda. Even its round corner towers find direct precedent in the square corner towers of previous English Palladian work such as Combe Bank.

Whatever the significance of Inveraray for the Gothic Revival, it was presumably responsible for the later introduction of crenellations to the local Palladian-derived seats of General John Campbell at Strachur Park of 1780–95 and Robert MacLachlan of MacLachlan at New Castle Lachlan of *c.* 1790, both in Cowal in Argyll. A further design, similar to Strachur Park and probably of the early 1780s, was planned for Campbell of Ardkinglas, but never built. The original house at Knockbuy, home of the Campbells of Knockbuy and later enlarged as Minard Castle, may have been more thoroughly crenellated, as indicated by a surviving rainwater-head, dated 1775, showing what one supposes to be a miniature of the house.[14]

Before ending this discussion of manifestations of the Palladian villa in Argyll, mention must be made of Barbreck, built in 1790 for another General John Campbell. Not only is this house a dignified example of the continued Campbell adherence to Palladianism, but it was highly unusual in integrating house and farm offices, setting the residential part of the house above the complex.[15] Such a hierarchy from cattle up to owners, all in reasonably close proximity, had precedent in antiquity and in Palladio but rarely in the age of agricultural improvement in Scotland. Sitting amid flat fields, this *villa rustica* with its attached barchessa is, in a very real sense, a Palladian villa.

In the more accessible locations of western lowland Scotland, from at least the 1750s the ubiquitous Palladian-derived smaller country house and the function of a rural retreat from urban pressures became increasingly merged in varying degrees. The enthusiasm for agricultural improvement and the creation of parkland, combined with the influx of new mercantile and professional wealth, often in the hands of younger sons of landed families, led to the creation of scores of genteel country houses – or villas, if you like, though the term may not have been used as part of their customary description – amid parkland. In Ayrshire, for example, few of these were very far from Ayr, Irvine, Troon, Kilmarnock,

Mauchline, Kilwinning, Stewarton and so on. Around the larger towns of Ayr and Kilmarnock, names such as Content, Bellfield, Rosemount and Belmont made their significant appearance. Names such as Belleisle and Rozelle indicated wealth from West Indian plantations. Though all such houses were reasonably elegant, few were of any great architectural significance. Many such as Belleisle, Dallers and Perceton, shared stock features. If these were not villas, then what were they?

Although the precursor of such Palladian houses in Ayrshire was John Adam's aloof and aristocratic Dumfries House in 1754–9, the bulk of genteel, pedimented boxes were built for lairds and lawyers, not earls. Speaking of the villas of the majority of Robert Adam's Scottish clients, James Macaulay refers to their owners as 'country lairds whose income and status depended upon the possession and working of their land'.[16] But against this obvious truth, sanctioned by Augustan values, was the inescapable phenomenon of new wealth enthusiastically adopting the 'conceit' of such values – along with its practical advantage as an investment – because, as in Classical times, the prestige of owning land was considerable. Thus, the explosion of the country villa in the second half of the eighteenth century can be seen in at least two lights: the pursuit of a cultural ideal, and the adoption of investment in land. The appearance of the suburban villa – a genteel house with grounds but no farmland on the edge of town – offered convenience and attainment of status and life-style without the economic basis of the country house (or of the country villa, should one say?).

The customary villa characteristics of relatively modest size, compactness and convenience of layout are often unconsciously applied to determine villa status. Size, however, is relative, as Pope appropriately declared: 'All vast possessions; just the same the case, whether you call them villa, park or chase'.[17] The idea that 'the villas at Foot's Cray and Mereworth . . . are the maxima of villas: beyond this the villa becomes a mansion'[18] is a later view coloured with knowledge of early nineteenth-century suburban villa development.

Disposition of plan and the provision of what J.C. Loudon hailed as 'all the essential comforts of a villa dwelling'[19] provide a more timeless attribute. Yet the subtext of exclusively middle-class ownership which one finds implied in John B. Papworth's *Rural Residences*[20] is very much a product of its time. So too, one must admit the seemingly valid, if contrasting, view that the villa could also represent an ideal in a less comfortable sense, as suggested by James Adam's (significantly unbuilt) 1755 design for a villa for Sir Thomas Kennedy (figs 12.4, 12.5).[21] The icy perfection of such a pavilion was not intended for even semi-permanent residence.

Precisely such a spirit runs through some of the more extreme villa plans of Robert Adam, though his houses were in fact usable. His triangular plan Walkinshaw in Renfrewshire was of this tendency. Several interesting caprices appear amid John Plaw's *Sketches for Country Houses, Villas and Rural Dwellings*.[22] The appeal was, therefore, not only to the country laird, the minister, or to the middle classes but to the sophisticated and to those in search of diversion and elegant amusement. Such a fast (and often aristocratic) life-style is hinted at as early as 1760 when the young Duchess of Northumberland visited Dumfries House: 'After Dinner we spent the Evening in very agreeable conversation. Ld

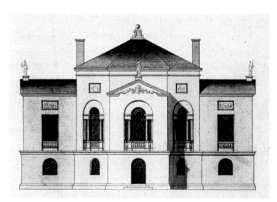

Fig. 12.4 *James Adam, Design for a villa for Sir Thomas Kennedy. Courtesy of National Trust for Scotland.*

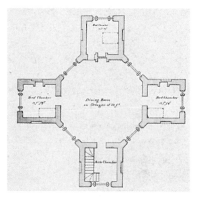

Fig. 12.5 *Plan for a villa for Sir Thomas Kennedy. Courtesy of National Trust for Scotland.*

Dumfries very drunk. Talked of being frisky and rummish.'[23] Two years later, the Duchess noted that 'Colonel Montgomerie expelled fr Dumfries House for being behind the window curtain with the Countess.'

THE GLASGOW URBAN VILLA?

Like Edinburgh, eighteenth-century Glasgow was densely packed. When Daniel Campbell built his Shawfield Mansion in 1711, 'set amid ornamental garden, shrubberies and orchard',[24] he set a new taste in terms of architectural style, for this was, as Frank Walker has said, 'a concetto whose provenance lay in the countryside of the Veneto'.[25] Moreover, it established the urban villa in eighteenth-century Glasgow as positively linked to rather than shying away from, the layout of its streets. Shawfield, as again Frank Walker has noted, existed in an 'axial relationship with the line of Stockwell Street running south to Glasgow Bridge'.[26] Thus the 'point-de-vue alignment' which placed the Buchanan, the Crawford and the Cunningham mansions at the end of the streets was also taken up by public buildings so that, according to the RIAS guide, 'comparable street layouts elsewhere in Britain do not exist'.[27]

Many of the merchants' villas, despite their setting, stood in grounds large enough to offer a degree of privacy and seclusion. The residence of George McCall on the west side of Queen Street was built in 1771 with a garden behind, which was large enough to allow several Victorian tenements to later occupy the site. 'Milton's House', Buchanan[28] tells us, looked down Queen Street 'from amid its tall rookery'.[28] It was only one of many such 'roomy and picturesque hotels, *entre cour et jardin*, with which our old Notables used to enliven our rich scenery'. A house of *c.* 1736 for baillie John Craig had a garden which even included a 'summer parlour of fine hewn stone, so that no carpenter or joiner in the kingdom has its parallel'.

Even before the major development of the new urban streets of the 'merchant city', tobacco lairds and other wealthy Glaswegians had built themselves 'streets of detached Palladian mansions of a type to be found nowhere else in Britain, exemplified by Miller, Virginia, Queen and Buchanan streets' (fig. 12.6).[29] The habit continued at least into the 1780s when the isolated Charlotte Street took shape. It is certainly curious to view old prints of these individual representations of *rus in urbe*, each with its own or shared wings, seeming to hold hands, lining both sides of the street. Charlotte Street was indeed conceived as an urban unit (built before the town had actually reached it). Its houses, one of which still survives, formed variations on several themes. Earlier developments such as Argyle Street, where Provost Murdoch's house stood, or Miller Street, where the residences enjoyed a more considerably detached status though they seemed to enter directly, or almost directly, from the street, were less unified in streetscape terms. Of these, only one villa survives. Also surviving in partially reconstructed form is a detached, pedimented urban villa of the 1790s in Blackfriar Street, amazingly just off High Street itself.

The magnificence of some of the Georgian town villas was legendary. William Cunninghame of Lainshaw's 1778–80 mansion, now wrapped in David Hamilton's Royal Exchange 'like a piece of granite embedded in some recent deposit', was reckoned 'the finest inside and out that Glasgow has yet seen'.[30] Also in Queen Street was the mansion of James Ritchie of Craigton, later owned

Fig. 12.6 Villa on Virginia Street, Glasgow.

by Kirkman Finlay. In Clyde Street, Allan Dreghorn's own 1752 Dreghorn Mansion survived until the 1970s, mouldering within a furniture store.

The unusual development of the Glasgow town villa, with its positive mix of urbanity and urbanism, owed a great deal to the nature of Glasgow and its trade. The lucrative tobacco trade allowed for leisure: as early as 1726, 'all the Merchants in Glasgow (excepting those who deal in exchange) are quite idle for one half or two thirds of the year'.[31] However, although very many availed themselves of the opportunity to buy a country retreat, the urban villa retained its hold, because the underdeveloped state of landward communications around Glasgow made a house conveniently close to the centre of town essential to business. Robert McLintock, a Glasgow merchant, in 1775 built the cottagey residence of Thornbank House as close to Glasgow as Partick 'for his country residence', a statement which seems absurd today considering the proximity of Partick to the city centre. Mr Gillespie, who enlarged the even closer North Woodside House in 1802, felt it necessary to have, 'for convenience . . . winter quarters in Garthland Street'. As late as the 1830s, the Govan road was so underused that it was not unknown that businessmen or merchants returning late might arrange to walk home with their neighbours 'for mutual protection'.[32]

The small world of Glasgow mercantile society encouraged competitive display; the four richest tobacco merchants – James Ritchie, Alexander Spiers, John Glassford and William Cunninghame – all bought country estates but retained impressive town houses in Glasgow itself.

THE GLASGOW COUNTRY VILLA

Compared with the extremes of rural and urban villas already described, the eighteenth-century spread of the Glasgow mercantile gentry into the surrounding countryside produced surprisingly little of interest, however well its largely unexceptional products may sit with the classic conception of country villas. Almost all are long gone, but a few may have been of interest, now almost exclusively glimpsed in the pages of *The Country Houses of the Old Glasgow Gentry*.[33]

Of these, Whitehall is particularly interesting and may have been an early example of a Palladian villa, with pyramid roof, Palladian window, Gibbsian doorcase and with later wings. It seems to have been built for the 'Virginia Don', John Glassford, who sold it in 1759.

Mount Vernon, Fairfield (at Govan) and Craigton had a few stylistic similarities, but Kelvinside House of 1750, the typical, small, eighteenth-century Palladian country villa, set in ornamental woods, was probably representative of the mass of merchants' country villas around Glasgow. Even commissions which may possibly be attributed to Robert or John Adam, such as Elderslie and Cochno, were of no great interest, though Robert Adam's Langside had an interesting forecourt formed by sharply advancing wings.

Greenbank, a very pleasant design, happily survives. It was built shortly after 1763 for Robert Allason, a Virginia merchant, and still retains its sylvan setting on the edge of the modern city. The dressed stonework is set against the antidote of harl, giving a strong Scots-Palladian character which harks back to Airds, Lochnell and even to Strathleven. It was probably designed by Allan Dreghorn.

THE EARLY NINETEENTH-CENTURY VILLA

During the late eighteenth and early nineteenth century, the villa architecture of the west coast abandoned Palladianism. As it did so, one senses a subtle movement towards understanding the villa in terms of a suburban or middle-class residence so that, by 1833, J.C. Loudon could declare that 'a villa should always form part of a village, and be placed, if possible, on rather higher ground'.[34]

But for the first twenty or so years of the nineteenth century, an area of overlap remained between villadom and the country house. It would be vastly stretching the point to claim the appellation of villa for John Paterson's Montgomerie House in Ayrshire of 1798–1804; but its miniature, Daisy Bank on the top of a ridge on the outskirts of nearby Tarbolton, fits precisely the contemporary understanding of the term, 'uniting architectural elegance with comfort, for an establishment within the confines of a moderate fortune'.[35] The same might be said for Braehead on the edge of Stewarton, with its tripartite front divided by pilasters framing relieving arches, making it possible to read the design as a Roman-inspired triumphal arch. But, since it was built as the manse, perhaps it should be described as 'villa-like'.

The middle ground is occupied by country houses such as Doonholm, remodelled c. 1818–20, set on the outskirts of Alloway in Ayrshire. Its low parapet and roofs seem almost to suggest that the archetypal Palladian box had been taken by its lugs and pulled out to provide an elongated profile. Even the minimally advanced and pilastered end bays can scarcely be held to terminate the façade which rolls through them, curving out of sight round the projecting bows.

In Ayrshire, Renfrewshire and around Glasgow, the mercantile gentry and their country cousins indulged a taste for such houses. Frequently they embodied similarities of design, each differing from the other by the articulation of the façade through seemingly endless variation of largely superficial detail, all lending surface modulation and movement to the façades.

Among these, an unknown number of which were designed by David Hamilton,[36] the most attractive were often the most reticent, using simple elements in a harmonious way. Near Glasgow, Shawfield – not the Shawfield in Glasgow – with roughdressed basement, curving steps to a simple opening cut into the wall plane, horizontal bands and a raised parapet by way of pediment, was a triumph of its kind. Moore Park, Govan, of c. 1805, despite its small scale (fig. 12.7), presented a lively front with advanced planes running vertically against the horizontal emphasis of cornice, raised band, fenestration and plinth. Lest the divisions become too regular, the horizontal band across the front terminates before the recessed corners, while the band on the side elevations set below the main-floor windows runs round into the recessed corners of the front.

This complex, yet unfussy, meshing of rhythm and emphasis occurs in comparable fashion at David Hamilton's Ralston (fig. 12.8), near Paisley, of 1810 where the recessed corners of Moor Park become full, wide bays. The repose this

Fig. 12.7   Moore Park, Govan, 1805.

Fig. 12.8   Ralston Park, Paisley, 1810.

brings is enlivened by playing with the detailing of the low parapet, so that the centre is indicated, all the while setting the chimney stacks laterally so that they appear as flat panels to further frame the entrance. Chimneys were also brought into compositional play at Fairlie House in Ayrshire, giving it the local name of 'Fairlie of the Five Lums'.

As Hamilton developed, he emerged out of the shadows and his grip on the patronage of the Glasgow mercantile élite served him well as they spread further afield. In this he was assisted by the interrelationships of many of the leading Glasgow families. An extreme case was that of the very well-connected Mungo

Nutter Campbell, who rose amid the Tory oligarchy to be Dean of Guild in 1823 and Provost in 1824. Campbell, according to Buchanan, had married firstly his cousin and then later his first cousin once removed 'so that Mungo Nutter, besides being John Campbell senior's partner, was his nephew, and his cousin's son, and his son-in-law, and his niece's son-in-law, and his son's brother-in-law, which is abusing the liberty of the subject'.[37]

When Mungo Nutter Campbell established himself in an estate in Cowal in the early 1830s, he was not merely retreating to the 'chaste and elegant' seaside mansion of Ballimore he built to the designs of David Hamilton; he was also following a pattern established by others such as Kirkman Finlay who had built Castle Toward in Cowal to Hamilton's designs in the 1820s. In point of fact, Mungo Nutter Campbell was not only related to Kirkman Finlay but also to the Cowal families of the Campbells of Glendaruel, the MacLachlans of MacLachlan and the Campbells of Otter from whom he had bought his Cowal property. He may, or may not, have been related to another Glasgow Lord Provost, James Ewing, for whom Hamilton in 1822 designed Castle House (fig. 12.9), a rampantly castellated marine villa in Dunoon in Cowal.

The remove to the seaside mansions of rural Cowal took Mungo Nutter Campbell and those like him at least one stop on the steamboat voyage beyond the destination of most of their social inferiors. All excepting, that is, the owner of Castle House in Dunoon who lived to regret his proximity to invasions of less socially elevated

Fig. 12.9 Castle House, Dunoon, 1822.

mortals.[38] In a remarkably short space of time other ranks of society hastened to follow as far as the growing villa and boarding-house communities throughout the Clyde estuary, which steamship and rail made increasingly accessible. Not all the subsequent rash of villa development was inferior or commonplace – witness the achievement of Alexander Thomson and C.R. Mackintosh – but the bulk subscribed to solid bay-windowed suburban domesticity from which the Arts and Crafts movement only partly rescued it. Consequently, travelling through the Kyles of Bute in 1926 on the *Columba*, Miss M.E.M. Donaldson was appalled to be brought 'face to face with replicas of commonplace suburban villas, dumped down, regardless of any sense of decency, in entirely incongruous surroundings'.[39] For her own rural retreat, she chose the furthest corner of Ardnamurchan, building Sanna Bheag in 1926–7 in local style (Fig. 12.10), allegedly down to including bottomless zinc pails as the chimney pots.[40]

It is doubtless appropriate to end a chapter in part devoted to perhaps extreme manifestations of the villa on such a note. Yet I hope that the point has been taken that 'the Georgian villa' can be understood in a number of different contexts, often overlapping to be sure, but each with its own quite independent nuances of meaning: the country villa, the villa of retreat and Horatian sentiment, the Palladian villa, the castellated Palladian villa, the *villa rustica* (as centre of a working farm), the suburban villa, the convenient villa, the middle-class villa, the elegant villa of caprice, the Glasgow urban villa, the mercantile villa, the marine villa and the (pejorative) commonplace villa. We now recognize these different species of Georgian villa and the characteristics which distinguish, relate and divide them!

Fig. 12.10 M.E.M. Donaldson, Sanna Bheag, Ardnamurchan, 1926–7.

13 The Edinburgh Villa Revisited: Function not Form[1]

Ian Gow

As you approach Edinburgh the scene wonderfully improves: it is cultivated landscape all around, abundant in wood and every cheering view. We peeped into Mr Dundas's grounds at Melville Castle, which is altogether superb and beautiful. There are few more smiling or more desirable places to be met with, here the owner dismissed his cares, and welcomed the unmixed pleasures of society. Here enjoyed

> . . . the happy hour,
> Of social freedom ill exchanged for power,
> And here uncumber'd with the venal tribe
> Smiled without art, and won without bribe.

We passed many fine seats on either hand – Lord Somerville's, the Duke of Buccleuch's at Dalkeith, Lord Lothian's &c. As we neared the capital the villas of course crowded upon us.

> *R.L. Willis*, Journal of a Tour from London to Elgin made about 1790
> *(Edinburgh, 1890)*

This short chapter derives in part from research originally carried out at Cambridge over twenty years ago, but I also want to pick up some of the more important threads raised in this volume. I especially want to home in on the inherent contradictions in the idea of the villa that were raised in Dr Howard's thoughtful chapter.

As a capital city and administrative centre, Edinburgh possessed ideal conditions for the creation of a villadom. Although the Court after 1603 and the Parliament after 1707 had followed the king of Scotland south to London, there were still a great many people who had of necessity to spend long periods in the city with its courts, commerce, schools and the complex mechanisms of assemblies and the marriage market. Because of the city's unusual topography, confined on its narrow ridge, a dense high-rise city had resulted whose living conditions were hardly ideal.

While the many drawbacks could be tolerated in the winter chill, in summer the insanitary conditions were less easily borne, as the published accounts of many visitors confirm. This very density had ensured that the real countryside was always conveniently close at hand. From an early period, the nobility and wealthier citizens had favoured self-contained houses set in parks and gardens near the city. Indeed the Canongate, straddling between the city and the Palace of Holyroodhouse, can be seen as an early villadom, whose many windowed houses looked south across extensive gardens to the prospect of Arthur's Seat.

It is remarkable how many Scots carried this fondness for villa life south when they were obliged to move to London, John Johnston at Twickenham, the Duke of Argyll at Sudbrook and Lord Mansfield at Kenwood being celebrated examples.

Unlike London or Glasgow, where villas spread along the banks of the navigable rivers, the Edinburgh villas were scattered throughout Edinburghshire, as Midlothian was formerly known, which was recognized in being rich in scenic beauties. The many hills and ridges provided terraced sites from which the dramatic silhouette of the city on its ridge between the castle and Arthur's Seat could be enjoyed.

The popularity of particular viewpoints resulted in concentric rings of ribbon development along the contours surrounding the city. Because some spots were deemed to be particularly healthy like Inveresk, the Montpelier of Scotland, or Morningside, where the city's lunatic asylum was to be especially sited, villa villages gradually accrued in the most choice locations. The fashion for sea bathing was to create a semi-independent town at Portobello from modest beginnings. Although there were many large estates near the city, the popularity of villas tended to create fragmented patterns of land-holding. This fragmentation was promoted by the peculiarities of the Scottish feudal system of land tenure where the owner of a large plot could expect an annual feu duty from the occupants of portions.

The character of the villadom was shaped by a number of influences. First, Scottish education was firmly rooted in the Classics and there was thus a dose of conscious neo-Classicism. The Latin inscription on Caroline Park, dating to 1685, claims that Viscount Tarbat's not inconsiderable mansion was to be viewed as but a *turgulum* or shepherd's cottage. Mavisbank bears Latin doggerel incised into its façade declaring it to be a *villa*, lest we were in any doubt (fig. 13.1). Lord Cockburn, in his *Life of Lord Jeffrey* (1852), refers to his friend's 'half town and half villa life' in a way that brings Pliny to mind.

This must be balanced against the almost all-pervasive Presbyterianism of the Established Church which favoured rural retreat for very different reasons. In 1738 Provost George Drummond wrote of his villa at Hailes:

This place has so many natural beauties and sweet solitary retirements, that if I were disposed to take pleasure in anything in time it would very much delight me. But although I was easy in my circumstances I habitually view myself as not at home in this world.[2]

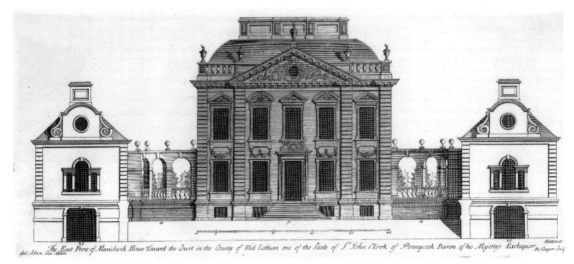

Fig. 13.1 *Mavisbank, designed by Sir John Clerk of Penicuik, c. 1723, from* Vitruvius Scoticus.

These philosophical incentives were balanced by purely practical functions. Sir John Clerk of Penicuik's children were brought up in the healthy environs of his first villa at Cammo rather than in the city. Villa gardens grew produce for the town and their grounds had room for livestock of various kinds.

To this cocktail of influences must be added the following of fashion which was no less persuasive and in Susan Adam's poem about a family party at Sunnyside, a villa which was to be redesigned into an almost Parisian elegance by her brother Robert, she gives the viewpoint of the more empty-headed citizenry:

> 'Tis vulgar to be seen in town
> The Beau Monde to the Country flown
> Betake themselves for want of betters
> To rural sports and fêtes champêtres.[3]

Since Edinburgh, before the New Town, must have been especially trying in the heat of even a Scottish summer, fashion and practicality here went hand in hand.

Changing architectural fashions seem to have altered their form at whim, and, at least in Edinburgh, there is no type. Because of the importance of the encircling gardens or park, the architectural element is in any case only a component in something more complex. The scale was a function of the owner's pocket. In Allan Ramsay's case, perched on a ledge on Castle Hill, the grounds were merely a window box with a view over real country, maintained at others' expense. Looking out towards the Forth and through its elevation, the view of the Forth was barely impinged upon by the building of the New Town in its immediate foreground. From my research in Edinburgh, this ideal of the real country, as against a suburban hinterland, seems to have been important, and *suburban* seems to have been reserved as a term of abuse for scruffy ribbon development at the main entrances to the city which were neither urban nor rural.

At the top of the scale, there were a whole series of what might be loosely dubbed 'secretaries of states' villas' as it was from Brunstane, Hatton, Caroline Park and later Melville Castle that much of the business of government and official entertaining was conducted during the summer. The lack of a type was also shaped by changing aspirations, and although Sir William Forbes's sumptuous villa at Colinton of 1801 was everything that a successful banker of the day required, the function of the house was not necessarily very different from much more modest early Georgian boxes when fewer public rooms and smaller parties were in vogue, just as fashions in laying out the grounds moved from the elaboration of the Baroque to the apparently naturalistic parkland of Brown. Perhaps most arrestingly, although some of the leading citizens of the 'modern Athens' may have possessed appropriately Grecian townhouses, they passed their summer leisure hours in their tower-house villas. Lords Jeffrey and Rutherford improved genuinely ancient tower-houses while their friend, Lord Cockburn, was also to employ Playfair to produce a Baronial pastiche at Bonaly.

Although I did not originally, perhaps, devote enough attention to the garden history aspect of my subject, I formed a vivid impression of their powerful impact as a group from travellers' accounts. The aesthetic of the villadom is encapsulated best in the *View of the Agriculture of Midlothian* (1795):

> Numberless villas in the vicinity of Edinburgh and Gentlemen's seats, all over the county, are seen beautiful and distinct, each in the midst of its own plantations. These add still more to the embellishment of the scene from the manner in which they were disposed; not in extended and thick plantations, which turn a country into a forest, and throw a gloom upon the prospect; but in clear and diversified lines, in clumps and hedge-rows.[4]

This can be partnered visually by a plate after a sketch by Alexander Campbell in his *Journey from Edinburgh* (1802), looking across the valley of the Water of Leith towards a line of villas and the villa-village of Trinity and the Forth, beyond which he described as a 'scene replete with such objects as characterise the lovely landscapes of Claude Lorraine'.[5] This was perhaps no happy accident because the mineral well in the foreground had been especially designed, by the artist Alexander Nasmyth, to this end, but the villas on the horizon were the result of individual enterprise with no planning controls and it is unthinkable today that we could trust our neighbours to produce a Claude from their random home improvements.

This added group value of often not especially interesting individual houses is clear from many visitors' accounts where a trip out in the villadom, as a Picturesque experience, was a standard way of rounding off a visit to the city's sites. Similarly residents would ride out into the villadom. The 'Journal' of Jessy Allan, in reality a series of letters retailing family news to her sister in India,[6] shows the important place of the villadom in the lives of women of the period. The Allans possessed a cottage for sea bathing at Leithmount ('it is really a snug place') where they often went for the day or sometimes stopped the night. From there they visited friends in neighbouring villas while she often had a horse saddled to call unannounced on friends in retreat at Inveresk.

The assumption that the villas as a group served as a form of public recreation is also highlighted by the case of Walter Ross who, having transformed a rather ordinary house at Stockbridge into a Scottish Strawberry Hill where a real Gothic tracery of antiquarian fragments was balanced by a Gimcrack painted window in trompe l'oeil, then affected annoyance when his house was treated as a tourist attraction. After polite advertisement had failed, spring-guns and mantraps followed. Eventually a human leg was obtained from the Infirmary and paraded through the streets clenched in one of the mantraps as a warning to the curious.[7]

This very popularity of the villadom posed its own threat and there are many references to the need to protect the amenity of individual villas against the threat of overdevelopment. As early as 1778 the owner of Eskgrove at Inveresk had to resort to camouflage:

> [We] went on invitation to dine with Mr Rae the advocate. His house is on the north-west end of the elevated ground on which the highest and pleasantest part of this town stands, and is entered to by a gate on the left hand or north-east side. . . . Mr Rae has a very pleasant neat house, with a semi-circular green plot of moderate size before it, skirted with young thriving trees which partly conceal the houses of the town that are too near, but Mr Rae purposes, after getting a certain high and unseemly one pulled down, to open or at least to cut and crop the trees in front of the house beyond the green in such a manner as to have a view of the beautiful cultivated country which is on the left or east of the vale that runs up the River Esk to Dalkeith etc. I thought this view might be opened without regard to the above said house which is on the right hand and will soon be concealed by trees. . . . The beauties of these grounds of Mr Rae's depend chiefly upon the skirtings of wood and flowering shrubs with which he has inclosed some of his fields.[8]

Because the site was so important it is pointless trying to seek to define the villa in purely architectural terms and even the site had a further dynamic transcending its actual dimensions because of the premium placed on a view from a terraced contour. In this respect, Edinburgh's villas were to be no different from those analysed by C.L. Frank, *The Villas of Frascati* (2nd edn, 1966). A striking feature of villas like West Warriston is the large area of glass on the prospect front to the south which commanded a view of Edinburgh. Robert Mylne described the entrance or north front, by contrast, as being 'cold and seldom used'.[9] This same three- and five-bay formula can also be seen at Hawkhill (fig. 13.2). William Adam's fascination with glazing can be seen in the State Drawing-room at The Drum where almost the whole wall to the south has been turned to glass. Because, in

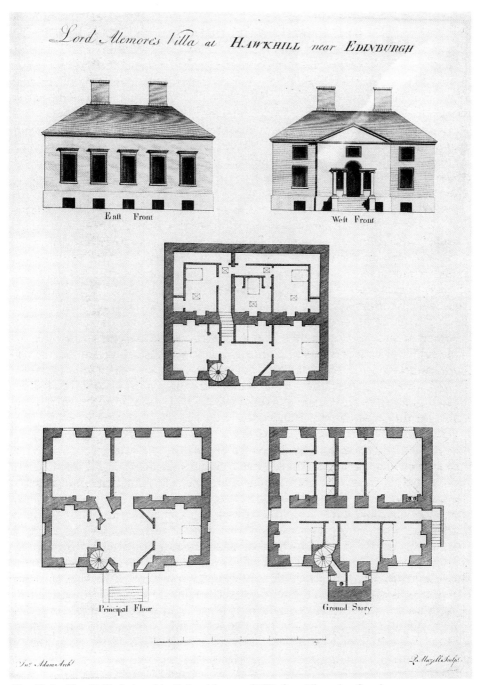

Fig. 13.2   Hawkhill, designed by John Adam, c. 1757, from Vitruvius Scoticus.

general, Scottish architecture is marked by a higher proportion of wall than window this does seem to be an important architectural characteristic of the villa, if a rather non-architectural one, tolerating, in two Adam villas, Milton and Minto, the Classical solecism of a four-bay frontage to maximize on the southern prospect.

Rather less readily defined is the strong tendency to miniaturization in the idea of the 'box' or, to give a common Edinburgh term, 'hut' which Margaret Tait first drew attention to in her article 'William's Hut'.[10] The idea of the hut was that it was a temporary residence in which only a simple life was possible; in the hands of an architect like William or John Adam, however, this tiny scale presented a formal challenge to which they responded with ingenious variations on intricate plans, of which Hawkhill was to be a particular perfect expression. Mavisbank, characteristically, began as such a small house that large wings had to be added almost immediately. At the hands of Robert Adam, who made several handsome contributions to the Edinburgh villadom, including Sunnyside, the simple hut became transformed into the more luxurious pavilion which is one of the many paradoxes surrounding the villa's inherent contradictions.

But at the same time as this formality was being promoted, at the end of the eighteenth century there seems to have been a consciousness that a distinctive vernacular style was passing away which gave rise to a crop of thatch around Eskbank, at the heart of the villadom. Although we now classify houses like Midfield as cottages *ornées*, their character remained true to their rustic origins. This clutch of houses seems to be firmly connected with Robert Adam and his brother-in-law, John Clerk of Eldin. The most famous of the group is Barony House, where the newly married Sir Walter Scott passed his summers and which was romantically and misleadingly described by later nineteenth-century commentators as an ordinary labourer's cottage (fig. 13.3).

The bucolic and diminutive mood of the villa is vividly conjured up in their very names, and there are few prizes for originality in the Edinburgh villadom with its Belvidere, Belmont and Bellvue. Suffixes include 'parks', 'banks', 'fields' and 'groves'. We have already mentioned the 'huts' which are far outnumbered by 'cottages' and 'cots'. While it is easy to be snobbish in the face of such banality the names are a testament to the very deep affection in which villas were held, with many being named to commemorate spouses. Mavisbank translates simply as 'thrush' bank. By contrast, there is no sign of a reciprocal affection for townhouses and those of the New Town were to become increasingly standardized and impersonal. This very personal involvement of owner and villa is reflected in the extent to which they tended to be disposed of on their deaths. They were not seen as more general family possessions to be passed on to the next generation: the new owner usually transformed it in his or her own image.

A possible definition of a villa may lie in an attitude of mind: a house is a villa if its occupant thinks it is. Behind this idea is the inherent contrast of the less attractive townhouse with all its social demands and business cares to highlight the agreeableness of the carefree villa, which is another of the concept's contradictions. Similarly, the villa avoids boredom because needs must ensures that the stop is finite. It is the architecture of leisure for pleasure. The definition of the villa has therefore to accept that it is only one half of a whole.

Fig. 13.3 Barony House, Lasswade. Summer house of Sir Walter Scott, from Homes &
Haunts of Sir Walter Scott, *1897.*

In Edinburgh a wide variety of different houses served as villas. Before he
acquired Craigcrook, Lord Jeffrey spent his summers in the decaying Baroque
splendour of Hatton (fig. 13.4), one of the late seventeenth-century 'secretary of
states' villas', and some of its romantic character was transferred in the early
improvements to Craigcrook which played up its ancient character. Although we
now see old towerhouses like Craigcrook as relics of an earlier age, with an
emphasis on defence, many of these small towerhouses surrounding Edinburgh
from the sixteenth century possibly bear direct comparison with pre-Classical
Medici villas and always functioned in a similar, city–centred mode.

If the popularity of the villa was promoted by its ability to be accessible to a
wide range of incomes because its essential equation of a small house in a garden,
with a view over land looked after by others, could be achieved so readily, the
villadom was marked by a much greater potential for social mixing than the
rigidly controlled 'sets' of the town and the exclusiveness of the Assembly Rooms.
It is quite difficult to pin this aspect down in predominantly middle-class
Edinburgh, although it is obviously characteristic of the Thameside villadom, but
it is of interest that it was while residing at Barony House that Scott came within
the orbit of his great kinsman, the Duke of Buccleuch, before they all decamped

Fig. 13.4   Hatton House, Midlothian, from John Slezer's Theatrum Scotiae.

to the Borders on the friendliest of terms, just as the struggling architect George Meikle Kemp, on a very constrained income, was able to gain a modest foothold with a tiny house on the fringe of Morningside, then, as now, a fashionable villa quarter.[11] This defrosting of social formalities could not but be promoted by the warmth of the holiday mood of the villa's temporary residents.

The very artificial distinction at one celebrated Edinburgh villa between the house of retreat and entertainment, separated only by the day of the week, is beautifully described in Cockburn's account of Lord Jeffrey at Craigcrook:

> Saturday, during the summer session of the courts, was always a day of festivity; chiefly, but by no means exclusively, for his friends at the bar, many of whom were under general invitations. . . . Our legal practitioners . . . are liberated earlier on Saturday; and the Craigcrook party began to assemble about three, each taking to his own enjoyment. The bowling-green was sure to have its matches, in which the host joined with skill and keenness; the garden had its loiterers; the flowers, not forgetting the wall of glorious yellow roses, their worshippers; the hill its prospect seekers. The banquet that followed was generous; the wines never spared, but rather too various; mirth unrestrained, except by propriety; the talk always good, but never ambitious; and mere listeners in no disrepute. What can efface these days, or indeed any Craigcrook day, from the recollection of those who had the happiness of enjoying them.[12]

On Sundays, however, the drawbridge was raised firmly and friends of the family knew that the Jeffreys were not to be disturbed. Because Lord Jeffrey was so famous as the editor of the *Edinburgh Review* there are many visitors' accounts of being entertained by him at Craigcrook. It is just possible that the meals served at the villa with their local fish, oatcakes and whisky were different in character to the extremely pretentious dinners of imported viands given in the private houses of the 'Modern Athens'. The concept of a lighter less formal decorative style for a summer residence was certainly familiar from the many published writings of the Edinburgh decorator D.R. Hay, who included Jeffrey among his many patrons.

Although the very success of the villadom was to contain the seeds of its own destruction, in that the city could only expand over the sites of destroyed villas, so tightly was the city constricted, the loss of amenity was a gradual process and there are several references to villa lovers buying up nearby fields to keep development at bay. A memorable example of the march of urbanization is provided by the way in which Robert Adam's elegant villa of Bellvue (fig. 13.5) became stranded in Drummond Place (fig. 13.6) and briefly served as the Excise Office. Lord Cockburn deplored the destruction of its woods. It is fascinating to see in the many engraved plans for proposed developments, the standard New Town terraces giving way to planned developments of villa quarters, obviously recalling Nash in Regent's Park, but also reflecting a traditional pattern of Edinburgh life.

It was the arrival of suburban railways that transformed the villa's fortunes in Edinburgh, because, for the first time, it was possible to use them as full-time

Fig. 13.5 Bellvue, designed by Robert Adam, 1774–5.

*Fig. 13.6   Bellvue House by Robert Adam, stranded in Drummond Place, 1829, from
Shepherd's Modern Athens.*

residences. Many villas were extended to provide more ample family and service
quarters at this time. Although the spawning Victorian full-time villas were to be
deplored by Robert Louis Stevenson ('They belong to no style of art, only to a
form of business much to be regretted. . . . And as this eruption keeps spreading
on our borders, we have ever further to walk among unpleasant sites, before we
gain the country air'),[13] these aesthetic drawbacks did not impair their
functioning as villas. Indeed, since the villadom had no planning controls, it is
possible to see in many villa developments an almost vernacular tradition
continuing, although bowing to contemporary fashions, as villas always have. The
main loss was that of the prospect, and as they crowded closer together a sense of
stress is visible in the obvious signs of walls being raised ever higher to preserve
privacy. These lofty walls, with their many courses, are characteristic of present-
day villadoms throughout Europe, whether in Edinburgh, Hampstead, Rome or
Florence.

Sadly, many contributors to this volume have dismissed the Victorian villa as
such a pale shadow of an aristocratic tradition as to be beneath contempt, but it
seems to me that behind these walls the villa still functions because its scale is as
capable of reduction as of Hadrianic expansion. It is a source of great pleasure in
Edinburgh to retain some contact with the seasons in the limited space of a
Victorian villa garden from spring bulbs to falling leaves, enlivened by the 1990s
fauna of magpies, grey squirrels and fearless foxes, and yet be only a bus ride, or
the occasional walk, from the very heart of the city. The villa may not readily
submit to formal definitions but there can be little doubt that it is one of the most
successful forms of housing ever invented and one which has proved unusually
exportable from the south to the furthest north and wildest west.

Notes

1. The Italian Renaissance Villa

1. Andrea Palladio, *I quattro libri dell'architettura* (Venice, Dominico de' Franceschi, 1570), book II, p. 45.
2. Ibid., book II, p. 46.
3. Ibid., book II, p. 45: 'quietamente si potrà attendere à gli studij delle lettere, & alla contemplatione; come per questo gli antichi Saui soleuano spesse uolte vsare di ritirarsi in simili luoghi.'
4. David Coffin, *The Villa in the Life of Renaissance Rome* (Princeton, NJ, Princeton University Press, 1979), p. vii.
5. Palladio, *I quattro libri*, book II.
6. Leon Battista Alberti, *On the Art of Building in Ten Books (De re aedificatoria)*, tr. Joseph Rykwert, Neil Leach and Robert Tavernor (Cambridge, Mass. and London, MIT Press, 1988), pp. 140–53; Myra Nan Rosenfeld (ed.), *Sebastiano Serlio on Domestic Architecture* (Cambridge, Mass. and London, 1978); Anton Francesco Doni, *Le ville* (Modena, 1566), ed. Ugo Bellocchi (Modena, 1969).
7. Doni, *Le ville*, p. 29; translation from James S. Ackerman, *The Villa: Form and Ideology of Country Houses* (Princeton, NJ, Princeton University Press, 1980), p. 109.
8. Doni, *Le ville*, p. 31; quoted in Ackerman, *The Villa*, p. 109.
9. Palladio, *I quattro libri*, book II, p. 45.
10. Ibid., pp. 18–19: 'il quale non mi è parso mettere tra le fabriche di Villa per la uicinanza ch'ella ha con la Città.'
11. James S. Ackerman, *Palladio* (Harmondsworth, Penguin Books Ltd, 1966), pp. 48–54 (with bibliography on p. 189); Howard Burns with Lynda Fairbairn and Bruce Boucher, *Andrea Palladio 1508–1580: The Portico and the Farmyard* (Arts Council exhibition catalogue, London, 1975); Michelangelo Muraro, *Venetian Villas: The History and Culture*, tr. Peter Lauritzen, John Harper and Stephen Sartarelli (New York, Rizzoli, 1986), pp. 53–66; Paul Holberton, *Palladio's Villas: Life in the Renaissance Countryside* (London, John Murray, 1990), pp. 156–63; Denis Cosgrove, *The Palladian Landscape* (Leicester, Leicester University Press, 1993).
12. C.L. Frommel, *Die Farnesina und Peruzzis architektonisches Frühwerk* (Berlin, Ernst Wasmuth, 1961); Felix Gilbert, *The Pope, his Banker and Venice* (Cambridge, Mass. and London, Harvard University Press, 1980).
13. Coffin, *The Villa*, p. 108.
14. Ibid.
15. See especially Richard Bentmann and Michael Müller, *Die Villa als Herrschafts-architektur: Versuch einer kunst- und sozialgeschichtlichen Analyse* (Frankfurt, Edition Suhrkamp, 1970), English edition: *The Villa as Hegemonic Architecture* (Atlantic Highlands, NJ, Humanities Press, 1992); and Muraro, *Venetian Villas*, pp. 47–54.
16. Palladio, *I quattro libri*, book II, p. 45. He was echoing similar recommendations by Alberti, *On the Art of Building*, pp. 140–1, 145.
17. The Villa Medici at Cafaggiolo lay near the Observant Franciscan monastery of San Francesco al Bosco. The Villa Medici at Fiesole lay on the hillside below the monastery of San Girolamo. All these buildings were remodelled for Cosimo il Vecchio by Michelozzo from about 1420 onwards. See Harriet McNeal Caplow, *Michelozzo*, 2 vols, Outstanding Dissertations in the Fine Arts (New York, Garland Press, 1977); Miranda Ferrara and Francesco Quinterio, *Michelozzo di Bartolomeo* (Florence, Salimbeni, 1984).

18. *The Letters of the Younger Pliny*, ed. Betty Radice (Harmondsworth, Penguin Books Ltd, 1963), p. 144.

19. Giuseppe Falcone, *La nuova, vaga, et dilettevole villa* (Brescia, 1559), p. 3; extract quoted in English translation in Ackerman, *The Villa*, p. 112.

20. Alberti, *On the Art of Building*, p. 141.

21. Coffin, *The Villa*, p. 170.

22. Palladio, *I quattro libri*, book II, p. 45.

23. Palladio, *I quattro libri*, book I, p. 52; Holberton, *Palladio's Villas*, pp. 206–28.

24. *The Commentaries of Pius II: Books VI–IX*, ed. Florence Alden Gragg (Northampton, Mass., Smith College Studies in History, 1951), p. 600.

25. Caplow, *Michelozzo*, vol. II, pp. 595–604; Ferrara and Quinterio, *Michelozzo*, pp. 73–8, 168–73, 176–85, 245–52; Ackerman, *The Villa*, pp. 66–73.

26. Caplow, *Michelozzo*, vol. II, pp. 604–6; Ferrara and Quinterio, *Michelozzo*, pp. 185.

27. Ferrara and Quinterio, *Michelozzo*, pp. 79–80, 253–5; Ackerman, *The Villa*, pp. 73–8.

28. Coffin, *The Villa*, pp. 101–2, 105–7.

29. Antonio Pinelli and Orietta Rossi, *Genga architetto: aspetti della cultura urbinate del primo 500* (Rome, Bulzoni Editore, 1971), pp. 121–34.

30. G. Fiocco, *Alvise Cornaro: il suo tempo e le sue opere* (Vicenza, Neri Pozza, 1965), pp. 47–57.

31. Fiocco, *Alvise Cornaro*, pp. 47–8.

32. Coffin, *The Villa*, p. 107; James S. Ackerman, *The Cortile del Belvedere* (Rome, Vatican, 1954); Arnaldo Bruschi, *Bramante*, tr. Peter Murray (London, Thames and Hudson, 1977), p. 100; Pinelli and Rossi, *Genga architetto*, pp. 143, 153–5; Roger Jones and Nicholas Penny, *Raphael* (New Haven and London, Yale University Press, 1983), pp. 226–34.

33. Ackerman, *The Villa*, p. 18.

34. Most of the correspondence relating to the building and gardens was addressed to or written by Eleonora. See Pinelli and Rossi, *Genga architetto*, pp. 305–35.

35. Letter of Cardinal Bembo to Duchess Eleonora, 19 December 1543 (Pinelli and Rossi, *Genga architetto*, p. 335).

36. See Ackerman, *The Villa*, pp. 120–3.

37. Alberti, *On the Art of Building*, pp. 119–20, 149.

38. Giorgio Vasari, *Lives of the Artists*, tr. George Bull, vol. I (Harmondsworth, Penguin Books Ltd, 1965), p. 312.

39. Rudolf Wittkower, *Architectural Principles in the Age of Humanism* (London, Studies of the Warburg Institute, 1949; many later editions), parts III–IV.

40. Ackerman, *The Villa*, p. 94.

41. Ibid., p. 73.

42. See L. Puppi, 'Il Barco di Caterina Cornaro ad Altivole', *Prospettive*, 25 (1962), pp. 52–64; Muraro, *Venetian Villas*, pp. 142–5.

43. Palladio, *I quattro libri*, book II, p. 45.

44. The villa was built for Paolo Almerico, former referendary to Pius IV, in 1566–9. See Lionello Puppi, *Andrea Palladio*, 2 vols (Milan, Electa, 1973), vol. II, pp. 381–3. The silhouette with its low stepped dome, the top-lit central hall (originally with an open aperture when visited by Inigo Jones) and the triangular staircases are all recognizable allusions to the precedence of the Pantheon.

45. Ackerman, *The Villa*, pp. 78–86 (with further bibliography).

46. A. Perosa (ed.), *Giovanni Rucellai e il suo Zibaldone*, vol. I, *Il zibaldone quaresimale* (London, Warburg Institute, 1960), pp. 20–3 (description of the Villa di Quaracchi).

47. *The Commentaries of Pius II*, pp. 597–600.

48. Philip Foster, 'Raphael on the Villa Madama: The Text of a Lost Letter', *Römisches Jahrbuch für Kunstgeschichte*, (1967–8), pp. 307–12; English translation in Jones and Penny, *Raphael*, pp. 247–8.

49. Ackerman, *The Villa*, p. 78; Holberton, *Palladio's Villas*, p. 136.

50. Book VI survives in two manuscript versions in the Avery Library of Columbia University, New York (see Rosenfeld (ed.), *Sebastiano Serlio on Domestic Architecture*); and in Munich (see Sebastiano Serlio, *Architettura civile: libri sesto settimo e ottavo nei manoscritti di Monaco e Vienna*, ed. Francesco Paolo Fiore (Milan, Edizioni il Polifilo, 1994), pp. 1–246).

51. Tacitus, *The Annals of Imperial Rome*, tr. Michael Grant (Harmondsworth, Penguin Books Ltd, 1959), p. 353.

52. Wittkower, *Architectural Principles*; Colin Rowe, *The Mathematics of the Ideal Villa and other Essays* (Cambridge, Mass. and London, MIT Press, 1976).

53. Ackerman, *The Villa*, p. 73.

54. See Marcello Faglio (ed.), *Natura e artificio* (Rome, Officina Edizioni, 1979); Claudia Lazzaro, *The Italian Renaissance Garden* (New Haven and London, Yale University Press, 1990), pp. 131–66.
55. Michel de Montaigne, *Journal de voyage*, ed. Fausta Garavini (Paris, Gallimard, 1983).
56. Quoted in Ludwig Heydenreich and Wolfgang Lotz, *Architecture in Italy 1400–1600*, tr. Mary Hottinger (Harmondsworth, Penguin Books Ltd, 1974), p. 396.
57. See especially on the Villa d'Este: Lazzaro, *The Italian Renaissance Garden*, pp. 214–42; and on the Villa Lante, ibid., pp. 243–69.
58. Palladio, *I quattro libri*, book II, p. 45.
59. Ibid., book II, p. 61; Burns *et al.*, *Andrea Palladio*, pp. 83–4.
60. Coffin, *The Villa*, pp. 193–5.
61. Richard J. Goy, *Venetian Vernacular Architecture: Traditional Housing in the Venetian Lagoon* (Cambridge, Cambridge University Press, 1989), pp. 206–7.
62. Palladio, *I quattro libri*, book II, p. 64.
63. Georgina Masson, *Italian Gardens* (London, Thames and Hudson, 1987), p. 144.

2. Villa Views and the Uninvited Audience

1. James S. Ackerman, *The Villa: Form and Ideology of Country Houses* (Washington, 1990), p. 156.
2. Jane Clark, 'For Kings and Senates Fit', *The Georgian Group Journal* (1989), p. 55.
3. David H. Solkin, *Richard Wilson: The Landscape of Reaction* (Tate Gallery, 1982), p. 214.
4. Ackerman, *The Villa*, p. 156.
5. See Adrian Tinniswood, *A History of Country House Visiting* (Oxford, 1989).
6. See Morris R. Brownell and Jacob Simon, *Alexander Pope's Villa* (Marble Hill House, 1980), and Giles Worsley, 'Jewels in a Rich Coronet' *Country Life* (14 October 1993), pp. 68–71.
7. Brownell and Simon, *Alexander Pope's Villa*, cat. 6.
8. Ibid., p. 35.
9. Ibid., p. 36.
10. Quoted in Tinniswood, *Country House Visiting*, p. 94.
11. Ibid., p. 97.
12. For illustrations and more detailed discussion of early images of Marble Hill and Kenwood see Julius Bryant, *Finest Prospects: Three Historic Houses* (Iveagh Bequest, Kenwood, 1986).
13. Ibid., p. 75.
14. Henrietta Pye, *Short Account of the Principal Seats in and about Twickenham*, pp. vi–ix.
15. Quoted in Julius Bryant, *Mrs Howard: A Woman of Reason* (Marble Hill House, 1988), p. 9.
16. Quoted in Bryant, *Finest Prospects*, p. 41.
17. Ibid., p. 111.
18. *Gentleman's Magazine*, 64 (1794), p. 182.
19. *The Builder* (12 July 1890).
20. James Thorne, *Handbook to the Environs of London* (London, 1876), p. 633.
21. See Bryant, *Finest Prospects*, cat. 62, 63.
22. Freeling, op. cit., p. 320.
23. Quoted in Bryant, *Finest Prospects*, p. 68.
24. John Macky, *A Journey through England* (London, 1714), pp. 42–3.
25. Illustrated in Bryant, *Finest Prospects*, p. 136 and cat. 75.
26. Ibid., p. 136 and cat. 76.
27. Ibid., pp. 109–10.
28. Ibid., p. 100.
29. Ibid., cat. 92, 95.
30. K. Garlick and A. Macintyre (eds), *The Diary of Joseph Farington*, vol. I (London and New Haven, 1978), p. 97.
31. J.C. Loudon, *Suburban Gardener, and Villa Companion* (1838), pp. 673–4.
32. John Harris, *The Palladian Revival: Lord Burlington, his Villa and Garden at Chiswick* (Royal Academy of Arts, 1994), p. 267.
33. Ibid. See also Jacques Carré, 'Through French Eyes: Rigaud's Drawings of Chiswick', *Journal of Garden History*, 2 (2) (1982), pp. 133–42 and Peter Willis, *Charles Bridgeman and the English Landscape Garden* (London, 1977), pp. 113–19, figs 129–42.
34. James Lees-Milne, *Earls of Creation* (London, 1986), p. 136. According to the same author's research at Chatsworth, in 1742 Pope sent Jonathan Richardson a ticket of admission, explaining that the paintings in the house were only shown on afternoons when the family was in residence. Reference kindly provided by Treve Rosoman.
35. *The Freemason* or *The Hyp Doctor*, 1 (13

November 1733); reference kindly provided by Dr Jacques Carré.

36. Paget Toynbee (ed.), 'Horace Walpole's Journals of Visits to Country Seats, &c', *The Walpole Society*, 16 (1927–8), pp. 9–80. For Chiswick see pp. 22–3.

37. W. Watts, *The Seats of the Nobility and Gentry in a Collection of the Most Interesting and Picturesque Views* (1779–86), pl. 30. Watts also notes, 'It is somewhat remarkable that persons are not admitted to see this place without tickets for that purpose, a ceremony, we believe, not observed at any other seat in the kingdom; and that upon admission you are prohibited from making any drawings.'

38. Quoted in T.J. Edelstein, *Vauxhall Gardens* (Yale Center for British Art, 1983), p. 12.

3. Jane Austen's Aversion to Villas

1. *Jane Austen's Letters*, ed. R.W. Chapman, 2nd edn (London, Oxford University Press, 1952, repr. 1969), p. 401.

2. *Pride and Prejudice* (1813), ed. R.W. Chapman, The Oxford Illustrated Jane Austen, vol. 2, 3rd edn (London, Oxford University Press, 1932, repr. 1971), p. 156.

3. *Letters*, p. 269.

4. Letter to G.H. Lewes, 11 January 1848, quoted by Elizabeth Gaskell, *The Life of Charlotte Brontë*, ed. Clement Shorter, World's Classics (London, Oxford University Press, 1919, repr. 1951), p. 282.

5. Richard Elsam, *An Essay on Rural Architecture &c.* (London, E. Lawrence, 1803, facsimile repr. 1972), p. 18.

6. *Minor Works*, ed. R.W. Chapman, The Oxford Illustrated Jane Austen, vol. 6 (London, Oxford University Press, 1954, rev. repr. 1969), p. 322.

7. J.C. Loudon, *An Encyclopaedia of Cottage, Farm, and Villa Architecture &c.* (1833), 3rd rev. edn (London, Longmans, 1839), p. 763.

8. *Letters*, p. 314.

9. Ibid., p. 465.

10. *The World*, 12 (22 March 1753).

11. Ibid., 15 (12 April 1753).

12. *Letters*, pp. 401–2.

13. *Emma* (1816), ed. R.W. Chapman, The Oxford Illustrated Jane Austen, vol. 4, 3 edn (London, Oxford University Press, 1933, repr. 1971), p. 7.

14. Ibid., p. 136.

15. *Minor Works*, pp. 380–1.

16. William Cobbett, *Rural Rides* (1830), ed. George Woodcock, Penguin English Library (Harmondsworth, Penguin Books, 1967), p. 402.

17. *Pride and Prejudice*, p. 18.

18. *Minor Works*, 'Edgar and Emma', p. 31.

19. *Pride and Prejudice*, p. 255.

20. *Emma*, p. 207.

21. *Northanger Abbey* (1818), ed. R.W. Chapman, The Oxford Illustrated Jane Austen, vol. 5, 3rd edn (London, Oxford University Press, 1933, repr. 1969), pp. 119–20.

22. John Ruskin, 'The Poetry of Architecture' (1837–8), Ruskin's Works (New York, Lovell, Coryell & Co., undated), p. 87.

23. *Mansfield Park* (1814), ed. R.W. Chapman, The Oxford Illustrated Jane Austen, vol. 3, 3rd edn (London, Oxford University Press, 1934, repr. 1970), p. 82.

24. *Sense and Sensibility* (1811), ed. R.W. Chapman, The Oxford Illustrated Jane Austen, vol. 1, 3rd edn (London, Oxford University Press, 1933, repr. 1971), p. 28.

25. Ibid., p. 72.

26. Ibid., p. 252.

27. *Letters*, p. 266.

28. *Persuasion* (1818), ed. R.W. Chapman, The Oxford Illustrated Jane Austen, vol. 5, 3rd edn (London, Oxford University Press, 1933, repr. 1969), p. 36.

29. Ibid., p. 123.

30. Ruskin, 'Poetry of Architecture', p. 101.

31. W.F. Pocock, *Architectural Designs for Rustic Cottages, Picturesque Dwellings, Villas, &c.* (London, J. Taylor, 1807, facsimile repr. 1972), p. 11.

32. *Persuasion*, p. 125.

33. *Mansfield Park*, p. 244.

34. Ruskin, 'Poetry of Architecture', p. 60.

4. John James

1. BL Add MS 32540 ff. 7v–8.

2. For further details on both Banckes and James, see the author's unpublished PhD thesis, *English Baroque Architecture: The Work of John James* (University of London, 1986).

3. Letter from James to Robert Harley, 24 October 1711, BL MS Loan 29/217 f. 556.

4. Contracts, drawings and accounts, Surrey Record Office, 176/19/1, KP6/27/4–5.

5. Nicholas de Salis, 'Richmond's Forgotten

House', *Country Life* (30 September 1982), and letter from the author, *Country Life* (2 December 1982).

6. Bodleian, MS Rawl. B376, ff. 8, 9, 20 October 1711.

7. James was clerk to Hawksmoor.

8. Papers in the Hampshire Record Office; and see Sally Jeffery, 'John James and George London at Herriard: Architectural Drawings in the Jervoise of Herriard Collection', *Architectural History*, 28 (1985), pp. 40–71.

9. Hampshire Record Office, Jervoise of Herriard Collection, 44 M 69, P1/18.

10. Hampshire Record Office, Jervoise of Herriard Collection, 44 M 69/E14.

11. See Sally Jeffery, *The Mansion House* (Chichester, Phillimore, 1993), p. 26, illus. 18A.

12. John Macky, *A Journey Through England*, vol. 1 (London, 1714), p. 36.

13. John Macky, *A Journey Through England*, vol. 2 (London, 1722), p. 63; Patricia Astley Cooper, *The History of Orleans House, Twickenham* (London Borough of Richmond upon Thames Library and Information Services, 1984).

14. See John Brushe, 'Wricklemarsh and the Collections of Sir Gregory Page', *Apollo* (November 1985), pp. 364–71.

15. PRO Pitt Papers, C108/415–424 and C110/28, 81.

16. PRO C11 118.16, C33 369 f. 335, IND 4148, IND 4183; BL Add MS 36046; Sally Jeffery, 'An Architect for Standlynch House', *Country Life* (13 February 1986), pp. 404–6.

5. *The Transformation of Lord Burlington*

1. All the necessary references and sources are in my *The Palladian Revival: Lord Burlington, His Villa and Garden at Chiswick* (Yale, University Press, 1994). However, I would like to single out R. Wittkower, 'Lord Burlington and his Work in York', *York Institute of Architectural Study, Studies in Architectural History* (York, 1954); and also Eileen Harris, *British Architectural Books and Writers 1556–1785* (1990), for its account (pp. 348ff.) of the *Fabbriche antiche*. I also

want to acknowledge Dr Edward McParland's forthcoming article on the New Junta.

6. *Poor Palladian or Not?*

1. The standard text on the subject is James S. Ackerman, *The Villa: Form and Ideology of Country Houses* (London, Thames and Hudson, 1990). It is worth noting here the title's use of the term 'villa' as a synonym for 'country house'. The work of David R. Coffin provides an essential complement to Ackerman, and is summarized in *The Villa in the Life of Renaissance Rome* (Princeton, Princeton University Press, 1979). I must acknowledge my debt to Coffin's work in this chapter. Two other short notices provide useful perspectives: Mark Girouard, 'What is a Villa?', *Town and Country* (New Haven and London, Yale University Press, 1992), pp. 235–8, and Pierre de la Ruffinière du Prey, *John Soane: The Making of an Architect* (London and Chicago, University of Chicago Press, 1982), pp. 265–9.

2. Ackerman's approach in *The Villa*, is representative, as he advances his discussion directly from the villas of the Medici to those of the Veneto, notably Palladio's, passing over the villas of Renaissance Rome.

3. On Woodlands see, for example, Maurice Craig, *Classic Irish Houses of the Middle Size* (London and New York, Architectural Press, 1976), pp. 76–9, and Dan Cruickshank, *A Guide to the Georgian Buildings of Britain and Ireland* (London, Weidenfeld and Nicolson, 1985), p. 59.

4. For this perspective on Pearce see the relevant discussion (chapter 2) in the Knight of Glin, *The Irish Palladians*, an unpublished study now on deposit in the Irish Architectural Archive, Dublin. This remains the most complete and authoritative introduction to the topic, both in detail and in general. As the text exists in a number of versions with different page numbers, references are noted by chapter and section.

5. Du Prey's conclusion remains equally valid today: 'what was acually *called* a "villa" and what *looks* like one to the modern critic's eye have, of necessity, no correlation', *John Soane*, p. 269.

6. *Georgian Society Records*, vol. V (Dublin, Dublin University Press, 1913), pp. 81–107.

7. Ibid., p. 88.

8. See in particular Glin, *Irish Palladians*, esp. chapter 8, 'Conclusion'.

9. For a general review see e.g. Christopher Hussey, 'Powerscourt, Co. Wicklow', *Country Life* (6 December 1946), pp. 1062–7; (13 December 1946), pp. 1158–61; (20 December 1946), pp. 1206–9. For more detailed critical and historical assessments see Glin, *Irish Palladians*, chapter 3, section 4, and David Griffin, *Powerscourt House Co. Wicklow: An Architectural Report Compiled for the National Building Agency Limited* (Dublin, Irish Architectural Archive, 1989) (unpublished report) and, more recently this author's preliminary unpublished report summarizing the present knowledge of the development of the fabric in light of more recent work on the house: Seán O'Reilly, *Powerscourt House Co. Wicklow: Report and Recommendations*, Architectural Heritage and History (Dublin, 1995).

10. Viscount Powerscourt, *A Description and History of Powerscourt* (London, Mitchell and Hughes, 1903), pp. 141–2.

11. Ilaria Toesca, 'Alessandro Galilei in Inghilterra', *English Miscellany*, 3 (1952), pp. 189–220 (p. 213).

12. The genesis of Castletown is relevant to this interpretation of Powerscourt but is too complex to be considered in detail here. In its more recent review by Giles Worsley ('Castletown House, Co. Kildare', *Country Life* (17 March 1994), pp. 52–7) the author presents Castletown as a simple variation, probably by Thomas Burgh, of designs available in *Vitruvius Britannicus*. If, as Worsley notes, the shape (rectangular) also bears a significant resemblance to, for example, Burgh's Library at Trinity College Dublin, the details of the library, together with those of the distinctly old-fashioned Steeven's Hospital, Dublin – in effect nearly contemporary with Castletown and still in a style more typical of the previous century (fairly described as 'the last kick of the seventeenth century' by Maurice Craig, *Dublin 1660–1860* (Dublin, Allen Figgis & Co., 1980), p. 97) – have nothing in common with Castletown. Consequently it is difficult to see how

Burgh could have been responsible for any significant aspect of Conolly's house. Some features from Castletown do have a correspondence with Burgh's documented work but these are more reasonably explained as Burgh's derivation from Castletown than by attributing Castletown to Burgh.

13. See especially the discussion of the house by Griffin, *Powerscourt House*.

14. NLI, Powerscourt Papers, MS 4875. See also the discussions in Griffin, *Powerscourt House*, and O'Reilly, *Powerscourt House*.

15. This generalization excludes lesser modifications, such as those to the windows, and lateral extensions.

16. Quoted in Griffin, *Powerscourt House*, p. 11.

17. Viewed from the lower terraces the discrepancy would have been less apparent, but numerous other views from the garden would have highlighted these imperfections.

18. See for example the discussion in Edward Malins and Patrick Bowe, *Irish Gardens and Demesnes from 1830* (London, Barrie & Jenkins, 1980), pp. 82–95.

19. John Rocque, *A Map of the County of Dublin . . .* (Dublin, 1762) and Thomas Reading, *A Map of the Demesne Land Belonging to Powerscourt . . .* (1740) (IAA, 89/62).

20. Coffin, *The Villa*, pp. 311–40. The evidence cited in O'Reilly, *Powerscourt House*, reinforces the argument concerning Castle's purposeful monumentality in the garden elevation, in that no medieval precedent for his tower-like bows has been identified. The gardens recorded by Reading, *Map*, may well derive at least in part from a pre-Georgian planting.

21. Ackerman, *The Villa*, pp. 92 ff.

22. See for example the complex history of the Villa Medici as reported by Coffin, *The Villa*, pp. 219–33.

23. See the recent discussion of this question in Niall McCullough, *Palimpsest: Change in the Irish Building Tradition* (Dublin, Anne Street Press, 1994), pp. 53–86.

24. The recurrence of what are generally referred to as pistol-loops at a comparatively late date is a curiosity of Irish architecture related to this question, though it should be said that the defensive purpose of such loops has been questioned.

Representing a similar mood is the door in Castle's early Georgian villa of Ballyhaise, Co. Cavan, described by the Knight of Glin as follows: 'An impressive fortress-like cast iron door with spyholes' (*Irish Palladians*, chapter 3, part 4).

25. Coffin, *The Villa*, pp. 140–4.
26. See, among other sources, Craig, *Classic Irish Houses*, pp. 102–3, and Girouard, *Town and Country*, pp. 109–20.
27. The original Diocletian windows were replaced by the present square tripartite windows in the later nineteenth century but they represent well the gestural Palladianism found also in the later English Baroque.
28. Coffin, *The Villa*, pp. 69–74.
29. The Knight of Glin, 'A Baroque Palladian in Ireland: The Architecture of Davis Duckart – I', *Country Life* (28 September 1967), pp. 735–9, and 'The Last Palladian in Ireland: The Architecture of Davis Duckart – II', *Country Life* (5 October 1967), pp. 798–801. See also Glin, *Irish Palladians*, chapter 7.
30. Richard Hewlings, 'James Leoni c.1686–1746: An Anglicized Venetian', in Roderick Brown (ed.), *The Architectural Outsiders* (London, Waterstone, 1985), pp. 21–44.
31. See for example Brian de Breffny and Rosemary Ffolliott, *The Houses of Ireland: Domestic Architecture from the Medieval Castle to the Edwardian Villa* (London, Thames & Hudson, 1975), pp. 141–2.
32. Dr Craig has recently identified the hunting lodge at Klemensworth, Sögel, Germany, as a possible source for Castlecor, sharing as it does both scale and exterior composition.
33. Referred to in de Breffny and Ffolliott, *The Houses of Ireland*, p. 142.
34. The complex geometrical patterning of Castlecor does appear in the English Palladian tradition, for example in the polygonal patterning of Halfpenny, but the matter requires further study.
35. For considerations of Pearce as a Palladian with various degrees of purity, see for example Howard Colvin and Maurice Craig, *Architectural Drawings in the Library of Elton Hall by Sir John Vanbrugh and Sir Edward Lovett Pearce* (Oxford, Private Printing, Roxburghe Club, 1964); Glin, *Irish Palladians*, chapter 2; and

Cruickshank, *Georgian Buildings*, p. 59.
36. As part of the more recent reassessment of Pearce see Edward McParland, 'Sir Thomas Hewett and the New Junta for Architecture', *The Role of the Amateur Architect: Papers given at the Georgian Group Symposium 1993* (Georgian Group, London, 1994), pp. 21–6. Here Dr McParland describes Pearce as 'a most uncomfortable Burlingtonian' (p. 25).
37. F. Elrington Ball (ed.), *The Correspondence of Jonathan Swift, D.D.*, vol. V (London, G. Bell and Sons, 1913), p. 295, where Swift writes to the Duke of Dorset on 30 December 1735 to say that 'Mr Jackson . . . hath built a family house, more expensive than he intended'.
38. Craig, *Classic Irish Houses*, p. 77.
39. Craig, ibid., considers that the belvedere derives from Coleshill 'in some fashion'.
40. For the Villa Lante at Bagnaia see for example J.C. Shepard and G.A. Jellicoe, *Italian Gardens of the Renaissance* (London, Ernest Benn, 1925; repr. London, Academy Editions, 1986), pls 26–9, and Coffin, *The Villa*, pp. 340 ff.
41. If considered in terms of English architecture the arrangement might be interpreted as a double-pile plan turned on its side. However, though simple in principle this re-orientation is radical in practice as it eliminates the hall, a fundamental theme in English domestic architecture.
42. H. Lebas and F. Debret, *Œuvres complètes de Jacques Barozzi de Vignole* (Paris, 1815), pls 46–7. See also the discussion by Coffin, *The Villa*, pp. 132–5.
43. Isaac Ware, *The Complete Body of Architecture* (London, 1756), Book III, ch. 24, p. 321.
44. I am indebted to Dr Edward McParland of Trinity College Dublin for his guidance through the collection. The collection is now in the Victoria and Albert Museum.
45. Colvin and Craig, *Architectural Drawings*, cat. no. 242a. The drawing is almost certainly after Vignola, though the precise connections between it, Pearce and the building are, as yet, unclear.
46. Coffin, *The Villa*, pp. 135–40.
47. The theme of the corridor as entrance had been explored at other levels in the architecture of sixteenth-century Rome. In the arrangement of the Villa Lante in

Rome – attributed to Giulio Romano and dating from about 1518 – the first intention was to have a central corridor running through the building (Coffin, *The Villa*, pp. 257–62). The scheme was altered during execution and would not have been known to Pearce.

48. See the discussion in Edward McParland, 'Edward Lovett Pearce and the Deanery of Christchurch', in Agnes Bernelle (ed.), *Decantations: A Tribute to Maurice Craig* (Dublin, Lilliput Press, 1992), pp. 130–33.

49. Colvin and Craig, *Architectural Drawings*, cat. no. 119. While these plans recall those of the Villa Lante in Rome they are also reminiscent of the style of corridor-access in Vanbrugh's designs, e.g. for Philip Vanbrugh's house at Greenwich (cat. no. 6), though here the arrangement appears to derive from the lateral entrance to the hall of an earlier English tradition.

50. Here I am excluding any consideration of his public works, though such a study should prove interesting.

51. Cruickshank, *Georgian Buildings*, and David Griffin, 'Ireland's Palladian Gem', *Irish Arts Review*, 3 (4) (Winter 1986), pp. 24–8.

52. I am indebted to Dr McParland for drawing this detail to my attention.

53. Francis Elrington Ball, *A History of the County Dublin . . .* (Dublin, Thom, 1902–20, repr. Dublin, Gill & Macmillan, 1979), vol. 3, p. 40. See also James Howley, *The Follies and Garden Buildings of Ireland* (New Haven and London, Yale University Press, 1993), pp. 206–9.

54. Ball, *Dublin*.

55. See Rocque, *Map of the County of Dublin*.

56. The roof may be a rebuilding (Howley, *Follies*, p. 207).

57. The window openings do not define a separate floor.

58. See, for example, the hunting lodge at Bagni di Tivoli, in Coffin, *The Villa*.

59. Personal communication through Edward McParland and with thanks to Sir Howard Colvin.

60. I would like to thank Professor Alistair Rowan, Desmond FitzGerald, Knight of Glin, David Griffin, John O'Connell, Peter Pearson and, in particular, Dr Edward McParland for their assistance, suggestions and interest. I would also like to thank John O'Connell for permission to reproduce his drawings of Woodlands.

7. 'Heretical and Presumptuous'

1. G. Wightwick, 'Sketches by a Travelling Architect', *Library of the Fine Arts*, 3 (1832), p. 39.

2. British Architectural Library [hereafter BAL], SMK 6/11.

3. F. Arundale, *The Edifices of Andrea Palladio* (London, privately printed, 1832), preface. Of the two seventeenth-century architects mentioned by Arundale only Inigo Jones had been to Italy. It is well known that Jones visited Palladio's Villa Rotonda (on 24 September 1613), Villa Thiene at Quinto (on 13 August 1614) and Villa Valmarana at Lisiera (see B. Allsopp (ed.), *Inigo Jones on Palladio*, 2 vols (Newcastle, Oriel Press, 1970), vol. 1, pp. 23, 30–1 and 29–30 respectively). But there is also reason to believe that he visited the Villa Cornaro at Piombino, since his observation that the ceilings of the small rooms and the spiral stairs were 'of timber becaus thear is no thick waale' (Allsopp, *Jones*, vol. 1, p. 28) provides information not to be found in the text of Palladio's *Quattro libri*.

4. For an interesting parallel study see P. Davies and D. Hemsoll, 'Sanmicheli through British Eyes', in J. Bold and E. Chaney (eds), *English Architecture Public and Private: Essays for Kerry Downes* (London, Hambledon Press, 1993), pp. 121–34.

5. An Irish exception to this is perhaps Edward Lovett Pearce. A copy of the 1601 edition of Palladio's *Quattro libri* in the BAL has annotations made as a result of a visit to the Veneto in the Spring of 1724 and attributed to Pearce by Miss L. Lang and John Harris (see H.M. Colvin and M. Craig, *Architectural Drawings in the Library of Elton Hall by Sir John Vanbrugh and Sir Edward Lovett Pearce* (Oxford, privately printed for the Roxburghe Club, 1964), p. xli). The book was displayed as Pearce's copy in the 1980 Vicenza exhibition *Palladio: La Sua eredità nel mondo* (Venice, Electa, 1980), p. 36. From the marginalia it can be established that Pearce travelled to probably twelve of the villas illustrated in Book 2 of the *Quattro libri* (see the entry on this copy in N. Savage, P. Nash et al, *Catalogue of the British Architectural Library Early Imprints*, 4 vols (London, Bowker-Saur, 1994), vol. 3 (forthcoming 1998)). I am grateful to Dr Edward Chaney for drawing my attention to this important volume.

6. For analyses of the annotations see P. Kingsbury, 'Lord Burlington's Architectural Theory and Practice', in R. White (ed.), *Lord Burlington and his Circle: Papers Given at a Georgian Group Symposium* (1982), pp. 2–24, and J. Harris, *The Palladian Revival: Lord Burlington, his Villa and Garden at Chiswick* (New Haven and London, Yale University Press, 1994), pp. 62–4.

7. R. Boyle, *Fabbriche antiche disegnata da Andrea Palladio* (London, 1730 [actually after 1736]), preface 'All'intendente lettore'; J. Clark, 'The Mysterious Mr Buck', *Apollo*, 129 (1989), p. 320.

8. Burlington also would have known of the Villa Rocca Pisani from V. Scamozzi, *L'idea della architettura universale*, 2 vols (Venice, 1615), vol. 1, p. 273, since an inventory of his library (compiled 1742–51) shows that he owned a copy.

9. J. Ackerman, *The Villa: Form and Ideology of Country Houses* (Princeton, Princeton University Press, 1990), p. 142.

10. Ackerman, *Villa*, p. 192.

11. A. Bolton (ed.), *Lectures on Architecture by Sir John Soane* (London, Sir John Soane's Museum, 1929), p. 117. For William Chambers's prior use of the ellipse and its origin in French neo-Classicism see chapter 9 in this book p. 100.

12. J. Soane, *Sketches in Architecture, Containing Plans and Elevations of Cottages, Villas, and Other Useful Buildings* (London, Taylor, 1793), introduction.

13. R. Wetten, *Designs for Villas in the Italian Style of Architecture* (London, James Carpenter, 1830 [plates dated 1829]). For an excellent recent study of the Picturesque villa and its literature see T. Mowl, 'The Williamane: Architecture for the Sailor King', in R. White and C. Lightburn (eds), *Late Georgian Classicism: Papers Given at the Georgian Group Symposium 1987* (1988), pp. 92–106. See also J. Archer, *The Literature of British Domestic Architecture, 1715-1842* (Cambridge, Mass., MIT Press, 1985).

14. Royal Institute of British Architects Drawings Collection [hereafter RIBA DC], L3/4, f. 44r (Villa Foscari, Malcontenta, including the side wing since demolished, fig. 7.1 here), f. 11r ('Farmer's House at Stra') and f. 11v (Villa Foscarini, 'Cavaliero a Stra').

15. Victoria and Albert Museum, Collection of Prints, Drawings and Paintings [hereafter V&A PDP], D.1479.13, 27 and 28: 'the famous Capra Casino (which for conspicuity I shall call the Burlington Casino, as copied by that noble architect at Chiswick) by much exceeded my expectations, although I had formed them pretty high from having seen Lord Burlington's. I think it the chef d'oeuvre of modern architecture of any kind, & that it is in point of invention as much as the art itself is susceptible of.'

16. Sir John Soane's Museum, A. Bolton (ed.), 'George Basevi . . . Home Letters from Italy and Greece 1816–1819', unpublished typed transcript [hereafter SM, Basevi Transcript], p. 141.

17. BAL, SMK 1/29 and 1/33.

18. RIBA DC, BaFam 1(a)3.7, f. 90.

19. Ibid.

20. SM, Basevi Transcript, p. 143.

21. In his proposed itinerary for a two-year tour of France, Italy and Greece, Wolfe set aside one month for visiting Vicenza, the same time as that allotted to each of the cities of Florence, Naples and Milan (RIBA DC, Wolfe Sketchbook 1). In fact Wolfe's and Barry's visit to the Vicentine region lasted two weeks (between about 12 and 28 June 1820, RIBA DC Ba/Fam 1(a)3.7, ff. 62–91), and this was longer than the few days most British architects spent there.

22. Arundale, *Edifices*, p. 26.

23. RIBA DC, Wolfe Sketchbook 10, f. 1r.

24. BAL, MyFam 4/21–6.

25. RIBA DC, Wolfe Sketchbook 10, ff. 1r and 18r–63v; RIBA DC, BaFam 1(a)3.7, ff. 62 and 75–92. According to Alfred Barry (*The Life and Work of Sir Charles Barry* (London, Murray, 1867), note on p. 60), Barry 'managed to hunt out every one' of Palladio's villas, but the evidence of Barry's and Wolfe's diaries does not bear out this assertion.

26. G.L. Taylor, *The Autobiography of an Octogenarian Architect*, 2 vols (London, Longman, 1870–2), vol. 1, p. 151.

27. SM, Basevi Transcript, p. 150.

28. A. Palladio, *I quattro libri dell' architettura* (Venice, 1570), Book 2, p. 47; RIBA DC, Wolfe Sketchbook 10, f. 56v (with sketch, fig. 7.2 here); RIBA DC, BaFam 1(a)3.7, f. 88 (with almost identical sketch). In the top left sketch on fig. 7.2 Wolfe omitted the

Villa Pisani's wing towers, which he found to 'compose with the pediment a profile too abruptly irregular to be pleasing in Roman architecture. It rather resembles the western front of a gothic Cathedral.'

29. F. Muttoni, *Architettura di Andrea Palladio Vicentino*, 8 vols (Venice, 1740–8). The east front of the Villa Pisani at Bagnolo, studied by Wolfe and Barry, appeared as plate 20. Vol. 5 of Muttoni's work (1744) was an edition of Book 2 of the *Quattro libri*, the plates being re-engraved in reverse (with some adjustments, including inversion). The measurements given are those of the *Quattro libri*.

30. O. Bertotti Scamozzi, *Le fabbriche e i disegni di Andrea Palladio*, 4 vols (Vicenza, 1776–83). There was a parallel French edition, and a second edition followed in 1786. A quarto edition was published in 1796, of which a facsimile has been printed (London, Alec Tiranti, 1968). At Vicenza in 1761 Bertotti Scamozzi had already published an illustrated guidebook to the city, *Il forestiere istruito delle cose più rare di architettura e di alcune pitture della città di Vicenza* (further editions 1780 and 1804). This contained a plan, section and elevation of the Villa Rotonda.

31. Bertotti Scamozzi, *Le fabbriche*, vol. 2, plate 1; Palladio, *Quattro libri*, Book 2, p. 19.

32. For the libraries of Chambers, Adam, Dance and Smirke see D. Watkin (ed.), *Sale Catalogues of Libraries of Eminent Persons: Vol. 4 – Architects* (London, Mansell with Sotheby Parke-Bernet, 1972). Information on the libraries of Soane and of the Royal Academy was kindly supplied by Eileen Harris and Nicholas Savage respectively.

33. BAL, MyFam 4/26; Palladio, *Quattro libri*, Book 2, p. 54. Mylne may have been following the lead given by Muttoni, who identified the now lost architectural fragment at Marocco as Palladio's part-built villa (Muttoni, *Architettura di Palladio*, vol. 1, part 2, p. 26. See H. Burns et al, *Andrea Palladio 1508–1580: The Portico and the Farmyard*, Arts Council of Great Britain, 1975, pp. 222–23.

34. V&A PDP, 7076.43. If the French (Paris Royal) foot is taken as 32.5 cm and the Vicentine as 35.7 cm, Chambers's measurements of the four corner rooms (26

ft 7 in by 16 ft 8 in) equal 8.64 m by 5.42 m. Bertotti's measurements of 24 ft 4 in by 15 ft 6 in equal 8.69 m by 5.53 m (Bertotti Scamozzi, *Le fabbriche*, vol. 2, plate 1). Bertotti's dimensions are the same as those given earlier in his *Il forestiere*, plate 6, though the plan there is, significantly perhaps, also provided with a scale of English feet. Chambers's study of the Villa Rotonda also included a (cut down) measured elevation showing the building up to the attic cornice (V&A PDP, 7073.13) and a number of other details (V&A PDP, 7074.75, 77 and 80, and possibly 7074.78 and 79). (See M. Snodin (ed.), *Sir William Chambers*, (London, V & A Publications 1996), pp. 120–21)

35. RIBA DC, H1/6, f. 13r.

36. RIBA DC, E3/54. Hardwick measured the four corner rooms of the villa at 28 ft 3 in by 18 ft 1¾ in. If the English foot is taken as 30.5 cm, these measurements equal 8.62 m by 5.53 m. Francis Arundale's published (English feet) measurements, *Edifices*, plate 11, gave the dimensions as 28 ft 1 in by 18 ft 1 in or 8.57 m by 5.52 m.

37. In the *Quattro libri* Palladio showed all four internal stairs as triangular in plan, but in the Villa Rotonda today, while the north and east stairs are indeed triangular (and built in timber), the west and south stairs are elliptical in plan and built in stone spirals. (I am grateful to my colleague, Mr Eamonn Canniffe, for confirming this information for me during his visit to the villa in July 1995.) The history of the stairs was discussed in C. Semenzato, *The Rotonda of Andrea Palladio*, Corpus Palladianum, vol. 1 (University Park and London, Pennsylvania State University Press, 1968), note 25 on pp. 31–2, p. 41 and plate 68. Semenzato established that the west stair was converted to an oval form in the first half of the eighteenth century and suggested that the south stair must have been likewise converted after 1786, because Bertotti rendered it as still triangular in the second edition of *Le fabbriche*, published in that year. Chambers's plan (fig. 7.3) shows that only the west stair was elliptical in 1755, and this is confirmed by the first plan of the villa published by Bertotti (*Il forestiere* (1761), plate 6). Hardwick's plan (RIBA DC E3/54), however, shows that a second stair (the south) adjacent to the first

had already been converted by the time of his visit to the villa in July 1779. In fact Hardwick's plan is erroneously orientated, the result no doubt of his having later drawn it up at large on the basis of rough memoranda taken on the site. It was Arundale's plan of the Villa Rotonda, published in 1832 (*Edifices*, plate 11) which was the first to be configured entirely correctly. For fuller illustration and discussion of these materials see my article 'Eighteenth-century Alterations to Palladio's Villa Rotonda' *Annali di Architecttura*, 7 (1995), pp. 177–81.

38. V&A PDP, 7073.24; RIBA DC, H1/6 f. 12v; Bertotti Scamozzi, *Le fabbriche*, vol. 2, pp. 52–3 and plates 43–5. Palladio's autograph sketch plan of the villa is RIBA DC XVII, 20A v. Chambers noted on his drawing: 'a pretty front designed by Palladio'. Two further buildings newly illustrated by Bertotti were the villas Forni and Piovene (*Le fabbriche*, vol. 2, p. 44, plates 33–35, and pp. 27–8, plates 16–17 respectively). Chambers had drawn the former (V&A PDP, E.3267–1934) and noted on it: 'At Casa Pioveni at Lonedo an Hexastyle Ionic Loggia in the manner of Palladio with a large flight of steps a poor performance.' The Villa Piovene is not currently accepted as a design of Palladio.

39. RIBA DC, Parke Sketchbook 1, f. 12r. See Bertotti Scamozzi, *Le fabbriche*, vol. 3, pp. 48–9 , plates 47–9. Palladio's authorship of this building is also confirmed by an autograph plan (RIBA DC XVI, 20A r).

40. J. Gwilt, *Notitia architectonica italiana, or Concise Notices of the Buildings and Architects of Italy* (London, privately printed, 1818), pp. 112–13. A list of Palladio's villas drawn up by a British architect who visited Italy in the 1780s can be found in Willey Reveley's manuscript 'Dictionary of Architecture' (BAL, ReW/1, ff. 49r–v). It contains only the Villas Malcontenta, Barbaro at Maser, Trissino at Meledo, Pisani at Montagnana (and Trissino at Cricoli). Reveley called all of these villas 'palaces', except for the fragmentary Villa Trissino at Meledo, which he referred to as a 'cassine'.

41. RIBA DC, Wolfe Sketchbook 9, ff. 34–9.

42. RIBA DC, Wolfe Sketchbook 10, ff. 61v–63r, with sketches of both.

43. Bertotti Scamozzi, *Il forestiere*, p. 49 and plate 15; *Le fabbriche*, vol. 2, pp. 50–1, plates 40–2; RIBA DC, BaFam 1(a)3.7, f. 76, with a thumbnail sketch very similar to Wolfe's.

44. RIBA DC, BaFam 1(a)3.7, f. 89; Palladio, *Quattro libri*, Book 2, p. 59. Actual state illustrations of the villa were given in Muttoni, *Architettura di Palladio*, vol. 1, part 2, plates 28–9. Bertotti's illustration of the Villa Valmarana, however (*Le fabbriche*, vol. 2, plate 39), did not show the building in its actual state. Bertotti 'improved' the elevation given in the *Quattro libri* by lowering the side bay towers and raising the roof line behind the portico. Barry's inability to accept the villa as a mutant work of Palladio mirrored the scepticism of Matthew Brettingham the Younger, recorded in a letter from Vicenza of 1754: 'NB ye Building markd for Palladio on ye Mapp at Lisiera, is positively not by him' (see S. Anderson, 'Matthew Brettingham the Younger, Foots Cray Place, and the Secularization of Palladio's Villa Rotonda in England', *Journal of the Society of Architectural Historians*, 53 (1994), p. 430).

45. See J. Harris, *Sir William Chambers: Knight of the Polar Star* (London, Zwemmer, 1970), p. 22. Chambers's elevation of the Villa Forni 'anglicized' the building by, among other things, showing its open loggia as enclosed (V&A PDP, E.3267–1934).

46. Bolton (ed.), *Soane Lectures*, p. 117. Ambrose Poynter also took the view that Palladio had 'degenerated into tameness in search of simplicity' (RIBA DC, C. Bell (ed.), 'Ambrose Poynter . . . Journal and Notes of Travels in the Ionian Islands, Sicily and Greece, 1821', unpublished transcript, p. 105).

47. J. Fleming, *Robert Adam and his Circle in Edinburgh and Rome* (London, John Murray, 1962), pp. 235, 241 and 273.

48. V&A PDP, D.444.88 and D.437.88 respectively.

49. BAL, SMK 1/32 and 1/33. Smirke's drawing of the Villa Rotonda is RIBA DC, CC12/68. In 1825 Smirke's brother Sydney also admired the villa's situation and sketched a plan of the terraces (RIBA DC, Shelf C3, Sydney Smirke Albums, vol. 3, p. 84), though in his letters Smirke reported that his paper had been 'soaked with rain' while he was attempting to draw

there, reminding us of yet another occupational hazard for the architectural student (BAL, SMK 6/11).

50. BAL, CoC Add. 1/38.

51. RIBA DC, Wolfe Sketchbook 10, f. 58r; RIBA DC, BaFam 1(a)3.7, f. 91.

52. RIBA DC, Wolfe Sketchbook 9, f. 39 and Sketchbook 10, f. 53v.

53. RIBA DC, BaFam 1(a)3.7, f. 91.

54. Bertotti, *Le fabbriche*, vol. 2, pp. 9–13.

55. RIBA DC, Wolfe Sketchbook 10, ff. 30v–33r; RIBA DC, BaFam 1(a)3.7, f. 85. Barry's pen and ink view of the Villa Rotonda (f. 84, fig. 7.6 here) is identical to one in pencil by Wolfe (RIBA DC Y8[7A]49). In 1816 Joseph Woods thought the Villa Rotonda was 'certainly Palladio's design . . . though Scamozzi lays claim to the honour of terminating it *with some alteration*; what this alteration was is not known. I willingly attribute to him the internal cornices of doors, chimneys, &c. which are heavy and inharmonious' (J. Woods, *Letters of an Architect from France, Italy, and Greece*, 2 vols (London, John and Arthur Arch, 1828), vol. 1, p. 242.

56. For many of the architects who travelled to Italy in the later Georgian period we have little documentation. Thus the proportion visiting Vicenza was probably much greater than the 30 per cent recorded.

57. The notes Chambers made on his plan of the Villa Rotonda, for example (V&A PDP, 7076.43, fig. 7.3 here), reappeared in his *Treatise on Civil Architecture* (London, J. Haberkorn, 1759), p. 56.

58. BAL, SMK 1/31 and BAL, CoC Add. 1/38. In 1821 Ambrose Poynter wrote: 'Palladio's Churches disappointed me exceedingly, they were the first of his works I had seen. I should be at a loss to know upon what [his] fame [stood] had I not been able to form another judgement from his works at Vicenza, though even there there are some, which, the sooner they tumble down the better for Palladio's reputation. Of the Villa Capra and the theatre it is impossible to speak too highly' (RIBA DC, Poynter Journal transcript, p. 124). Earlier (p. 111) Poynter called the Rotonda 'a capo d'opera – deserves all the praise that has ever been given to it'.

59. SM, Basevi Transcript, pp. 135–6.

60. Gwilt, *Notitia architectonica*, p. 113. See also Woods, *Letters*, vol. 1, p. 239: 'My object in stopping at Vicenza was to examine the buildings of Palladio, the first of modern architects.'

61. Wightwick, 'Sketches', p. 39.

62. I am glad to acknowledge that in preparing this chapter I enjoyed every assistance from the staffs of the Royal Institute of British Architects (British Architectural Library and Drawings Collection) and of Sir John Soane's Museum. I am especially grateful to Stephen Astley, of the Collection of Prints, Drawings and Paintings at the Victoria and Albert Museum, for permitting me to examine drawings by William Chambers in the process of being catalogued and thus usually unavailable to students.

8. *Villa Variants*

1. The inscriptions in the Adam volumes often seem to have been added when the volumes were made up after Robert and James Adam's deaths, most probably by the one surviving brother, William Adam, or else by his niece, Susan Clerk. For a discussion of this topic see Alistair Rowan, *Designs for Castles and Country Villas by Robert and James Adam* (Oxford, Phaidon Press Ltd, 1985), pp. 10–13.

2. *Vitruvius Scoticus* (Edinburgh and London, *c.* 1812), pls 109 and 110.

3. Scottish Record Office, West Register House, Mar and Kellie papers GD 124/14.

4. *Catalogue of the Drawings Collection of the Royal Institute of British Architects – S*, ed. Margaret Richardson (Farnborough, D.C. Heath Ltd, 1976), pp. 86–7.

5. This scheme is illustrated as fig. 73 in *RIBA Drawings Collection – S*.

6. Colen Campbell, *Vitruvius Britannicus*, vol. II, pl. 51.

7. Ibid., vol. III, pl. 41.

8. Ibid., vol. II, pl. 88.

9. Ibid., vol. III, pl. 47.

10. James Gibbs, *A Book of Architecture* (London, 1728), pls 40 and 55.

11. Ibid., pls 59 and 60.

12. Ibid., pl. 61.

13. *Vitruvius Scoticus*, pl. 45.

14. John Adam's use of Ware as a source for his own work is neatly illustrated by a letter written to the 2nd Earl of Hopetoun in connection with the completion of the front hall and state rooms at the house,

where he recommends 'great lightness be studied in the ornaments of the ceiling and cove. That in Ware page 21 seems to be a good model', and again for the chimney-piece: 'Ware page 22 is thought will do well for this room'; see John Fleming, *Robert Adam and his Circle in Edinburgh and Rome* (London, John Murray, 1962), p. 92.

15. Isaac Ware, *The Complete Body of Architecture* (London, 1st edn, 1756), pl. 35.

16. John Summerson, 'The Idea of the Villa: The Classical Country House in Eighteenth-century England', *Journal of the Royal Society of Arts*, 107 (1959), pp. 539–87.

17. Ware, *Complete Body*, pls 47–8 and 54–5.

18. Ware's remarks on country houses, quoted here and below, are taken from chapter 24, 'Of the General Distribution of Apartments', pp. 321–4.

19. Ibid.

20. Ibid., pls 56 and 57.

21. For a plan of Paxton House see Alistair Rowan, 'Paxton House, Berwickshire', *Country Life* (August 17, 24 and 31, 1967). This shift downwards in the scale of a country house is neatly illustrated in Scotland at the same time as Paxton House by the building in 1757 of the house for James Boswell's father Lord Auchinleck in Ayrshire, an unorthodox rectangular block with a curious four-bay centre under a pediment on the garden front, which so far remains without a convincing attribution to any architect.

22. For Taylor's villas see Marcus Binney, *Sir Robert Taylor: From Rococo to Neo-Classicism* (London, George Allen & Unwin, 1984), pp. 39–54.

23. The standard reference work on the Adam brothers is Arthur Bolton, *The Architecture of Robert and James Adam* (London, Country Life, 1922). All the villas designed by the Adam brothers, which were built, are illustrated and discussed in David King, *The Complete Works of Robert and James Adam* (Oxford and London, Butterworth and Heinemann Ltd, 1991). This volume is invaluable for the detailed documentation of all the known buildings and architectural features designed by the Adam brothers. Mersham le Hatch is treated on pp. 113–55 and at pls 145–50.

24. Both these designs are illustrated in Rowan, *Castles and Country Villas by Adam*, pls 6 and 7.

25. The analogy between the Admiralty screen and Captain Pitts's villa is not as apt as may appear, as Captain Pitts was not in the Navy but served in the Royal Engineers.

26. For Kirkdale see Rowan, *Castles and Country Villas by Adam*, pls 20 and 21.

27. Ibid., pl. 12.

28. Ibid., pl. 3.

29. For Moreton Hall see King, pp. 125–9.

30. Sir John Soane's Museum, *Adam Drawings*, vol. 10, f. 183.

31. Rowan, *Castles and Country Villas by Adam*, pls 26 and 27.

32. Ibid., pl. 28.

33. *The Works in Architecture of the Brothers Robert and James Adam*, vol. III (Priestley & Weale, 1822) pls XVI and XVII.

34. The staircase in a villa could, according to Ware, be placed either off the hall to one side or – and he seems to think this has a better effect – in the middle of the house in a direct line with the front hall. In Taylor's villas it frequently has this location, sometimes with a second service stair beside it. In his smaller houses Adam regularly makes use of a top-lit staircase in the very centre of the plan directly behind the entrance hall; this is a planning device which has a long tradition in Scottish architecture, going back to his father, William Adam, and also to Lord Mar. In some of his most economical designs the entrance hall and stair are fused into one. Adam appears to have developed this arrangement early, in advance of its more general acceptance by many designers in the early nineteenth century.

35. Rowan, *Castles and Country Villas by Adam*, pls 14 and 15.

36. Ibid., pl. 35.

37. George Richardson, *New Designs in Architecture* (London, 1800), pls XXXIII–XXXV.

38. Ibid., Introduction, p. ii.

39. George Richardson, *The New Vitruvius Britannicus*, 2 vols (London, 1802–8 and 1808–10), vol. I, pls XIX–XXI.

40. Ibid., p. 6.

41. David Laing, *Hints for Dwellings* (London, 1800), pls 23 and 24.

42. Rowan, *Castles and Country Villas by Adam*, pls 56 and 57.

9. Soane's Concept of the Villa

1. Arthur T. Bolton (ed.), *Lectures on Architecture by Sir John Soane* (London, 1929), p. 151.
2. Soane Museum SDR vol. 39, *Italian Sketches 1779*.
3. On Castell, see Eileen Harris and Nicholas Savage, *British Architectural Books and Writers 1556–1785* (Cambridge, 1990), pp. 149–54.
4. Soane on Castell, *Villas of the Ancients*, p. 32 (Soane Museum Archives 1/90/21).
5. Ibid.
6. Bolton, *Lectures*, p. 150.
7. Soane Museum, Drawer 62.1,2.
8. See Peter Willis, *Charles Bridgeman and the English Landscape Garden* (London, 1977), pp. 48–50.
9. Bolton, *Lectures*, p. 18.
10. Soane on Castell, *Villas of the Ancients*, p. 19 (Soane Museum Archives 1/171).
11. Palatial aviaries recurred in the Baroque period. Soane may have known the one at the Villa Borghese, Rome, built in 1617–19 from designs by Rainaldi.
12. Soane Museum Archives 1/170, 'The magnificent aviary of Varro', from Bernard de Montfaucon, *L'antiquité expliquée*, vol. III (Paris, 1719), part 1, pp. 114–35 and pl. LXXVII.
13. Bolton, *Lectures*, p. 150.
14. Soane on Castell, *Villas of the Ancients*, p. 15 (Soane Museum Archives 1/213).
15. Bolton, *Lectures*, p. 114.
16. Ibid., p. 115.
17. Ibid., p. 117.
18. Bolton, p. 115.
19. See Alvar Gonzalez-Palacios, 'The Prince of Palagonia, Goethe and Glass Furniture', *Burlington Magazine*, 112 (August 1971), pp. 456–60.
20. Soane Museum AL Soane Case 156, Lecture 6 1819, f. 42.
21. Burdon's reply of 2 February 1819 is in Soane Museum Archives, Private Correspondence III.B.2.14.
22. Soane Museum AL Soane Case 156, Lecture 6 1819, f. 42.
23. Johann Wolfgang von Goethe, *Italienische Reise*, in *Goethes Werke*, ed. Erich Trunz, vol. XI (Munich, 1989), pp. 242–7.
24. On this point, see Anthony Blunt, *Sicilian Baroque* (London, 1968), p. 155.
25. Soane Museum AL Soane Case 156, Lecture 6 1819, f. 42.

26. Apart from the celebrated view of the garden front in his *Vedute di Roma*, Piranesi illustrated numerous antique columns, capitals, friezes, vases, candelabra and caryatids in the possession of Cardinal Albani in his *Vasi* and *Della magnificenza*.
27. The building history of the Villa Albani is still uncertain. Joachim Gaus, *Carlo Marchionni: Ein Beitrag zur Römischen Architektur des Settecento* (Cologne, 1967), is inadequate, and the best account is in Herbert Beck and Peter C. Bohl (eds), *Forschungen zur Villa Albani: Antike Kunst und die Epoche der Aufklärung* (Berlin, 1982). For a brief but suggestive survey, see Joseph Rykwert, *The First Moderns: The Architects of the Eighteenth Century* (Cambridge, Mass., and London, 1980), pp. 342–55.
28. Soane Museum Drawer 45.1.7, and Drawer 45.3.43.
29. Victoria and Albert Museum, 3436.189. See *Catalogue of Architectural Drawings in the Victoria and Albert Museum*. Pierre de la Ruffinière du Prey (ed.), *Sir John Soane* (London, 1985), p. 28 and pl. 2.
30. A point made by William O. Collier, 'The Villa of Cardinal Alessandro Albani, Hon. F.S.A.', *Antiquaries Journal*, 67(2) (1987), pp. 338–47.
31. On the detailed survey of the Villa Albani by Pierre-Adrien Pâris, a near contemporary of Soane, see Alain-Charles Gruber, 'La villa Albani vue par un artiste du XVIIIe siècle', in Georges Brunel (ed.), *Piranèse et les français* (Rome, 1978), pp. 281–92.
32. Soane Museum, 'Original Sketches Miscellaneous Architectural Subjects', Item 135 recto.
33. On this bathroom, see Mark Girouard, 'Country House Plumbing 2', *Country Life*, 164 (1978), pp. 2218–20.
34. John Soane, *Designs in Architecture* (London, 1778), pl. 34.
35. On the Malvern Hall bathroom, see du Prey, *Catalogue*, where he suggests, wrongly in my view, that 'Soane designed a room perhaps intentionally recalling the decadently lavish Parisian baths' (p. 53).
36. Ibid., p. 57 and pl. 24.
37. Soane Museum Archives, *Italian Sketches and Mem[emoranda]. J. Soane 1779*.
38. John Soane, *Memoirs of the Professional Life of an Architect* (London, 1835), p. 15.

39. See Pierre de la Ruffinière du Prey, *John Soane: The Making of an Architect* (Chicago and London, 1982), p. 116.

40. Bolton, *Lectures*, p. 45.

41. John Soane, *Designs for Public and Private Buildings*, 2nd extra-illustrated edn (London, 1832), pl. xxxiv**.

42. For a suggestion that the design is related to garden buildings at Stowe, see Michael McCarthy, 'Thomas Pitt, Piranesi and Soane: English Architects in Italy in the 1770s', *Apollo*, 36 (December 1991), pp. 380–6.

43. Soane, Royal Academy Lectures.

44. Ibid.

45. According to George Tappen, *Professional Observations on the Architecture of the Principal Ancient and Modern Buildings of France and Italy* (London, 1806), p. 98.

46. Bolton, *Lectures*, p. 117.

47. Bolton, p. 116.

48. Though this design was unexecuted, a version was realized by James Wyatt at Bowden, Wiltshire, in 1796.

49. A point made by du Prey, *John Soane*, p. 120 and fig. 6.

50. See Dorothy Stroud, 'Sir John Soane and the Rebuilding of Pitzhanger Manor', in Helen Searing (ed.), *In Search of Modern Architecture: A Tribute to H.-R. Hitchcock* (Cambridge, Mass., and London, 1982), pp. 38–51.

51. Soane, Royal Academy lectures.

52. John Soane, *Plans, Elevations, and Perspective Views of Pitzhanger Manor-House and of the Ruins of an Edifice of Roman Architecture* (London, 1802), pp. 4–5.

53. George Dance's richly decorated dining-room and drawing-room forming a wing which Soane had originally intended to replace.

54. George Richardson, *New Vitruvius Britannicus*, vol. II (London, 1808), p. 9.

55. Soane Museum AL Soane Case 170, ff. [134]–135.

56. *The Champion* (10 and 24 September 1815). Though critical of 13 Lincoln's Inn Fields, George Soane was probably echoing language that his father had used about the building.

57. Soane Museum Archives 1/2/52, 'Query 5th lecture' (paper watermarked 1808).

58. It should be pointed out, however, that much of the sculpture now at the Villa Albani was introduced from 1868 by the Torlonia family, the present owners.

59. See Peter Thornton and Helen Dorey, *A Miscellany of Objects from Sir John Soane's Museum* (London, 1992), p. 71.

60. Alison Kelly, *Mrs Coade's Stone*, (Upton-upon-Severn, 1990), pp. 86 and 188.

61. Victoria and Albert Museum, 3436.187.

62. Anna Riggs Miller, *Letters from Italy*, 2nd edn, 2 vols (London, 1777), vol. II, pp. 298–9.

63. Soane Museum, Private Correspondence, Lady Miller to John Soane, 23 July 1780.

10. A Family Affair

Cres= *Crown Estate papers held at the Public Record Office.*

1. A full list of works carried out by Decimus Burton (1800–81) appears in H. Colvin, *A Biographical Dictionary of British Architects*, 3rd edn (New Haven and London, Yale University Press, 1995), pp. 194–9.

2. James Burton had built to his own designs. Most notable is his Russell Institution (1802) in Bloomsbury, which was not very well received. It is discussed in J. Summerson, *Georgian London* (Harmondsworth, Penguin Books, 1978), p. 171.

3. James Burton's work in Bloomsbury is discussed in Summerson, *Georgian London*, pp. 169–73.

4. The Burtons also designed and/or built several other buildings in Regent's Park, including Cornwall Terrace and Cumberland Terrace: these are discussed in Summerson, *Georgian London*, pp. 183–4. Decimus also went on to design the Colosseum (1823–7) for Thomas Horner, and the Zoological Society Gardens (1826–41).

5. A brief study has been made principally of James Burton's work at St Leonards: J. Manwaring Baines, *Burton's St Leonards* (Hastings, Hastings Museum and Art Gallery, 1990).

6. For a full discussion of the Regent's Park project see J. Summerson, *The Life and Work of John Nash* (London, MIT Press, 1980), pp. 114–29, and A. Saunders, *Regent's Park* (London, Bedford College, 2nd edn 1981), chs 4–5.

7. James Burton took up many of the leases on the buildings on Regent Street. These are discussed in Summerson, *Georgian London*, pp. 186–8.

8. For a fuller discussion of the notion of the

Picturesque in the creation of the royal parks in London during the early part of the nineteenth century see D. Arnold, 'Decimus Burton and the Urban Picturesque', in D. Arnold (ed.), *The Picturesque in Late Georgian England* (London, Georgian Group, 1995), pp. 51–6.

9. Leigh Hunt, *The Townsman*, 2, 3 and 4, reprinted in *Political and Occasional Essays*, ed. L. and C. Houchens (1963), pp. 289–90, as quoted in Saunders, *Regent's Park*, p. 117.

10. For a fuller discussion of the motivation behind George IV's vision for London see D. Arnold, 'Rationality, Safety and Power: The Street Planning of Later Georgian London', in D. Arnold (ed.), *The Georgian Group Journal 1995* (London, The Georgian Group, 1995), pp. 37–50.

11. See D. Arnold, 'The Arch at Constitution Hill: A New Axis for London', *Apollo*, CXXXVIII, No. 379 (September 1993), pp. 129–33.

12. For a fuller discussion see E.C. Samuel, *The Villas in Regent's Park and their Residents* (London, The Marylebone Society, 1959).

13. Letter from Alexander Milne, Secretary to the Commissioners of the Office of Woods and Forests, to John Nash, quoted in Saunders, *Regent's Park*, p. 94.

14. Cres 24/3.

15. In 1823 Charles Arbuthnot, the Chief Commissioner of Woods, recommended Decimus Burton for the work in the royal parks on the basis that his 'plans for the other improvements of the parks [i.e. Regent's] had met with so much approbation', Cres 8/16 f. 3.

16. See Manwaring Baines, *Burton's St Leonards*.

17. See J. Mordaunt Crook, 'The Villas in Regent's Park, 1 and 2,' *Country Life*, 143, pp. 22–5 and 84–7.

18. There appears to have been an unhappy collaboration between C.R. Cockerell and Decimus Burton. This is outlined in Saunders, *Regent's Park*, pp. 23–4.

19. For a fuller discussion of the use of Picturesque ideals in the urban plan of London and the relationship of the individual to these landscapes see Arnold, 'Decimus Burton'.

20. Time, not distance, was the important factor here, and good communication to the centre via Regent Street made this possible. This is discussed in Arnold, 'Rationality, Safety and Power', p. 42.

21. Cres 6 122 ff. 90–1.

22. Cres 6 131 f. 47.

23. Cres 6 122 f. 170.

24. Saunders, *Regent's Park*, p. 16 states that this villa can only be attributed to the Burtons, but the Cres papers cited above clearly state that James Burton took up the lease in 1818. Moreover, the application by Decimus Burton to add an Ionic portico so soon after the start of the project implies he was the architect.

25. It is unclear whether Lance was speculating on the Burtons' speculations, did not like life in Regent's Park or if he simply ran out of money, but he did move out very quickly.

26. Cres 6 131 f. 66.

27. Cres 6 137 f. 248/255.

28. Cres 6 137 f. 248.

29. Saunders, *Regent's Park*, p. 23.

30. Ibid.

31. For a discussion of the term villa see Pierre Ruffinière du Prey, *Sir John Soane: The Making of an Architect* (Chicago, University of Chicago Press, 1982), pp. 265–95.

32. This is discussed more fully in the chapters by Philippa Tristram and Lindsay Boynton elsewhere in this volume.

33. This is suggested by Saunders, *Regent's Park*, p. 24.

34. Ibid., p. 23.

35. Decimus Burton had an excellent reputation for working within budget and using a competent professional workforce who kept costs down. This was partly responsible for his success as an architect and must have been learnt from his father's working practice. His expert running of contracts undoubtedly appealed to the Offices of Woods and Works.

36. A drawing for The Grove is held in the collection at the Victoria and Albert Museum, D.1310–1907.

37. This was executed by J. Henning, a member of Decimus Burton's regular workforce. Henning had made casts of the Elgin Marbles when they were housed in the courtyard of the Royal Academy on their arrival in London.

38. A folio volume containing the ten drawings Burton exhibited at the Royal Academy are

in the collection of the Architectural Association.

39. These have been discussed elsewhere in this volume, especially in the chapter by Alistair Rowan. For a fuller discussion of these examples and the nature of this type of dwelling see du Prey, *Sir John Soane*, ch. 13.

40. See Manwaring Baines, *Burton's St Leonards*.

41. This estate in Tunbridge Wells was designed by Decimus from 1828 onwards for John Ward MP. Burton also designed a splendid villa for Ward, Holwood House, Keston, Kent, in 1823–6. Drawings for Holwood are in the V & A, D.1894, 1895–1907.

42. This work was carried out for Lord Midleton. Papers and designs relating to the project are held at the Surrey County Record Office.

11. The Marine Villa

1. James Ackerman, *The Villa* (1990), esp. pp. 42, 52, 56–8.

2. John Archer, *The Literature of British Domestic Architecture 1715–1842* (1985), pp. 59, 62, 67–8.

3. Emily J. Climenson (ed.), *Passages from the Diaries of Mrs Philip Lybbe Powys of Hardwick House, Oxon, AD 1756 to 1808* (1899), p. 265.

4. Archer, *Literature*, *passim*.

5. Following the great fall of 1799 at the west end (100 acres), there were major falls in 1810 and 1818 at the east end (30–50 acres). See Sir Henry C. Englefield, *A Description of the Principal Picturesque Beauties, Antiquities, and Geological Phoenomena of the Isle of Wight* (1816), p. 144; J.L. Whitehead, *The Undercliff of the Isle of Wight* (1911), p. 3.

6. Misprinted 'trravelle' in the original text.

7. Ann Radcliffe, *Gaston de Blondeville, to which is prefixed A Memoir of the Author, with extracts from her journals*, 4 vols (1826), i, pp. 50 ff.

8. Jane Austen, *Mansfield Park*, vol. I, ch. 2.

9. The writer appears to have confused Knowles, a farmhouse, with Puckaster Cottage. The latter is the name given by all other contemporary sources.

10. H.P. W[yndham], *A Picture of the Isle of Wight* (1794), pp. 66, 82; John Green, 'Recollections' (written 1847), in the Ventnor newspaper, the *Isle of Wight Mercury*, 9 July 1890.

11. Sir Richard Worsley, *History of the Isle of Wight* (1781), pp. 202–3; Wyndham, *Picture*, p. 79; J. Hassell, *A Tour of the Isle of Wight* (1790 edn), p. 1.

12. *Letters from the Year 1774 to the Year 1796 of John Wilkes Esq. addressed to his daughter, the late Miss Wilkes*, 4 vols (1804), iii, p. 229; iv, p. 46.

13. Some secondary sources state 'during his first term as Governor', i.e. 1764–6, e.g. John B. Marsh, *Steephill Castle, Ventnor, Isle of Wight*, privately printed and published (*c.* 1907), without pagination. Worsley said 'soon after he became Governor', which is ambiguous since Stanley was reappointed for life in 1770 (Worsley, *History*, p. 144). According to Whitehead, (*Undercliff*), he acquired the estate in 1770. The *Dictionary of National Biography* (hereafter *DNB*) gives 1770 as the date of building. However, the *Southampton Guide . . . also the Isle of Wight* (Southampton and London, 1774) gives the impression of an established place in the context of visitors, and it may be that Worsley was referring to Stanley's original term.

14. J. Hassell, *A Tour of the Isle of Wight*, 2 vols (1794), i, pp. 212 ff.; Worsley, *History*, p. 201; Radcliffe, *Gaston de Blondeville*, p. 76; *Southampton Guide* (1776 edn); Wyndham, *Picture*, p. 74; E.W. Brayley and John Britton, *The Beauties of England and Wales*, vi (1805), p. 379.

15. The Rev. W. Gilpin, *Observations on the western Parts of England, relative chiefly to Picturesque Beauty. To which are added, A Few Remarks on the Picturesque Beauties of the Isle of Wight* (1798), p. 309.

16. *Southampton Guide*, p. 59.

17. Hassell, *Tour*, i, p. 213; Wyndham said the vase was about fifteen years old (*Picture*, pp. 75–6). The vase was said to be modelled from Michelangelo by the late Mr Bacon: its subject was the story of Agathocles of Syracuse (*Sporting Magazine*, Sept. 1806, p. 269).

18. Radcliffe, *Gaston de Blondeville*, p. 80.

19. Marsh, *Steephill Castle*.

20. Marsh, ibid., stated that the new castle was built between 1833 and 1835. But a Brannon engraving exists dated 1833 (H.M. Colvin, *A Biographical Dictionary of British Architects 1600–1840* (1978), p. 715).

'Large and ugly' was my own reaction to the building at close quarters before its demolition; cf. the illustrations in Marsh, *Steephill Castle*; it was more ornamental from a distance.

21. G. Brannon, *The Pleasure-visitor's Companion to the Isle of Wight* (Wootton Common, 1839), pp. 29, 37.

22. John Alman, *The Correspondence of the Late John Wilkes, with his Friends, Printed from the Original Manuscripts in which are Introduced Memoirs of his Life*, 5 vols (1805), v, p. 77.

23. Wilkes, *Letters*, iv, pp. 1–2; illustrated in *Gentleman's Magazine*, 74 (1804), p. 17, which remarked that it was a universal attraction for visitors to the Island, but 'more from the celebrity of the owner than from the elegance of the architecture'.

24. British Library (hereafter B.L.) Add.MS.30.866: china, books, glasses, liquor sent in May; tea, coffee, chocolate, carpets in June.

25. Ibid. 16.7.1789 and Michaelmas 1790 (fos 162, 165, 169v) for Wilkes's gardening outlay; Climenson (ed.), *Lybbe Powys, p. 266*; Wilkes, *Letters*, iii, p. 272; iv, p. 113.

26. B.L. Add.MS.30.866, f. 146v; Wyndham, *Picture*, p. 55.

27. B.L. Add.MS.30.866, f. 166. Sir Richard Worsley contributed £14 worth of stones for the tomb, but they were rough and 'workmanship is the thing' (William Taylor to Wilkes, B.L. Add.MS.30.874, f. 26); books: besides Greek, Latin, French and English classics, there was light reading – the *Works of Rabelais* and *Les liaisons dangereuses* (B.L. Add.MS.30.893).

28. *Gentleman's Magazine*, 74 (1804).

29. Almon *Wilkes*, v, pp. 78 ff.; Climenson (ed.), *Lybbe Powys*, p. 266; Brayley and Britton, *Beauties*, p. 383; Wilkes, *Letters*, iv, p. 33. The Etruscan Room measured 23 ft 4 in × 13 ft 8⅛ in × 11 ft high, plus a recess 6 ft 11¼ in × 3 ft 1½ in; cf. the Large Room 18 ft × 24 ft × 13 ft high, plus a recess for a sideboard (B.L. Add.MS.30.866, f. 146v). Wilkes's builder/factotum, William Taylor of Newport, excused his taking three weeks to fit the canvas 'as I think of being particularly nice in so elegant a room as your Tuscan room will be' (B.L. Add.MS.30.873, f. 198). According to a ?caretaker this had been Wilkes's smoking room and used to be hung with fine tapestry – but this hardly

squares with the prints; this visitor denigrated the room as 'extremely paltry, and in the worst possible taste', without allowing for the deterioration of wood/canvas constructions over a decade after Wilkes's death (Louis Simond, *Journal of a Tour and Residence in Great Britain During the Years 1810 and 1811*, 2 vols (Edinburgh, 1817, 2nd edn), ii, p. 310.

30. B.L. Add.MS.30.866, f. 146v.

31. Hassell, *Tour*, ii, Contents, 'Villa of Mr Wilkes'; ii, p. 21, 'this villa'.

32. Wilkes and Worsley were frequent companions at Appuldurcombe, Sandham Cottage and elsewhere in the Island (B.L. Add.MS.30.866, e.g. entries for 25, 27, 38/8/1788; 10, 31/12/88; 5/1/89; 21, 26, 31/7/89; 9, 16, 25, 30/8/89; 3/9/89.

33. Wilkes, *Letters*, iv, pp. 102–3. Murray's *Handbook for Travellers in the Isle of Wight*, ed. Rev. G.E. Jeans (1898 edn), p. 42 makes two significant errors in citing this passage: (a) the year is given as 1781; (b) the phrase 'as I am told' is omitted.

34. B.L. Add.MS.30.866, f. 159.

35. I.e. the original building: in Sir Richard's time William Lambert made drawings for a new kitchen, servants' hall and rooms above (Lincolnshire Archives Office [hereafter LAO], Bradford 2/1/6). Subsequently there were two major additions: in the earlier one the house was 'considerably enlarged, and ornamented in the old English style with elaborate bargeboards and pinnacles' (G. Brannon, *Picture of the Isle of Wight*, 1846, p. 75). The painting (fig. 11.3) was formerly in my possession but was accidentally destroyed. It was small – about 12 × 8 in – and bore an ink inscription on the back stating that it was by Buckler. I think J. or John was specified, and the date (1797).

36. Wyndham, *Picture*, p. 70.

37. William Lambert's status as builder is established by his being in charge of repairs at Appuldurcombe and Sea Cottage in 1804; by his taking off the roofs of the wings at Appuldurcombe and renewing the roofs without damaging the picture collection; he made drawings for additions to Sea Cottage; there are regular payments to him by Sir Richard between 1789 and 1803 (see Sir Richard's account at Hoare's Bank, entries for 29/10/89; 12/10/91; 24/3/92; 27/4/92; 18/9/92; 27/12/92;

23/2/93; 28/2/93; 19/3/93; March 1798; Jan. 1802; March 1802 (to Elias Lambert), Feb. 1803. At Sir Richard's death Lambert claimed £684 15s 6¹/₂d against his estate (LAO Bradford 2/1/6). Sir Howard Colvin kindly confirmed that Lambert did not appear as an architect in the forthcoming third edition of his *Dictionary of British Architects*.

38. The inventory of 1805 lists the rooms as follows: dining-room, breakfast room, housekeeper's room, kitchen, passage and staircase, drawing-room, best bedroom, dressing-room, back bedroom, back bedroom (LAO Bradford 2/2/10).

39. The inventory lists furniture including the following: *dining-room*, Wilton carpet 24 × 17 ft, 3 chimney ornaments, 2 china vases, a gilt fox head, chimney glass in slips 2 ft × 3 ft 9 in, large pier glass in gilt frame, 13 glazed prints, 4 chintz window curtains lined, fringed, with tassels, a handsome mahogany sideboard, a mahogany dining table, a rich inlaid pembroke table, a lady's work table richly inlaid, a large silver gilt cup in leather case, vase form and handles, two corner inlaid bookcases with veined marble tops, two china jugs, a marble bust, two spy glasses, twelve painted elbow chairs with horsehair cushions and covering; *breakfast room*, Wilton carpet 15 × 14 ft, a small silver-mounted barrel and silver stand, a small china ornament, two brass gilt greyhounds, a pier glass in slips 5 ft × 2 ft 6 in, 14 painted views in gilt frames, 1 fruit piece over chimneypiece, 2 paintings of cattle on the floor, a beautiful inlaid firescreen with Chinese painting on it, a rosewood lady's worktable richly inlaid with burnished gold, an elegant inlaid pembroke table, 2 mahogany card tables, a hand organ by Longman & Co., 6 painted chairs, 2 elbow ditto, with cane seats, 2 easy chairs and coverings, a sofa bedstead and coverings, 2 window curtains lined, fringed, with tassels, a marble dog trough and stand; *housekeeper's room*, a mahogany desk, ditto china cupboard, ditto dumb water, ditto claw table, 3 painted chairs, 2 elbow ditto, oval pier glass; *passage/staircase*, 2 barometers, mahogany stool and dirt brush, easy chair and covering, a bureau bedstead; *drawing-room*, Axminster carpet 16 ft 4 in × 15 ft 6 in, 5 chimney ornaments, chimney glass 3 ft 6 in × 3 ft 6 in; 14 prints in burnished gold frames, 2

mahogany bookcases, one with glazed doors and one with plate glass door, a large mahogany claw table, a rich inlaid Camp table, a set of mahogany tables, 6 painted chairs, 2 elbow ditto, with cane seats, dressing stool ditto, 2 easy chairs, one flat [?] ditto, with horsehair cushions and coverings, 4 window curtains lined, fringed, with tassels; *best bedroom*, mahogany four-post bedstead with chintz hangings lined and fringed and 3 matching window curtains, a painted chest of drawers and wardrobe, a box dressing-glass, a pier glass in gilt frame, 12 drawings in gilt frames (views in the Island), a mahogany pembroke table, richly inlaid, with cover, a circular table in two parts, a plain black vase, table ornaments, china figures, a rifle gun; *dressing-room*, Wilton carpet 11 × 9 ft, mahogany bookcase, richly inlaid, with glass doors, ditto inlaid with burnished gold, ditto chest of drawers, pier glass in slips and gilt frame, 2 glazed prints in gilt frames, 5 painted chairs, 1 elbow ditto, with cane seats, a mahogany dressing table, a spinning wheel and stool, a guitar and case; *back bedroom 1*, four-post bedstead with cotton hangings, a mahogany night stool, a ditto pot cupboard, a ditto card table, a ditto dressing table, 5 painted chairs; *back bedroom 2*, 5 drawings, small pier glass in shades, backgammon board, blunderbuss. (LAO Bradford 2/2/10).

40. B.L. Add.MS.30.874, f. 62. Sir Richard had planted some very ordinary trees in 1791 and 1792, probably for shelter (LAO Worsley MS.55/14).

41. LAO Worsley MS.55/13. I can find no such reference in Suetonius's *Twelve Caesars*.

42. LAO Worsley MS.55/10v, 12v, 13.

43. B.L. Add.MS.30.874, f. 62, dated 29.1.1792.

44. R. Warner, *History of the Isle of Wight* (1795), pp. 301 ff.; *Sporting Magazine* (Sept. 1806), pp. 267–8.

45. Brayley and Britton, *Beauties*, p. 377.

46. Letter dated 17.8.1793 endorsed 'Admit the Bearer to see Appuldurcombe Park & the Sea Cottage' (Isle of Wight Record Office, JER/WA/39/6); Wyndham, *Picture*, p. 72.

47. T. Barber, *Picturesque Illustrations of the Isle of Wight* (first published 1843; 1850 edn, p. 78).

48. The Duke's visit was recalled in his letter of thanks to Sir Richard for the gift of vol.

II of *Museum Worsleyanum* (LAO Worsley MS.31). The folklore may be sampled in The Rev. Edmund Venables, *A Guide to the Isle of Wight* (1860), p. 245. All such stories are traceable to John Green (see note 10), *Isle of Wight Mercury*, 4 June 1890.

49. E.g. Godshill Vestry Meeting 17.11.1777 (MS. in Isle of Wight Record Office); Chale, see *Proceedings of the Isle of Wight Natural History and Archaeological Society* for 1936 (vol. II, part vii, 1937).

50. It measures 4 ft 4 in long and 137 cm high. See A. Michaelis, *Ancient Marbles in Great Britain* (Cambridge 1882), p. 238; A.H. Smith, *A Catalogue of Antiquities in the Collection of The Earl of Yarborough at Brocklesby Park* (London, printed for private circulation, 1897), no. 91 gives a detailed description, and points out that in the bow section the beak is mostly modern, the head of an animal is modern, and on the foredeck the highest part of the turret is also modern (pp. 29–30). John Wilton-Ely, *Piranesi* (catalogue of the Arts Council of Great Britain exhibition, 1978, p. 112) incorrectly calls Sir Richard Worsley Sir Charles, and gives Brocklesby Park as the house where this sculpture originally belonged instead of Appuldurcombe Park, or more precisely the Sea Cottage; also Catalogue no. 302. I am unable to find the *Mus. Wors.* reference. The errors are repeated by Alvar Gonzales-Palacio in A. Bettagno, *Piranesi: incisioni-rami-legature* (catalogue of exhibition, Fondazione Giorgio Cini, 3rd edn, 1981, pp. 67–8), who adds that this ship was subsequently used by modellers at the Sèvres manufactory; fig. 378 illustrates the end-on view. Wilton-Ely follows Piranesi in describing this as a trireme, despite its having only two tiers of holes for oars: I understand that there is controversy as to whether a third bank operated from the gunwales, and note that Smith avoided the contentious 'trireme', settling for 'Roman ship'. Since Piranesi did not number the engravings in *Vasi e candelabri*, or even paginate the book, reference has been a problem. Happily it has been solved by the modern numbering supplied in John Wilton-Ely, *Giovanni Battista Piranesi: The Complete Etchings* (San Francisco, 1994): vol. II, no. 1000 is the side view, no. 1001 the end-on view. I owe this last reference to

Professor Wilton-Ely. The photograph (fig. 4) was taken by the University of Cologne for its research project on Classical sculpture in English country house collections. I am indebted to the late Earl of Yarborough who lent me the negative and to the present Earl for kindly renewing permission to publish.

51. LAO Bradford 2/2/10; 2/4/21. Richard Ford William Lambert was the 7th Earl of Cavan in the Irish peerage. The Doric greenhouse has sliding sashes to ground level. It measures approximately 9 × 5 yd. The Marine Villa and the Elizabethan Cottage (now renamed Lisle Combe) were earlier this century both owned by the late Mrs Alfred Noyes. When she sold the former, she altered the boundary and retained the Doric greenhouse.

52. Englefield, *Picturesque Beauties*, pp. 74–5.

53. See the article in *DNB*; also L.O.J. Boynton, *Appuldurcombe House* (1967). Cf. Brannon, *Picture*, p. 75 which refers to Sea Cottage as 'long celebrated as the favourite retreat' of Sir Richard and his house-keeper/mistress of eighteen years. (LAO Bradford 2/4/3).

54. LAO Worsley MS.55 (a commonplace book, or notebook, mostly not in Sir Richard's hand): *As You Like It*, II.1.12.

55. John Sturch, *A View of the Isle of Wight, in Four Letters to a Friend* (4th edn, 1791), pp. 10–11; Hassell, *Tour*, Contents: 'the cottage of St. Boniface, the villa of Col. Hill'.

56. LAO Bradford 2/2/10.

57. LAO Bradford 2/2/9. The address in 1807, 'Marine Villa, Isle of Wight', suggests that it was then unique in the Island (ibid., 2/8/3). Its situation was regarded as important for its letting at more than its real value (ibid., 2/8/17).

58. G. Brannon, *Vectis Scenery* (Wootton Common, 1839 edn), p. 41; Brannon, *Picture*, p. 77.

59. Wyndham, *Picture*, p. 66; G. Brannon, *The Sequel of Brannon's Views in the Isle of Wight* (Wootton Common, *c.* 1822); *Brannon's Picture of the Isle of Wight* (Wootton Common, 1846), p. 78.

60. *Brannon's Picture*, p. 77.

61. See *DNB*.

62. Brannon, *Sequel*; Brannon, *Picture*, p. 77: 'vines and peaches flourish'.

63. R. Ackermann, *The Repository of Arts,*

Literature, Commerce, Manufactures, Fashions, and Politics, 25 (1826), pl. 20 at p. 190.

64. Brannon, *Vectis Scenery* (1825 edn), p. 19.
65. Ibid., p. 20; see also the 1832 edn.
66. Ibid. (1825), p. 17.
67. Ibid.
68. Ibid., p. 16.
69. Ibid.; Montague Guest and William B. Boulton, *The Royal Yacht Squadron* (1903), p. 60.
70. Ackermann, *Repository*, 38 (1827).
71. See *DNB*; Guest and Boulton, *Royal Yacht Squadron*, p. 47; H. Colvin, *A Biographical Dictionary of British Architects 1600–1840* (1978), p. 585; Henry Stuart, Cardinal York, was the last male descendant of James II.
72. Brannon, *Picture*, p. 75.
73. *Wanderings in the Isle of Wight, by the Author of 'The Old Sea-Captain'* [G. Mogridge] (1846), pp. 63–4.
74. The Rev. Edmund Butcher, *The Beauties of Sidmouth Displayed . . .* (Sidmouth, 1810), pp. 58–9.
75. Ibid., 3rd edn (Sidmouth, *c.* 1820), p. 44.
76. Reproduced in L. Fleming and A. Gore, *The English Garden* (1979), p. 180: the original source is not given. I owe this reference to Professor John Wilton-Ely.
77. Simond, *Journal of a Tour*, vol. 2, pp. 308–9.
78. Englefield, *Picturesque Beauties*, p. 87.
79. Engravings seen recently in the Isle of Wight portfolio at Messrs Sanders, High Street, Oxford. That of Osborne after rebuilding was by T. Barber.

12. The Villas of Scotland's Western Seaboard

1. I am grateful to James Macaulay for bringing this quotation to my notice. Its source is: James Greig (ed.), *The Diaries of a Duchess: Extracts from the Diaries of the First Duchess of Northumberland 1716–1776* (1926).
2. 'Every moment of the vacation that could be spared from the circuit was spent by him at Auchinleck, of which he was passionately fond', A. Allardyce, *Scotland and Scotsmen in the 18th Century* (1888), quoted in: James Macaulay, *The Classical Country House in Scotland 1600–1800* (1987), p. 126.
3. A. Allardyce, *Scotland and Scotsmen*,

quoted in: James Macaulay, *Classical Country House*, p. 32.
4. Macaulay, *Classical Country House*, p. 35.
5. The date of Ardmillan's transformation from a 'palace' wing is unfortunately unknown. The paucity and small size of windows, the white harl and the 'odd' arrangement of pilasters and pediment do have a certain Italian quality. If Ardmillan's remodelling dated from the late-seventeenth century, it would have considerable interest; if from, say, the 1730s, it would merely seem inept!
6. Frank Arneil Walker, *The South Clyde Estuary: an Illustrated Architectural Guide to Inverclyde and Renfrew* (1986), p. 69.
7. 'Yt. what time I shall have done heer, I will be heartily tyred of ye Highlands', SRO, GD18/5009, quoted in: James Macaulay, *Classical Country House*, p. 96.
8. RCAHMS, *Argyll: An Inventory of the Monuments*, vol. 2, *Lorn*, pp. 30–1.
9. Macaulay, *Classical Country House*, p. 96.
10. Quoted in: Ian G. Lindsay and Mary Cosh, *Inveraray and the Dukes of Argyll* (1973), p. 30. This intricately researched book with its invaluable notes to the text is the source of most of the information in this paragraph.
11. Ibid., p. 358, n. 123 and p. 76.
12. Ibid., p. 366, n. 229.
13. Andor Gomme and David Walker, *Architecture of Glasgow*, 2nd rev. edn (1987), p. 51.
14. I am grateful to Ian Fisher, researcher with RCAHMS, for bringing the significance of these crenellated houses to my attention. See: RCAHMS, *Argyll: An Inventory of the Monuments*, vol. 7, *Mid Argyll and Cowal* (1992). It is interesting to note that although Robert MacLachlan of MacLachlan was son of a Jacobite, he was reunited with his lands and reconciled with Campbell culture by the intercession of the 3rd Duke of Argyll (ibid., p. 245).
15. Ibid., pp. 25 and 320–5 for description and plans of Barbreck.
16. Macaulay, *Classical Country House*, p. 153.
17. Alexander Pope, quoted in *Johnson's Dictionary*.
18. '1842 Gwilt *Archit.*', quoted in: *The Oxford English Dictionary*, vol. XII (1933), p. 204.
19. John Claudius Loudon, *Encyclopaedia of Architecture* (1833), quoted in: *The Oxford English Dictionary*, vol. XII (1933), p. 204.

20. John B. Papworth, *Rural Residences* (1818).
21. Plans with NTS; photographic copies in NMRS. See also: Michael C. Davis, *The Castles and Mansions of Ayrshire* (1991), p. 40.
22. John Plaw, *Sketches for Country Houses, Villas and Rural Dwellings* (1800).
23. Greig (ed.), *Diaries of a Duchess*.
24. Frank Arneil Walker in: Peter Reed (ed.), *Glasgow: The Forming of the City* (1993), p. 25.
25. Ibid. (Others might suggest a more direct relationship to the work of Roger Pratt than to the Veneto.)
26. Ibid.
27. Charles McKean, David Walker and Frank Walker, *Glasgow: An Illustrated Architectural Guide* (1989), p. 4. The suggestion has been made, however, that a similar arrangement did exist at Piccadilly, London.
28. The source for all the information and quotations in this paragraph is: John Buchanan, *The Old Country Houses of the Old Glasgow Gentry*, rev. edn by John Guthrie Smith and John Oswald Mitchell (1878).
29. McKean, Walker and Walker, *Glasgow* (1989), p. 4.
30. Buchanan, *Old Country Houses*.
31. Letter from George Bogle to Roger Bogle, 1726, quoted in: T.M. Devine, *The Tobacco Lords* (1990), p. 9.
32. Buchanan, *Old Country Houses*.
33. Ibid.
34. Loudon, *Encyclopaedia of Architecture*, quoted in: *The Oxford English Dictionary*, vol. XIII (1933), p. 204.
35. Papworth, *Rural Residences*, p. 74.
36. The recent *Catalogue to the David Hamilton Architectural Drawings Exhibition in the Hunterian Art Gallery, University of Glasgow, 29 April–24 June 1995* is virtually the only published treatment of Hamilton's suburban villas, an aspect of his work not greatly explored in Aonghus Mackecknie (ed.), *David Hamilton, Architect: Father of the Profession* (1993). Michael C. Davis, *Castles and Mansions of Ayrshire* (1991) deals with Ayrshire examples.
37. Buchanan, *Old Country Houses*. Buchanan also made reference to Campbell's 'kenspeckle' middle name, mentioning that after a disagreement with local Tories, Campbell refused to take any side in an election. Consequently, he was dubbed 'Mungo Neuter Campbell'.
38. In 1835 he attempted, unsuccessfully, to exclude the public from Castle Hill. See: Frank Arneil Walker with Fiona Sinclair, *North Clyde Estuary: An Illustrated Architectural Guide* (1992), p. 122.
39. M.E.M. Donaldson, *Further Wanderings Mainly in Argyll* (1926), p. 3.
40. For a satirical description of a visit to a thinly disguised Sanna Bheag, see Compton MacKenzie's magnificent farce, *Hunting the Fairies*.

13. The Edinburgh Villa Revisited

1. I am conscious that this chapter on the Edinburgh villa is necessarily a *réchauffé* of research I carried out for my Cambridge undergraduate thesis. My choice of subject had its origins in then current conservation concerns. James Simpson had just published an article in the Scottish Georgian Society's *Bulletin* (1972), deploring the recent destruction of Hawkhill with its landscape frescoed dining-room which had been designed by John Adam for Lord Allermoor, *c.* 1757. Then we were all very concerned for poor Mavisbank, designed by Sir John Clerk of Penicuik with the assistance of William Adam in 1723. The most romantic of ruins, Mavisbank cast a spell as powerful as Manderley on all who braved a visit or merely glimpsed it from a safe eminence above Polton. Happily Mavisbank's fortunes appear much more promising today and I had the pleasure of writing it up for *Country Life* (20 August 1987).

   Back in 1975, however, both these buildings appeared exceptional as isolated examples of villas in the Edinburgh context, but I was inspired by my Italian Renaissance supervisor, Caroline Elam, and my lecturers Howard Burns and Deborah Howard, to test the then current typology of the Italian Renaissance villa, particularly as codified by Ackerman, against the Edinburgh evidence. I was also fortunate to be given by Marcus Binney, another of my supervisors, an extremely thought-provoking typescript discussing the social world of the Thameside villadom. I was thus particularly well equipped to be let loose on the Edinburgh villadom which had been my natural habitat for the previous twenty years and whose charms had, I felt, been insufficiently recognized in comparison to the praise that was then being conventionally lavished on Edinburgh's Old and New Towns.

In my research I was to benefit greatly from both the National Monuments Record of Scotland and the long run of *The Book of the Old Edinburgh Club*. It therefore seemed appropriate to publish my findings in the new series of the *BOEC* which was launched in volume 1, 1991. Rather than repeat that paper, the following is merely a summary of my findings, offering the Edinburgh evidence as a contribution to the general debate about the villa promoted by this conference. Anyone wishing to pursue the Edinburgh villa in detail must repair to the *BOEC*, which also gives the sources of the following quotations.

2. Diary of Lord Provost George Drummond, Edinburgh University Library, MS.Dc.1.82–3.

3. Scottish Record Office GD18/4477.

4. George Robertson, *General View of the Agriculture of the County of Midlothian* (Edinburgh, 1795).

5. Alexander Campbell, *A Journey from Edinburgh through Parts of North Britain*, 2 vols (London, 1802), vol. 2, p. 191.

6. William Park, 'Extracts from the Journal of Jessy Allan, Wife of John Harden, 1801–1811', *Book of the Old Edinburgh Club*, 30 (1959), pp. 60–118.

7. Cumberland Hill, *Historic Memorials and Reminiscences of Stockbridge*, 2nd edn (Edinburgh, 1887).

8. [Melvill White], 'Notes of a Visit to Edinburgh, 1778', *Book of the Old Edinburgh Club*, 25 (1945).

9. Scottish Record Office, Mylne Papers, Diary of a Visit to Edinburgh, 1780, GD1/51/37.

10. Margaret Tait, 'William's Hut', *Book of the Old Edinburgh Club*, 30 (1959), pp. 31–5.

11. Thomas Bonnar, *Biographical Sketch of George Meikle Kemp* (Edinburgh, 1892).

12. Lord Cockburn, *Life of Lord Jeffrey*, 2 vols (Edinburgh, 1852), vol. 1, pp. 236–7.

13. Robert Louis Stevenson, *Edinburgh: Picturesque Notes* (1906), p. 124.

Index

Page numbers given in italic refer to illustrations